THE MAGNIFICAT®
YEAR OF MERCY
COMPANION

~

Edited by Father Peter John Cameron, O.P.

DECEMBER 8, 2015 TO NOVEMBER 20, 2016

Table of Contents

Legend of Elements

Sunday – Poetry

Monday – Meditation

Tuesday – Saints

Wednesday – Catechesis

Thursday – Witness

Friday – Scripture

Saturday – Devotion

Devotions

Prayers

Catechetical Essays

Table of Contents

Red Line Section

EDITORIAL

Father Peter John Cameron, O.P.

WITH JOY WE ENTER INTO the Extraordinary Jubilee of Mercy, which Pope Francis calls "a special time for the Church, a time when the witness of believers might grow stronger and more effective" (*Misericordiae Vultus* 3).

The first sign of civilization

It is reported that a student once asked the famous anthropologist Margaret Mead, "What is the earliest sign of civilization in any given culture?" According to the story, the questioner likely expected Mead to say a tool, a weapon, a piece of pottery, an artifact of domestic life, etc.

Instead, the anthropologist answered: "A healed femur" (the big leg bone between the hip and the knee). A healed femur shows that someone took care of the injured person. Someone else had to step in to carry out the work of hunting and gathering until the individual's fractured leg healed. For Mead, the first sign of civilization was *the evidence of compassion*.

Pope Francis has called for the Extraordinary Jubilee of Mercy to make that primordial sign of civilization plain and far-reaching in the world again.

How to use this book

The pope has proclaimed a Jubilee of Mercy because, as he writes, "at times we are called to gaze even more attentively on mercy so that we may become a more effective sign of the Father's action in our lives" (MV 3). To assist with that attentive gaze, MAGNIFICAT is pleased to offer this *Year of Mercy Companion*.

You will find within something for each day of the Jubilee Year, and much more as well. Sundays are set apart by the forty-nine original poems written for this book. On Mondays you will read an array of meditations on the theme of divine mercy. Tuesdays bring an encounter with the saints of mercy. Wednesdays offer thoughtful catechetical essays addressing the most salient points of the theology of mercy. Thursdays are dedicated to witnesses of mercy, whether they be found in history, the present day, or literature. Fridays reflect on the notion of mercy as it appears in Sacred Scripture. And Saturdays stand dedicated to prayerful devotions of many sorts.

Also, in the "Red Line Section" of the book you will discover reference materials for the Jubilee Year that you will want to return to again and again: essays on the meaning of a Jubilee Year, the conditions for gaining the Jubilee Year indulgence, the Jubilee Calendar of Events, a Little Office of Divine Mercy, a Year of Mercy Penance Service, and more.

Merciful like the Father

Pope Francis tells us that this special Holy Year is a time "to bear the weaknesses and struggles of our brothers and sisters" (MV 10), an occasion to "open our eyes and see the misery of the world, the wounds of our brothers and sisters" (MV 15).

We can do so when we recall how much God looked upon our own wounds and misery with untellable, unlimited love and mercy. Let us pray for the grace to be effective signs of the Father's mercy to others, with the assurance given by Doctor of the Church Saint Francis de Sales:

> Do not look forward in fear to the changes in life;
> rather, look to them with full hope that as they
> arise,
> God, whose very own you are,
> will lead you safely through all things;
> and when you cannot stand it,
> God will carry you in his arms.
> Do not fear what may happen tomorrow;
> the same understanding Father who cares for
> you today will take care of you then and every day.
> He will either shield you from suffering
> or will give you unfailing strength to bear it.
> Be at peace,
> and put aside all anxious thoughts
> and imaginations.

Then, "touched by [God's] compassion, we also can become compassionate towards others" (MV 14). ❦

*J*ESUS CHRIST IS THE FACE of the Father's mercy. These words might well sum up the mystery of the Christian faith…. We need constantly to contemplate the mystery of mercy. It is a wellspring of joy, serenity, and peace. Our salvation depends on it. Mercy: the word reveals the very mystery of the Most Holy Trinity. Mercy: the ultimate and supreme act by which God comes to meet us. Mercy: the fundamental law that dwells in the heart of every person who looks sincerely into the eyes of his brothers and sisters on the path of life. Mercy: the bridge that connects God and man, opening our hearts to the hope of being loved forever despite our sinfulness.

At times we are called to gaze even more attentively on mercy so that we may become a more effective sign of the Father's action in our lives. For this reason I have proclaimed an Extraordinary Jubilee of Mercy as a special time for the Church, a time when the witness of believers might grow stronger and more effective….

With our eyes fixed on Jesus and his merciful gaze, we experience the love of the Most Holy Trinity.

– *Misericordiae Vultus* 1-3, 8

What Is Mercy?

MERCY IS THE FORM LOVE TAKES when it encounters misery. It is first of all a form of love because it wants what is good *for the one who is loved*. Keeping this in mind can keep us from some subtle and corrupting mistakes. For example, Saint Thomas Aquinas points out that mercy is a Godlike virtue because it involves the strong showing pity to the weak, and from this truth someone may delight in showing "mercy" precisely because it allows him to highlight his own superiority on both a spiritual and a material level. But this isn't really mercy. It's just pride dressing up as mercy. It's the sort of pride that Saint Francis de Sales said would make the poor "hate you for the very bread you give them."

Mercy is not condescension. Instead it is a kind of restoration. Imagine someone of royal lineage who has recently fallen upon hard times. He is wandering and lost and perhaps suffering from a form of amnesia. He cannot tell you his name. If you encounter this person, you feel compelled to restore something lost. You don't love the fact that he doesn't have access to who he really is. You love what he is and who he is, and so you strive to restore who he really is.

Or imagine a young person lacking judgment, experience, and knowledge. If you love this young person, you don't love her poverty in these matters. You love her and what she could be with the proper instruction and guidance, and therefore you want to free her from her present limitations. This is the gift of mercy, and it is rooted in profound respect.

This way of putting things makes a difference, because one could place the stress elsewhere. One could, for example, stress the fact that mercy is contrasted with justice. It is an undeserved gift, and hence to receive it marks one forever as one of the "undeserving poor." To receive mercy would, in that case, also be to receive a form of contempt.

God knows us as he intends us to be; his sons, his daughters, his friends. He knows that he has fitted us for himself and that no other destiny for us will do. When he knows us as sinners and as unable to secure our own deliverance from our sins, he knows us as needing his mercy. But this mercy is, in a way, called for, not by reason of our own merits, but because of his own fatherly affection for us and because he sees the change in us that his father's love will produce. His mercy reflects God's true judgment on us as being not his "undeserving poor" but his own beloved children.

– Father John Dominic Corbett, o.p.

ADAM AND EVE HAVE EATEN of the fruit of the forbidden tree. At first they felt as if they had been raised to deity, but that was mere intoxication, a drunken illusion. They seal their guilt with an act of lust, and fall into a troubled sleep. When they awake they are truly naked:

> Innocence, that as a veil
> Had shadowed them from knowing ill, was gone;
> Just confidence, and native righteousness,
> And honor from about them, naked left
> To guilty shame.   (Milton, *Paradise Lost*)

"He covered," says Milton, "but his robe / Uncovered more."

All seems lost. The Son has judged them and pronounced sentence, yet his first act after that was one of mercy. He clothed their bodies with skins, and their souls with the stirrings of penitence. Says Adam to Eve:

> What better can we do, than to the place
> Repairing where he judged us, prostrate fall
> Before him reverent, and there confess
> Humbly our faults, and pardon beg, with tears
> Watering the ground, and with our sighs the air
> Frequenting, sent from hearts contrite, in sign
> Of sorrow unfeigned, and humiliation meek.
> Undoubtedly he will relent, and turn
> From his displeasure; in whose look serene,
> When angry most he seemed and most severe,
> What else but favor, grace, and mercy shone?

Words of wisdom for us all.

– Anthony Esolen

IT BEGINS BY SAYING, "This is your lucky day." Often I receive an email informing me that millions of dollars are being held in my name in a foreign country. To receive the treasure I need simply contact the sender with my personal financial information. Most people realize this is a scam and delete the message. However, I once met a man who fell for it and was nearly ruined.

In the Letter to the Ephesians, Paul reflects on how choices made out of greed or selfishness can lead to our ruin. Sin deadens our good judgment and leaves us spiritually poor. But then Paul offers the message: every day can be our lucky day. In reminding us that *God is rich in mercy* (cf. Eph 2:4), Paul says that no matter how bankrupt we may feel because of our sins, God continues to invest mercy into our lives.

We've all trusted a voice that has led us astray. We've made a choice that seemed convenient. It may have not lead to our ruin, but it caused pain or hurt. The guilt that follows can kill our spirit. But our spirit can be renewed when we trust the voice of faith that assures us—every day is a lucky day for those who trust in his mercy.

– Monsignor Gregory E. S. Malovetz

A Scriptural Litany of Mercy

Throughout the ages, almighty God has manifested his unfailing mercy.

℟ *Lord, have mercy on us.*

O infinite, divine mercy, you are:

◖ Beauteous Creation brought forth from the abyss of nothingness. ℟

◖ The breath that turned muddy clay into a living human being. ℟

◖ The leather garments that clothed sinful man and woman. ℟

◖ The ark that saved Noah from the cataclysm of the flood. ℟

◖ The rainbow—sign of your covenant with the earth. ℟

◖ The halt put to building the haughty Tower of Babel. ℟

◖ The everlasting covenant made with Abraham. ℟

◖ The angel who stayed Abraham's knife above his son Isaac. ℟

◖ The stairway shown to Jacob in a dream. ℟

◖ The forgiveness Joseph offered to his treacherous brothers. ℟

◖ The hope of liberation promised in the burning bush. ℟

◖ The miraculous passageway through the parted Red Sea. ℟

◖ The authority of Moses and the attained Promised Land. ℟

◖ The manna in the wilderness for those facing famine. ℟

◖ Flowing water to drink from a rock in the desert. ℟

◖ The gift of the tablets bearing the Ten Commandments. ℟

◖ The Ark of the Covenant. ℟

◖ The certainty that filled Joshua to serve God alone. ℟

◖ The strength of Samson. ℟

◖ The tenderness that moved Ruth to stay with Naomi. ℟

◖ The voice that beckoned Samuel in the nighttime. ℟

◖ The kingly anointing of Saul. ℟

◖ David's defeat of the Philistine Goliath. ℟

◖ The Temple built by Solomon. ℟

– Father Peter John Cameron, o.p.

The Question (Lk 3:10-18)

"Might you be the Christ?"
We ask without knowing
to the picture
on the wall,
the open lily
in the pot,
the bourbon
on the shelf,
the stranger
down the hall.
We ask it
of the verse
as it focuses our cry:
Might these be the words
that can lead me
from my thirst?
That can satisfy my mind?
Or are they flat and dry
like the chaff
that will be burned,
that no one stirs
for a return,
that captures mercy
with a line?

– Rita A. Simmonds

A S WE CAN SEE IN SACRED SCRIPTURE, mercy is a key word that indicates God's action towards us. He does not limit himself merely to affirming his love, but makes it visible and tangible. Love, after all, can never be just an abstraction. By its very nature, it indicates something concrete: intentions, attitudes, and behaviors that are shown in daily living....

In order to be capable of mercy, therefore, we must first of all dispose ourselves to listen to the Word of God. This means rediscovering the value of silence in order to meditate on the Word that comes to us. In this way, it will be possible to contemplate God's mercy and adopt it as our lifestyle.

Let us not fall into humiliating indifference or a monotonous routine that prevents us from discovering what is new! Let us ward off destructive cynicism! Let us open our eyes and see the misery of the world, the wounds of our brothers and sisters who are denied their dignity, and let us recognize that we are compelled to heed their cry for help! May we reach out to them and support them so they can feel the warmth of our presence, our friendship, and our fraternity! May their cry become our own, and together may we break down the barriers of indifference that too often reign supreme and mask our hypocrisy and egoism!

– *Misericordiae Vultus* 9, 13, 15

Saint Thérèse of Lisieux

THÉRÈSE († 1897) ENTERED the Lisieux Carmel at fifteen and died there at age twenty-four of tuberculosis. At that time, many Carmelites were offering themselves as victims to God's justice. Thérèse died having offered herself as an oblation to God's mercy. But she was in the business of saving souls long before this.

Thérèse was only fourteen when she heard of Pranzini, a criminal convicted of having committed three murders on one night. The newspapers were full of information about him, including reports of his total lack of repentance. Thérèse wanted to obtain this grace for him. She felt certain that Jesus could heal Pranzini all at once, as he had healed the repentant thief as he hung on the cross. She prayed for him, took on penances for him, had a Mass offered. "I wanted at all cost to prevent him from falling into hell," she said.

Thérèse had full confidence that Jesus would hear her, but, for her own consolation, she asked for a sign. When the papers arrived with news of Pranzini's execution, Thérèse rushed to read them. There it was, in black and white: just before he was to meet the executioner, Pranzini had called out, "Bring me a cross." Witnesses confirmed that he pressed his lips to it three times. Thérèse called Pranzini "my first child."

– Lisa Lickona

The Relationship between Justice and Mercy

SAINT THOMAS SAYS that if there were some sin God was unwilling to forgive even though the sinner wanted forgiveness, then God would—impossibly—be overcome by man. This counter-factual is a key to many things.

If our sin could outrun the mercy of God, then the scope of Christ's redemption would be quite other than what we think it is. Christ dies for all sins of all sinners from the dawn of Eden to the twilight of Armageddon. Saint Thomas' counter-factual supposes a divine will at odds with itself: it envisages some sin Christ dies to efface as somehow withdrawn from the divine purpose that sent him into the world.

Because the death of Christ is figured in the New Testament as a price paid for our sins, it is counted as a manifestation not only of divine mercy but also of divine justice, wherein Christ fulfills the just requirements of the law. But justice is fulfilled only in such a way as to display the divine mercy all the more. It is better *for us* that Christ fulfills the just requirement of the law and so makes satisfaction for our sins. It is better and so more merciful because it opens up a way for us, too, to share in the work of reparation. The Lord Jesus makes us friends with him in his own work of saving us.

Christ's redemption not only fulfills the original purpose of creation but fulfills it according to the very idea of creation. We don't usually think of creation as an act of mercy, but Saint Thomas thought of it so. Evidently, there is no justice according to which an unreal creature claims being from God. Bringing the whole being of the creature out of nothing is rather a kind of mercy to the creature: it saves him from the darkness of non-being; it brings him into the warmth and the light of what is, positively reflecting the divine goodness. And the manner of the redemption, in which mercy triumphs over justice, imitates the original manner of creation itself.

Creation is also an imitation of the Father's generation of the Son (and the procession of the Spirit from both Father and Son). The assertion of the perfect equality of the Persons one to another, an upshot of the Arian controversy, shows us a kind of "justice" to be observed in the Trinity. But this just equality is a result of a logically prior generosity or "mercy" whereby the Father begets the Son by giving him all that he is and has. The "justice" of the equality of the Persons, in other words, is founded in the "mercy" of the processions, a mercy, a goodness, a generosity than which nothing more primordial can be thought.

– **Father Guy Mansini, o.s.b.**

Beaten, betrayed, and hung from a cross, he cries out to his Father to forgive us. He cries out for my salvation and covers me in his mercy. I weep at the price paid for my eternity, humbled by his graciousness, and long to live his command: *"Be merciful, just as [also] your Father is merciful"* (Lk 6:36).

I focus my thoughts on him and yearn to exist in a place where it is his face, not mine, that shines through every encounter. I seek his direction and pray his will be done. I cast out my fear of making a mistake, and pray, if I miss an opportunity, he will afford me one more chance. Despite my prayers and pleas, at times I find fault, press on in *my* timing, and become consumed with worldly desires. I breathe the tainted air of judgment, wallow in what I've decided should've been, and fixate on my needs. Even though I am blinded and lose sight of his commands, he stands firm.

The weight of the world leaves me exhausted, and the realization that I have strayed chokes me. I fall to my knees and beg for forgiveness. In that instant—that very moment—he renews and reminds me of a love far greater than worldly definition. He does not begrudge missed opportunities and selfish actions. He is merciful, and restores footing. He forgives and wipes clean my stains. He is love, and stands vigil over my life.

– Jennifer Hubbard

A MAN I KNOW HAS LIVED most of his life trying to deal with the pain he experienced in his relationship with his mother while growing up. Trying to come to terms with this he studied and considered much, yet this issue continued to overwhelm and obsess him. One day I said to him, "Hey, look, you just have to forgive her. That's all."

But where does the ability to forgive come from? If the hurt we have received seems to have stolen our lives from us, has darkened our days and twisted our choices, how is it possible simply to set this aside? Something has to happen. We have to beg for something we cannot produce ourselves, ask that our entreaty be met by grace that overcomes death itself.

This is the mercy that the Holy Spirit proclaims through the mouth of Zechariah in his blessing song at his son's circumcision (Lk 1:76-78): John the Baptist *"will go before the Lord/…[announcing]…/ forgiveness of [our] sins,/ because of the tender mercy of our God/ by which the daybreak from on high will visit us."*

Something of that daybreak must have reached my friend, because his mother called me one day to say that he had stopped by just to hug her silently. Mercy consists not simply in working things through but in begging for the grace to embrace our lives and to be grateful for everything.

– Father Vincent Nagle, F.S.C.B.

A Scriptural Litany of Mercy

Throughout the ages, almighty God has manifested his unfailing mercy.

℟ *Lord, have mercy on us.*

O infinite, divine mercy, you are:

◖ Elijah's unlimited jar of flour feeding the widow. ℟

◖ Elijah's victory over the prophets of Baal. ℟

◖ The tiny whispering sound Elijah heard on the mountain. ℟

◖ The cure of Naaman the leper. ℟

◖ The new eyesight given to Tobit. ℟

◖ The conquering might of Judith. ℟

◖ The intervention of Esther that saved her people from destruction. ℟

◖ The valor of the mother with her seven martyred sons. ℟

◖ The compassion shown to Job. ℟

◖ The shepherd sung of by the Psalmist. ℟

◖ The lover sought in the Song of Songs. ℟

◖ Divine Wisdom, overlooking sins so that people may repent. ℟

◖ The comfort proclaimed by the Prophet Isaiah. ℟

◖ The expiation of guilt proclaimed by the Prophet Isaiah. ℟

◖ The wolf and the lamb grazing together. ℟

◖ The voice that formed us in our mother's womb. ℟

◖ The new law within us, written on our heart. ℟

◖ The new heart and new spirit replacing our stony heart. ℟

◖ The spirit and flesh put on once-dry bones. ℟

◖ The rescue of the young men from the fiery furnace. ℟

◖ The espousal to the Lord of the unfaithful wife. ℟

◖ The fish that swallowed Jonah, saving him from drowning. ℟

◖ The preaching of Jonah, converting the great city of Nineveh. ℟

◖ The Day of the Lord foretold by the prophets. ℟

– Father Peter John Cameron, O.P.

The Visitation (Lk 1:39-45)

Our souls leapt
suddenly sanctified
at the voice of the Virgin—
her hidden divinity
swelling inside.

At the sound of her voice
the heart
we didn't know
beat a solid pound,
hit a kindred note.

She came to us
"in haste"
like the wind
carrying the sea,
and poured
into our laps
the teeming gifts
she couldn't keep.

She is voyager and star—
the brightest of our race.
She grows our harbored hope
beneath her billowed cape.

– Rita A. Simmonds

*O*NLY WHEN I DISCOVER that [God] loves me in spite of all my infidelities, when I really discover the mercy of God to me, only then shall I discover the true, compassionate face of Jesus: only then shall I discover that I was a captive, I was the oppressed. He comes to break the yoke. I am the one who had the yoke on my shoulders and yet did not know it: I was blind.

Now you have liberated me…; you have made me free…. [Jesus] comes to make us free, to give us the freedom of the Spirit. He takes away the yoke which crushes our shoulders. This doesn't mean that he liberates us from worries or administration, these are our problems. But he renders these problems very light if we let the Spirit come into us. *"Come to me, all you who labor, and rest."* All you who labor in administration, put your worries in the hands of Jesus.

If we are firmly convinced how weak and incapable we are, how our decisions are frequently tainted by egocentric motivations, how unfaithful we are to the Spirit, how sinful and unloving we really are, he will transform our hearts and give us a new strength. Conscious of our weakness, we must at the same time maintain a living and burning hope, and a confidence that he is with us; that he helps us, that he loves us and guides us. Then we can begin to live without too much worry.

– Jean Vanier

Saint John Bosco

JOHN BOSCO († 1888) was nine when he received his calling in a dream: he was to be an apostle to youth. At this very young age he began to seek out other boys, amazing them with his magic tricks or his juggling skills. From the fun, John moved effortlessly into catechesis. Soon, he had his friends praying the rosary.

After seminary and ordination, John was assigned to Turin, Italy, where the world had lately changed. Families had migrated to the city for factory work. Often young boys were untended, wandering the streets with no place to go. Crime was common. Don Bosco first befriended little lonesome Bartholomew Garelli and his few comrades. More and more boys began to come to his weekly "Oratory": catechesis, Mass, games, and outings. Soon John was taking in homeless boys and finding ways to train them for jobs. Money was always in short supply, but his pious mother came to help. Just when the work seemed too much, other young men joined him, the first Salesians.

Love and the sacraments were the pillars of John's "system." He told the boys: "My children, jump, run, and play and make all the noise you want, but avoid sin like the plague and you will surely gain heaven." And he told his followers: "As far as possible avoid punishing…. Try to gain love before inspiring fear."

– Lisa Lickona

"*I* WAS HUNGRY AND YOU GAVE ME FOOD" (Mt 25:35). Nothing but the literal meaning of these words should be accepted. This statement may shock us, and yet a deep conviction in faith that Christ himself is present in the poor must be our primary motive in performing the corporal works of mercy. Any interpretation of Matthew 25 and the corporal works that would diminish or dilute Jesus' words, reducing them to symbolic evocations, contradicts his own clear statements. It is he whom we feed in the poor.

That is how saints understood all the corporal works of mercy. Mother Teresa is a contemporary example: "We should not serve the poor like they were Jesus. We should serve the poor because they are Jesus." In giving food to the hungry, whether we realize it or not, we place ourselves before the concealed presence of Christ himself, who has chosen to become one with the poor. The action directed to a real human person is always, inseparably, also touching a hidden but real presence of Christ himself.

Third-world poverty demands a first thought in this regard. Famine can be a tragic reality for the parched countries that suffer drought, as in Somalia a few years ago. The Gospel asks us to be mindful of this suffering, not to forget, not to wait until the next dry season in order to take notice. The world's poorest do not disappear simply because the journalists and cameras have departed.

There is another thought, however, to ponder regarding the hunger of the poor. The downtrodden lives that we brush up against in our cities may face no risk of starvation. Another form of hunger hides within these lives. Mother Teresa became very aware of this other hunger, even as her own experience was rooted in harsh third-world poverty. "Poverty doesn't only consist of being hungry for bread…. We need to love and to be somebody for someone else." I remember a day more than thirty years ago when she visited the soup kitchen run by her sisters in the South Bronx. She entered the long room lined with tables on either side. Many knew her already, greeted her, reached out their hands to her. She made her way slowly, exchanging hellos. As she reached the last table, she took a quick step to the left and bent down to one man. She placed her hand on his arm, spoke some words in his ear. Then she turned and addressed the crowd.

I looked to see who had received this special attention. He was the only old man in the room, a lonely figure in a Bronx soup kitchen. Hungry in soul, needing more than bread, this worn old man provoked the act of love from the saint of Calcutta.

– **Father Donald Haggerty**

"I DON'T KNOW WHAT DAY IT IS," says the old man, awake in the morning and delighted to find himself still among the living. "I don't know anything at all. I am quite a baby" (Charles Dickens, *A Christmas Carol*).

Every speaker of English knows his name: Ebenezer Scrooge. Everyone knows he is a changed man. He is no longer the ruthless collector of bad debts. He will keep Christmas in his heart till the end of his days.

But we don't read our Gospels closely enough. For Scrooge really is quite a baby. When he and the Ghost of Christmas Yet to Come invisibly visited the Cratchit family, mourning for Tiny Tim, the older boy Peter was reading to the other children:

And he took a child, and set him in the midst of them.

Dickens didn't need to quote the rest. His readers could supply it. Unless we are converted, and become as little children, we shall not enter the Kingdom of heaven.

Scrooge had driven from his door a choir of children singing the old carol "God Rest Ye Merry, Gentlemen"— and we should be merry, because Jesus our Savior is born among us, "to save us all from Satan's power when we were gone astray." The Child comes, to make us children.

Scrooge can testify to that.

– **Anthony Esolen**

The Gift (Lk 2:1-14)

It's Christmas Eve and we will travel
a long way on a cold night
thinking of the twinkling lights,
the golden bulbs, the heirloom crèche,
the smell of sweets and spice.
A hearty greeting at the door!
The family, friends in velvet clothes
of red and black and gold with bows.
The hugs, the kiss, the Christmas wreath.
In we'll go, and sing and glow
and eat our ham and beef.
We'll join loud fun as one by one
we find our gifts beneath the tree.
We'll toast and tease before the hearth,
kick off our heels, amused and warm—
embraced, enwrapped in Christmas charm.

Now we arrive, and all is hushed.
The place is cold. We see our breath.
The cow and pig have not been killed.
There're lambs and goats alive as well.
The place is full of foreign folk,
battered guests and tattered hosts.
The floor is dirt. There is no tree.
No one has offered food or drink.
We've traveled far but cannot sit.
We see a light and just one Gift.
Is this one Gift for all to share?
This scene is death to Christmas cheer.

I stood and thought of all I'd missed—
until I knelt before the Gift.

– Rita A. Simmonds

A Scriptural Litany of Mercy

Throughout the ages, almighty God has manifested his unfailing mercy.

℟ *Lord, have mercy on us.*

O infinite, divine mercy, you are:

◖ The angel's announcement to the Blessed Virgin Mary. ℟
◖ The *Fiat* of the holy Mother of God. ℟
◖ The courage convicting Saint Joseph in his sleep. ℟
◖ The tidings of Good News to the shepherds in the fields. ℟
◖ The star guiding the Magi to the Bethlehem manger. ℟
◖ The tender will awaited by the long-suffering leper. ℟
◖ The healing of all those afflicted and sick. ℟
◖ The silencer of the storms at sea. ℟
◖ The expeller of demons. ℟
◖ The paralytic's ability to walk. ℟
◖ The sight given to the blind. ℟
◖ The hearing given to the deaf. ℟
◖ The hundredfold sprouting from the well-sown seed. ℟
◖ The deliciousness of Cana's wondrous wine. ℟
◖ The new beginning in Christ's call, "*Follow me.*" ℟
◖ The multiplied loaves for famished multitudes. ℟
◖ The desire that moves us to change and become like children. ℟
◖ The thirst of the Samaritan woman at the well. ℟
◖ The garment's hem within reach of the hemorrhaging woman. ℟
◖ The urgency dispatching the shepherd in search of lost sheep. ℟
◖ The buoyancy by which Peter walks on the water. ℟
◖ The life restored to the widow of Nain's dead son. ℟
◖ The welcome given the sinful woman who washes Jesus' feet. ℟
◖ The miraculous change promised us all in the Transfiguration. ℟

– Father Peter John Cameron, O.P.

A Prayer for All Families (Lk 2:41-52)

Heavenly Father,
Who called Your only Son
in obedience
away from the caravan
to Your House,
have mercy on our families.
Like Mary and Joseph
whose twelve-year-old son went missing,
we are often anxious and upset,
and we cannot comprehend
Your Will.
Let the family
be the place
where Your only Son is free to dwell.
Have mercy on us all:
the intact
the extended
the broken
the blended
the dysfunctional
the upended.
Bring Salvation to our steps
and let us open our door
and embrace
the strange and holy family
of Nazareth.

– Rita A. Simmonds

*W*HAT A DEPTH OF THOUGHT unreels from the words of Psalm 33: *Let your mercy, O Lord, be upon us, as we have hoped in you* (Ps 33:22).... Indeed, someone might inquire: "How far can we count on God's mercy?" For although in itself it is infinite and limitless, yet we, as created beings, can partake of it only in a limited, finite way.

The above-quoted words of David...provide us with an answer: *Let your mercy, O Lord, be upon us according to the measure of our hope in you*. In other words, the amount of mercy obtained by us from God corresponds to the greatness of our hope in him. The more we trust in God, the more abundantly shall we draw from the treasures of his mercy. The measure is, therefore, in our own hands since it depends on the hope we have in the Lord.

If we remind God of our hope, we can obtain from him ever more and more. God wishes us to appeal to him with confidence because such a confession of faith and hope in his mercy is an unending hymn of praise of his infinite perfection. Saint John of the Cross remembered this well, saying that God never refused him any grace when he implored him with the words of Psalm 119, *Be you mindful of your word to your servant: in which you have given me hope* (Ps 119:49). Is that "Word of God" anything other than his mercy revealed to us?

– Servant of God Father Hyacinth Woroniecki, O.P.

Saint Marguerite D'Youville

MARGUERITE († 1771) was twenty-nine when her husband François died. She soon learned that François, who lived by trading liquor with the Indians in Montreal, had squandered all of their money. She was left with two little ones to care for. Perhaps all of this would have been unbearable had she not met a Sulpician priest three years earlier who introduced her to the Confraternity of the Holy Family. She had learned to entrust all to God's providence.

And so the poor widow gathered her strength and found a way to provide for her sons. And she gave from what little she had, tending to the poor, who were all around her. In 1737, she brought a blind woman home. A month later, three friends pledged to help Marguerite serve the poor from her house. The constant comings and goings of the indigent set her neighbors' teeth on edge. They feared that the worst excesses of François' liquor trade were continuing under Marguerite. They dubbed the women the "Grey Sisters," "grey" in French being slang for "drunken."

Years later, when the sisters had overcome every obstacle—dire poverty, fires, resistance of the authorities—to continue to serve the poor, Marguerite insisted that they remain the "Grey Sisters." That name, she said, would "remind us of the insults of the beginnings, and keep us humble."

– **Lisa Lickona**

"*I WAS THIRSTY AND YOU GAVE ME DRINK*" (Mt 25:35). Among the corporal works of mercy identified by Jesus in Matthew 25, this action in particular compels an immediate thought of his Passion. The words invoke a link to the last moments of Jesus' agony on the cross, when he himself cried out the words "*I thirst*" (Jn 19:28). John's Gospel recounts that sour wine was then placed on a branch of hyssop and lifted to the lips of Jesus, who received it and shortly after died.

The connection between Matthew 25 and Jesus' own cry of thirst on the cross is necessary to ponder if we are to realize fully the significance of all the corporal works of mercy. In his words of thirst on the cross, a great mystery confronts us. A divine act may have taken place, not just the human cry of suffering from a man parched and bleeding to death.

In these words on the cross, which echo precisely the earlier statement in Matthew 25, Jesus in a divine act may have identified himself near his death with the suffering of all the poor until the end of time. If that is so, we have a deeper insight into what is meant by Jesus' statement that in each of the corporal works, we do an action to him. "*Amen, I say to you, whatever you did for one of these least brothers of mine, you did for me*" (Mt 25:40).

A mysterious and yet very real proximity to the Passion of Jesus awaits us in every encounter with a poor person. Actions of love seeking to relieve the sufferings of the poor are in truth a real contact with Jesus in his Passion. In the lives of the poor, in other words, he mysteriously prolongs his Passion in our midst. As the French philosopher

Blaise Pascal remarked, Jesus continues to suffer his agony until the end of time, and precisely in the suffering of the poor. This truth of course remains concealed from our sight, like the mystery of the Eucharist. But it is a truth that changes our lives once it is embraced.

Relieving the parched thirst of a poor person acquires an exquisite beauty in this light. It demands a sense of sacredness. On numerous occasions I have witnessed sisters of the Missionaries of Charity sitting on the edges of beds in their homes for AIDS patients or in their homes for the dying in Ethiopia or Calcutta, fully concentrated in this action of gently administering some water by spoon or in a glass to a dying person. They seemed to take no notice of anything but their action, fully absorbed, as though praying. The sacredness of those acts compares in my mind only to the lifting of a chalice of the Precious Blood of Jesus to a devout soul at Mass.

– **Father Donald Haggerty**

A LONELY WEAVER WALKS HOME in the darkness, on Christmas Eve. The best he receives from his fellow villagers is pity, not love. He had been cast out unjustly from his native town and had never recovered. He settled far away, devoting his time to amassing gold, earned by his single-minded diligence, keeping his heart locked up. Gold was his only friend. Then someone robbed him of that too.

He enters the house and sits by the fire, and in the glooming light he glimpses something yellow near the hearth—is it his gold, returned? His heart pounds. The yellow seems to glow and grow greater.

"He leaned forward at last," writes George Eliot, "and stretched forth his hand, but instead of the hard coin with the familiar resisting outline, his fingers encountered soft, warm curls. In utter amazement, Silas Marner fell on his knees and bent his head low to examine a marvel—it was a sleeping child—a round, fair thing, with soft yellow rings all over its head."

Might we call it unplanned parenthood? It surely is unanticipated mercy. The need to be in control of one's life, the control that Silas sought from gold, shuts out the possibility of mercy, which is never the result of our planning. It is always a gift.

– Anthony Esolen

THE SHEEP AND GOATS in the parable of the last judgment ask Jesus, *"When did we see you hungry and feed you...a stranger and welcome you?"* (Mt 25:37-38).

In our busyness, how easy it is to treat people who need our assistance and attention as interruptions. A person is easily reduced to an obstacle in my way.

When my concern has been how much time they are taking, or other things I have to do, or what I will do once I am "finished" with them, I am blinded to the real presence of the person.

How different it has been when I have been welcoming, and have entered into relationship with the person in need. So often I have been amazed that I am not able to solve the person's problem, but that a real good has come from the listening and being with.

I don't have many regrets regarding things or projects that remained unfinished, but I do have many memories of times I wish I had been more attentive, more present to a person.

What does this tell me? Those "needy" people who interrupt my life are Christ's mercy toward me.

The phenomenon of the sheep and the goats is not just something of the end time; its truth resonates now, in this life.

Mercy is not just for the end; mercy accompanies us on every step of our journey to our destiny.

Mercy, who is Jesus, is really present now.

– Father Richard Veras

A Scriptural Litany of Mercy

Throughout the ages, almighty God has manifested his unfailing mercy.

℞ *Lord, have mercy on us.*

O infinite, divine mercy, you are:

◖ The command to take up our cross and follow Christ. ℞
◖ The invitation to discipleship offered to the rich young man. ℞
◖ The water and the wine applied by the Good Samaritan. ℞
◖ The words traced in dirt at the absolution of the adulteress. ℞
◖ The unique, longed-for voice of the Good Shepherd. ℞
◖ The hunger of the starving prodigal son. ℞
◖ The running of the father to reunite with his lost son. ℞
◖ The robe and ring of the forgiving father. ℞
◖ The certainty impelling the tax collector to pray in the Temple. ℞
◖ The guest who makes himself at home in Zacchaeus' house. ℞
◖ The summons raising Lazarus from his four-day-old tomb. ℞
◖ The beauty awakening the five wise virgins. ℞
◖ The largesse prompting the poor widow in the Temple. ℞
◖ The gaze of love cast on Peter at the point of his denial. ℞
◖ The gleam of Christ-washed feet. ℞
◖ The friendship bestowed by the Son of God. ℞
◖ The dwelling place prepared for us in the Father's house. ℞
◖ The Presence alive in the Last Supper Bread and Wine. ℞
◖ The offer to Simon the Cyrenian to help carry Christ's cross. ℞
◖ The forgiveness to those holding hammers on Calvary. ℞
◖ The assurance of paradise to every begging Good Thief. ℞
◖ The priceless gift given to us in the Motherhood of Mary. ℞
◖ The saving blood and water pouring from the Crucified's side. ℞
◖ What is greater than darkness, sending the women to the tomb. ℞

– Father Peter John Cameron, O.P.

The Star of Mercy (Mt 2:1-12)

The brightest star is a knowing star,
present and light years away.
It travels the blue-black sky
moving herds of peoples
and herds of stray;
it moves wise souls to follow
with precious gifts in tow,
makes loners leave their havens,
the rich, their comfort zones.
It precedes the heads of state
and stuns their minds with fear.
It fills the poor with hope
and makes their waiting clear.
This brightest star is mercy
for it takes us to the place
we've wanted for all ages
but couldn't entertain:
The tiny cave that holds the Life
we never would've found
without the sign that shocked the night
and bent us to the ground.

— Rita A. Simmonds

*G*OD'S JUSTICE REQUIRES that he give the creatures whose nature he himself endowed with intelligence all that is needed by them to fulfill the God-imposed demands, and to achieve the God-assigned aims. Also, his justice requires that, in case they fulfill those demands, a proper reward be given and, in the event of their slighting and setting aside God's demands, a proper punishment be meted out to them....

However, God is not only the Maker and Lord... but he is also man's Father and best friend. Therefore, between God and ourselves there exist not only relations that are based on justice, but also those relations which are proper to God's fatherhood and friendship towards man; they reach much deeper because they are based on love. Love as the bond of family life... regulates sharing [all goods] not according to the measure of strict justice but according to the measure of mutual love of parents and children.

We should apply those fundamental notions also to our relations with God.... The essence of justice consists in giving that which is strictly due; but the essence of mercy is to take into account not only that which is strictly due, but also weaknesses, infirmities, and defects of all kinds, and in considering them, to give more than is required by merit and to punish less for offenses than the guilt deserves.

– Servant of God Father Hyacinth Woroniecki, O.P.

Saint Basil the Great

BASIL († 379) spent his youth at Athens and Constantinople, receiving a superior education among sages. But when he returned home after years of study, nothing attracted him so much as the austere life of his sister, Macrina. She convinced him to leave the world. "One day, like a man roused from deep sleep," he later wrote, "I turned my eyes to the marvelous light of the truth of the Gospel...and I wept many tears over my miserable life."

Basil threw himself into prayer and fasting. He founded a monastery on his own family's land, composing for the monks his famous Rule. Solitary prayer became his pursuit—until the day he was elected bishop of Caesarea in Cappadocia, in present-day Turkey.

As bishop, Basil continued to father his monks. He tended to the beauty of the liturgy and defended the Church's true teaching. And he gave bread to the poor. Moved by their infirmities, Basil gathered all the sick poor together under the eaves of a single structure—the Basiliad, perhaps the first hospital. Basil exhorted the Christians "not to be more cruel than beasts...by taking over what people possess in common or by grabbing what belongs to all." And he told them: "All the destitute look to our hands just as we look to those of God when we are in need."

– Lisa Lickona

"*I WAS NAKED AND YOU CLOTHED ME*" (Mt 25:36). Again we encounter a link between a corporal work of mercy and the Passion of Christ. This time Jesus' words in Matthew 25 recall the hour when the Roman soldiers, before nailing Jesus to the cross, stripped him of his clothing, divided it among themselves, and then rolled dice to determine the owner of the seamless tunic. The indignity Jesus suffered in this public humiliation offered the few pious onlookers little recourse but to avert their eyes. Perhaps some wanted to give their own cloak to him but could not. Others, we know, mocked him.

And what do we do ourselves to our Lord if we ignore the ragged presence of the poor in the streets of our cities? Saint Teresa of Ávila remarked, "Little honor is ever done to the poor." We should consider that statement. Clothing the naked ought not to mean simply discarding unusable, worn-out clothes in dust bins for the poor.

"If my gift is not to prove a source of humiliation," wrote Pope Benedict, "I must give to others not only something that is my own, but my very self. I must be personally present in my gift." The biting cold that pierces the homeless poor during winters offers an easy opportunity. A clean blanket, a warmer hat, new gloves or woolen socks, a heavy sweater or coat—it is not difficult to make a personal gift. We may not be able to share our dining table, but surely most closets await some emptying and a personal sacrifice for a poor person.

Third-world poverty is of course a graver condition of deprivation. A contribution to assist poor children—clothing or in other ways—can be considered in the light of

Matthew 25 as a gift to the Christ child, born in Bethlehem homeless and poor.

Such a gift raises yet a further possibility, since it is inseparable from love for the Virgin Mother. Like all mothers of poor children, she was touched herself by acts to her child. In heaven now, the same may be true.

Certainly children can teach us something important in this matter. I remember a mother and child staying some years ago at a Harlem shelter. The four-year-old daughter seemed to laugh and smile at everything in that shelter. But the greatest look of pleasure I saw on this little girl's face came on a cold winter day when she took her cap from her own head and placed it carefully on the bare head of a smaller boy about to go outside with his own mother. Her mother observed it all and did not stop her. The little girl's beautiful eyes were enough to ward off any intervention. It was a lesson of pure happiness in the act of self-giving.

– Father Donald Haggerty

A SCENE FROM SHAKESPEARE'S *As You Like It*.

The good Duke Senior has been supplanted by his brother and driven into the Forest of Arden, where he and his loyal men live exposed to the elements, which tell them "feelingly" how frail they are. A noble youth named Orlando has also been driven from home by a wicked brother, and he arrives in the forest with his loyal servant Adam, more than eighty years old. "Though I am old, yet I am strong and lusty," Adam had pleaded. "I'll do the service of a younger man." Orlando agreed, in mercy to the "good old man" and his faithful love.

But the woods have yielded nothing to eat, and Adam is near death. Orlando sets off in desperate search of food, till he meets Duke Senior and his men. The Duke promises him help, and when Orlando returns, carrying Adam in his arms—we are all Adam, aren't we?—the Duke shows the honor that faithfulness is due: "Welcome. Set down your venerable burden/ And let him feed." So he does, while one of the men sings these bittersweet words:

> Blow, blow, thou winter wind,
> Thou art not so unkind
> As man's ingratitude.

Compared with the repayments of man, even the stiff winds of God's winter are kind.

– Anthony Esolen

JESUS' FIFTH BEATITUDE—*"Blessed are the merciful"*—embodies a major part of the Christian message. The paradox is that mercy is evidently offered on the principle of stern justice. The mercy we show is precisely the mercy we receive. For most of us, this appears a little concerning. It is not easy to forgive. The human heart is petty-minded, a connate master of grudge-holding.

The parable of the unforgiving servant makes this unpleasant point quite well. Here Luke comes wonderfully to the rescue. *"Forgive and you will be forgiven./ Give and gifts will be given to you; a good measure, packed together, shaken down, and overflowing, will be poured into your lap. For the measure with which you measure will in return be measured out to you"* (Lk 6:37-38).

The picture is not of a miserly God, who weighs out every ounce. God is more like a friendly grocer who stuffs as much within the measuring cup we bring as he possibly can, then heaps it up until it is spilling out. There is a real proportion between what we do and what we get; we make our own measuring cup; but such justice is always—thank God!—slanted generously toward mercy.

– Father Anthony Giambrone, O.P.

Your mercy is hope,
Lord Jesus, the first light of our eyes and our hearts,
all good deeds, life and immortality are from you.
Turn with compassion toward me
and make my soul return to you rejoicing.
For without you I cannot be transformed anew,
and if your will is not in sympathy with me,
I am unable to save myself since I am condemned
        to death.
And if you, my guide, did not show me the way,
marking the footsteps on the path that leads to you,
I would fall into the abyss on the right and the left.

I am not proud, for I am justly scorned.
I am not arrogant, for I am blameworthy.
I am not haughty, for I am abandoned.
I do not boast, for I am reduced to silence.
I do not rebel, for I am mocked.
I do not rejoice, for I am pitiful.
I do not justify myself, for I am wicked.

For you alone give life to thinking beings.
And you alone maintain order in the cycle of creatures.
And you alone are my salvation, as the Psalmist said,
and you proclaim in joyous voice the good news,
which resounds in the ears of the attentive
        of all ages—
*"Come to me, all you who labor and are heavy laden,
and/ I will give you rest and cleanse you of your sins."*

                                        – Saint Gregory of Narek

"Every valley shall be filled in" (Is 40:4)

Every valley shall be filled in?
When Lord? When?
My heart is a cavern
that echoes Your Name.
Your Name is the cry
I have stopped crying out,
but the echo remains.
My heart is the place
of the echo.
The place
of Your Name.
Your absence is
a catalyst,
my cry is the refrain:
The valley sings
Your Name.
It echoes
a refrain.
Your Name's
my cry contained.
Once the valley
kept my cry
it bounced from side to side.
The cavern frames my cry
and keeps Your Name
alive.
My heart
is the valley.
The void resounds
Your Name!

– Rita A. Simmonds

*G*OD'S LOVE AND MERCY are acts of his holy will; under the name of mercy come all those manifestations of love which tend to remove any wants, needs, pains, sufferings, in a word, any deficiencies.

It follows, therefore, that in the broad sense all exterior works of God, that is, the whole of the created world, is a result of divine mercy or, in other words, that divine mercy is at the very foundation of creation. Indeed, the greatest possible want is the want of being or the want of existence; therefore, the act of creation, meaning the act of calling something into being out of non-being, is the first and most fundamental act of God's mercy upon which all his other acts are based. Even divine justice, which rules over the created world, has God's mercy for its starting point, for the world owes its existence to mercy.

Mercy is not limited to the very first act of calling the world into being. Since creatures have no reason for their being in themselves and are finite and limited in their perfections, they carry a germ of non-being in themselves from which their wants and needs arise. Therefore, divine mercy exercises a constant vigil over creatures; preserves their being; makes up for their wants; heals their wounds, and supplies new strength.

– Servant of God Father Hyacinth Woroniecki, O.P.

Saint Peter Claver

CARTAGENA, Colombia, was the center of the slave trade in the 17th century. Slaves were bought for so little in Africa and resold for so much in Cartagena that a trader could lose half of his slaves in transit and still make a profit.

Not even the warnings of the popes made a dent in the machinery of the slave trade. So what could one missionary do? Jesuit priest Peter Claver († 1654) had no hope of changing the system. But he plunged right into it, bringing light into the literal darkness of the holds of the ships that arrived daily. Peter, by nature a timid soul, went into those fetid holes of death and disease. He held in his hands every sweet and good thing he could find: brandy, tobacco, bread, lemons. He brought medicine for their wounds. "We must speak to them with our hands before we speak to them with our lips," he explained. Then he would show them pictures from the life of Christ, the one who had died for their sins. So that the catechesis was not in vain, he extended the apostolate to the plantations themselves. In forty years he baptized some 300,000 slaves.

Peter taught them simple prayers. We might make them our own. "Jesus Christ, son of God, you will be my father and mother and all my good." And: "Lord, I love you much, much, much."

– Lisa Lickona

SHELTERING THE HOMELESS is an example of how different a corporal work of mercy is from a mere social service. The cities of America have for some decades funded public shelters for the homeless, which, despite good intentions, are commonly shunned by the homeless themselves. The typically large dormitories are unrestful places of noise late into the night, of petty thievery and occasional violence. Many homeless in New York prefer the hard seat of a subway train on a cold winter night.

The corporal work of mercy is necessarily different, and more than a physical assistance. For a roof and bed alone do not have sympathetic ears for the soul of another. Many fine Catholics who have given their time and sleepless nights as volunteers in shelters run by parishes or religious congregations discover quickly how real are the lives of the poor.

Always, it seems, the homeless come to shelters unaccompanied, alone. They have used up family and friends, often by their own failures in life. Their isolation and despair, with nowhere to turn and no hopeful prospect in sight, burns at the heart of their poverty. "The biggest disease today is not leprosy or cancer or tuberculosis," said Mother Teresa, "but rather the feeling of being unwanted, uncared for, deserted by everybody."

The work of mercy in this case requires awareness of this quiet despair afflicting homeless people. It cannot stop at pity, which is so often detached from real compassion. We must allow ourselves to be moved by the plight of another and bend down in heart to the other. Availability, discrete sympathy, openness to conversation—these are the true measure of charity in sheltering the homeless. If ever we befriend a homeless person, even more if we share our faith in the act, we may contribute to a soul's salvation. Touching the soul of another is the ultimate fruitfulness of this work.

Yet we are not always the one who gives the gift in these settings. I never will forget one man who stayed for two weeks in the Missionaries of Charity shelter in the Bronx—within days the sister in charge compared him to Saint Benedict Labre—indeed his appearance was similar. Most of the nights he slept on the floor outside the locked chapel. He was quite sane and extremely well read, a scientist from Texas who had worked for the US military in the production of nuclear weapons. His stay in New York was only to await a friend's assistance before a trip to France and entry into a Trappist monastery. It was a deep lesson for me how much may be hidden underneath a threadbare appearance.

– Father Donald Haggerty

IN THE 13TH-CENTURY *Quest of the Holy Grail*, a crippled knight drags himself to the altar and falls to the ground before it. "Gracious Lord God," he begs, "who through this Holy Vessel that I now set eyes on hast performed so many miracles in this and other lands, Father, look on me in thy mercy and grant that I may presently be healed of my infirmity so that I too may undertake the Quest wherein all worthy men are entered." He then pulls himself up to the table with all his strength, to kiss it. And he knew relief from his suffering, says the author of the romance, and with a great groan he cried, "Ah! God, I am healed!" Then he fell into a sweet restorative sleep.

Another knight lies nearby, neither awake nor asleep. It is the courtly and sin-burdened Lancelot. He too receives mercy, as a voice from heaven: "Lancelot, harder than stone, more bitter than wood, more barren and bare than the fig tree, how durst thou presume to venture where the Holy Grail abides? Get thee hence, for the stench of thy presence fouls this place."

The words wring his heart and make him weep like Job, "groaning and cursing the day he was born." But the Lord, the only physician of the soul, is even now working another miraculous cure.

– Anthony Esolen

SHE STARES AT THE MIRROR as the dress is fitted and pinned. The gown my niece is to wear as the maid of honor in her sister's wedding is beautiful, but not a style she would ever choose. She frowns and then wonders aloud, "What if I just showed up wearing something else?"

From a prison cell, Paul writes to the Colossians, explaining to them what Christian life should look like. Since they have put on the garments of the baptized, Paul insists it is not enough for them simply to know about Jesus or speak about faith. Christians must put on the virtues that were seen in the life of Jesus. When those who are in the world look at Christians, they must see Jesus staring at them. This is the meaning of discipleship.

Paul encourages the Colossians to *clothe yourselves with heartfelt mercy* (Col 3:12). The sense here is that mercy must be shown particularly to the destitute and afflicted. It is the work of discipleship to offer clothing, food, and shelter to those in need. But if we do this without mercy, we show up clothed as volunteers. The moment we look into the heart of the needy and see ourselves is the moment we are clothed with something called mercy.

– Monsignor Gregory E. S. Malovetz

Lord Jesus, compassion, weeping for your sufferings, is a grace: faced with the spectacle of your cross, I cannot by my own power draw cries of grief from my stony heart, for, alas, it has become terribly hard! But at least I can ask you for compassion: I owe it to you, but if I am to be able to give it to you, I must first ask you for it. I have to ask you for everything I owe you.

O God, I beseech you, let us follow your example. The more we suffer and the more we are tempted, the more we should pray. In prayer is our only help, our only strength, our only consolation. We pray that the pain and power of temptation will not paralyze our prayer. We must look for our Savior who is there, close to us, and we must talk with him. He is before us, looking lovingly upon us, straining to hear us, telling us to speak to him, telling us that he is there, that he loves us. And we have no word for him, not a glance to give him. Let us gaze on him, talk to him constantly, as one does when one is in love, as our Lord is doing now to his Father. The deeper into agony we fall, the more necessary it is for us to throw ourselves into the embrace of our beloved, pressing ourselves against him in uninterrupted prayer. O God, give me this grace—the grace to follow your example by fulfilling so compelling and sweet a duty.

– Blessed Charles de Foucauld

The Wine to Come (Jn 2:1-11)

"My hour has not yet come."

But the hour is imminent.
We fill our jars to the brim
and pray that the feast
doesn't have to end.

The miracle has been granted.
Fine wine freely flows.
All the guests are happy.
The waiters are amazed.

Only the mother tastes
a trace of peculiar grape.
Her palate is familiar
with flavors undefined.
She weighs the phrase,
the swirling sip
that's tinged her mind.

"My hour has not yet come."

But the hour is near
to press the fruit of the vine.
Only then shall we truly taste
the goodness of the wine.

– Rita A. Simmonds

*T*HE ONE CONCLUSION DRAWN from all these facts is that the first and the main reason for the Incarnation of the Word of God is divine mercy, which is divine love condescending to creatures to deliver them from their wants and miseries. Of all the miseries afflicting mankind, the state of the fallen human nature resulting from the sin of Adam and Eve takes the first place, and is rightly considered the greatest misfortune of the world, because it affected man, the crown of creation. Man, a most noble being, was created in the image and likeness of God to spread the glory of the Creator by intelligent acts of his reason and will. But since the time of original sin, he was constantly realizing that he was not doing the good which he himself willed, but rather the evil which he hated (Rom 7:15). That desperate situation called for God's mercy, which could not remain insensible to man's misery.

In his eternal decrees God heard the cry of mankind. Even though he permitted the sin which was to drive mankind into such a desperate situation, at the same time he determined a plan of rescue which was to enrich mankind even more than before the fall and to give a perfect satisfaction to the requirements of divine justice.

– Servant of God Father Hyacinth Woroniecki, O.P.

Saint Marianne Cope

IN 1883, MOTHER MARIANNE († 1918) of the Sisters of Saint Francis in Syracuse, New York, received a letter from a priest who was seeking help for those who were suffering from Hansen's disease in the Hawaiian Islands. She was one of fifty religious superiors to receive the priest's request, and the only one to answer it. Having tended the sick in hospitals in Syracuse and Utica, Marianne had grown in holy confidence. "I am not afraid of any disease," she declared, "hence, it would be my greatest delight even to minister to the abandoned 'lepers.'"

Marianne and six sisters made for Honolulu, where they were given care of a receiving station for the lepers. The patients were sleeping on straw mattresses; the rooms were rife with lice and bedbugs. But the sisters did not fear to come close to the patients, to bathe them, to change their bedsheets. Soon, the hospital was a different place.

Then the patients were forced by the government to move to a colony on Molokai. Father Damien, who had been serving the lepers there, was now on his deathbed. Marianne came to his side and promised to continue the work. Her sisters shivered as they saw Damien dying, but Marianne reassured them. To this day, not one of the Franciscan sisters who have served on Molokai has contracted the disease.

– Lisa Lickona

"*[I was] ill and you cared for me*" (Mt 25:36). Occasions for visiting the sick can be endless inasmuch as illness displays so many variations. The debilities of old age, the sorrows of cancer and disease, of mental and emotional trials—the occasions are plentiful if only we have the heart for great love. And who has not an opportunity often in a friend or family member?

Yet the personal challenge in this corporal work of mercy requires a concentrated spiritual effort. Saint Augustine described it in this way. One must become as if sick oneself in drawing close to the sick, not as though having the same affliction, but by considering with sympathy how one would desire to be treated if sick oneself. This capacity to identify ourselves with the sick person's suffering is not to experience an identical pain. But it does entail drawing near to a primary need of the sick person.

The very sick person often suffers the depressing worry of being a burden to others. To encourage them, to shine hope on a possible recovery, to show our enjoyment of being in their company—these are true acts of mercy. The sick need to know from our own love for them that they have lost nothing of their essential attractiveness.

"Do not be ashamed of the flesh of your brother," Pope Francis has said. "In the end, we will be judged on our ability to draw close to 'all flesh.'" The words suggest, among other things, a need to overcome a repugnance that can rise up from contact with grave illness. For a deeper truth is always available. The wounded flesh of the sick person hides another presence. "When you attend to the wounds and bruises of the poor, never forget they are Christ's wounds"

(Mother Teresa). Jesus has chosen to unite himself with the person in his illness, just as he unites himself to all the sufferings and distress of the poor. And every gravely ill person, even someone we have known for long years, is always now a poor person. Our reverence for that same person, encountered in a different manner, must acknowledge this hidden presence of our Lord.

There are quiet signs of this at times. I recall a woman I knew in Harlem who in old age finished her life in a Catholic hospital for terminally ill cancer patients. She was not there long. But during that time this woman, who had often been agitated when I visited her Harlem apartment, could speak now only of gratitude to God for all the goodness he had showered on her life and also of her love for me. I had not heard either comment previously. It was her way perhaps of leaving behind a very fine blessing.

– Father Donald Haggerty

GOD SLEEPS IN RWANDA is a documentary featuring five Tutsi women who survived the Hutu massacre of 1994.

One, Severa Mukakinia, watched the Hutus butcher all seven of her children. She'd been gang-raped so many times she'd lost count. She'd been left for dead, dumped in a local river.

But she didn't die. She lived to discover that she was pregnant from one of the genocidal rapes.

Many people counseled her to have an abortion. She had access to abortion.

But this woman who'd been unspeakably violated in so many ways retained the will to give, to serve. She retained the fierce inner strength to resist the terrible temptation to return violence with violence.

After much thought and much prayer, she came to a conclusion: The child is innocent. Why should the child suffer for the crime of its father?

She decided to give birth to the child.

While violence, in all its forms, continued to rage, she had the baby. That's the backwards "triumph" of Christ who, when he said, *"The last shall be first, and the first shall be last,"* must surely have been thinking of people like Severa Mukakinia. Let us pray that we have always among us a single small human being, looking neither to the left nor the right, with the heart to act out of love.

She named her baby daughter Akimana: Child of God.

– Heather King

IF THERE WAS HOPE FOR SAUL, there is hope for all. That is a large measure of the message Paul sees in his conversion. Saints like to call themselves the greatest of all sinners. Paul's claim on the title is unusually strong, however. He was, in fact, *once a blasphemer and a persecutor and an arrogant man* (1 Tm 1:13). Yet Paul also explains that he received mercy because he acted *ignorantly in unbelief*. This is quite remarkable.

Paul's unbelief was in a real way his gravest sin, the foundation of all the others. Paul studied the Scriptures and awaited the Messiah. As a Pharisee he even believed in the resurrection of the dead. Yet, somehow his heart was closed to Christ the Lord.

The ignorance of unbelief, however, is a darkness God alone can illumine. And the Lord spread his merciful light when he blinded Paul with his radiant and living presence. Jesus' mercy to Paul, in other words, came as the ultimate personal encounter. Paul's knowledge of the Christ was no longer a matter of mere human learning—in the end more ignorance than knowledge. Mercy came as the voice and vision of the one risen from the dead.

– Father Anthony Giambrone, O.P.

My Lord, I believe, and know, and feel, that you are the Supreme Good. And, in saying so, I mean, not only supreme Goodness and Benevolence, but that you are the sovereign and transcendent Beautifulness. I believe that, beautiful as is your creation, it is mere dust and ashes, and of no account, compared with you, who are the infinitely more beautiful Creator. I know well that therefore it is that the angels and saints have such perfect bliss, because they see you. To see even the glimpse of your true glory, even in this world throws holy men into an ecstasy. And I feel the truth of all this, in my own degree, because you have mercifully taken our nature upon you, and have come to me as man. The more, O my dear Lord, I meditate on your words, works, actions, and sufferings in the Gospel, the more wonderfully glorious and beautiful I see you to be.

And therefore, O my dear Lord, since I perceive you to be so beautiful, I love you, and desire to love you more and more. Since you are the One Goodness, Beautifulness, Gloriousness, in the whole world of being, and there is nothing like you, but you are infinitely more glorious and good than even the most beautiful of creatures, therefore I love you with a singular love, a one, only, sovereign love.

– Blessed John Henry Newman

Today's Worship (Lk 4:14-21)

Today is the day
the Lord has come.
He enters our service
becomes our worship
remains with us.
He stands and reads,
reveals his call
unrolls his self
breathes our ancient hope,
winnowing our souls
with revolution
captives freed
oppression lifted
blindness healed!
We finally see
what we have heard.
We've finally heard
what we have read.
The scroll is rolled.
It is finished.
The Lord sits down
and bows his head.

– Rita A. Simmonds

[*I*SAIAH] ASSURED ISRAEL…: *Behold the hand of the Lord is not shortened that it cannot save: neither is his ear heavy that it cannot hear. But your iniquities have divided between you and your God: and your sins have hid his face from you that he should not hear* (Is 59:1-2*).

This does not mean that God does not want to hear us, but that sometimes he wishes us to wait before our prayer is heard: *The Lord waits that he may have mercy on you, and therefore shall be exalted sparing you: because the Lord is the God of judgment. Blessed are all they that wait for him* (Is 30:18).

Indeed, we must learn to await God's mercy as he had waited for our conversion. A time to quiet down is needed after the tumult and chaos caused by sin in our soul, and God provides this time to the sinner when he wishes him to await his mercy.

The sinner should not, then, become impatient or discouraged or, still worse, complain and give in to doubts about the divine mercy, but he should remember the God-inspired words of Isaiah: *If you return and be quiet, you shall be saved. In silence and in hope shall your strength be* (Is 30:15).

– Servant of God Father Hyacinth Woroniecki, O.P.

---

* All quotations are from the Douay–Rheims Bible.

Saint Francis de Sales

FRANCIS DE SALES († 1622) was the bishop of Geneva, Switzerland, when Calvinism, with its grim view of salvation, had drawn many away from the Church. With gentle persistence, Francis preached, ministered, and witnessed to his scattered flock. He wrote the *Introduction to the Devout Life* and a *Treatise on the Love of God*.

Many lay people who read Francis' writings came to see, for the first time, that holiness was accessible to them. Devotion, Francis taught, was for every person, in any state of life. "Do as little children do," Francis told them, "who with one hand cling to their father, and with the other gather blackberries along the hedges." And what should we do when we have let go of our father's hand and fallen down? "Lift your heart up gently whenever it falls," Francis counseled. "Humble yourself before God, but do not be astonished by your fall since it is not surprising that weakness is weak, frailty is frail, and misery is miserable."

But Francis never dwelt on failure. A woman who was a notorious prostitute came to confess to him. After receiving absolution, she collapsed in the confessional, struck with horror at what she had done. Francis rose, came to her, and asked her to stand. Then the bishop himself knelt down. In awe, he told her that he was on his knees before her in this way because he was now in the presence of a soul without sin.

– Lisa Lickona

"*[I was] in prison and you visited me*" (Mt 25:36). A prison may be the last place people expect a sacred encounter. Understandably so. The high prison walls posted by guards, the thick cordons of barbed wire, the sealed electrical gates—none of this is for show. The inside of high security prisons surely encloses a level of depravity that is best left unstated.

Yet that is not the entire reality. No sin, as we know, and no accumulation of evil is beyond the pale of God's grace and forgiveness. Indeed, ask a Catholic prison chaplain and he is likely to affirm that the sacramental confession of a Catholic inmate never fails to renew his love for the priesthood in a profound way. Where there is desperation and a setting of evil, there is bound to be much hidden working of grace. It might be said that God himself does not forget to live this corporal work of mercy, using his own instruments as means of grace.

In the summer of 1987, Mother Teresa paid a visit to San Quentin's death row section, a visit described afterward by one man awaiting execution. The inmates in this section known as "the shelf" were gathered together where Mother Teresa greeted them individually and gave each one a Miraculous Medal of Mary.

The inmate recounted that at one moment she turned to a nearby sergeant and said for all to hear: "What you do to these men, you do to God." The sergeant, said the inmate, was affected for "a whole day and a half." Cynicism may have clouded the inmate's perception, or maybe the words of Mother Teresa did in fact deliver only a passing shock.

And yet it is Jesus himself who includes in Matthew 25 the example of imprisonment in his identification with suffering humanity. There is no mention that this truth is confined to innocent or repentant prisoners. Jesus unites himself with suffering in whatever form it takes, though not with any evil present in a human person. And certainly he is in search of souls.

We ourselves may be unable to enter into prisons, but even if we cannot fulfill this corporal work of mercy in a concrete manner, we still should make a serious effort to live it. This can be done by intentions in our prayer. Those in prison have usually sinned much, and they need much prayer. In many cases the salvation of their souls is in a precarious state of uncertainty. They are also often quite forgotten. Cut off from our attention, they may receive little prayer from us. They are the poorest of the poor in that sense. Perhaps we may find one day that this work of intercession was one of our most important works.

– Father Donald Haggerty

"On what compulsion must I? Tell me that"
(The Merchant of Venice, *William Shakespeare*).

THE SCENE IS A COURT in Shakespeare's Venice, or rather any place at all, where what is called the "real" world, a world of inflexible law and compulsions, encounters the truth about human frailty, sin, and the mercy of God. Shylock the Jew is demanding his pound of flesh, to be carved from the body of his enemy Antonio. They had sealed a loan of three thousand ducats by bond, and by the terms so nominated Antonio is "a forfeit of the law," having not repaid it within the due time. Shylock is eager to exact the penalty.

More than Antonio's life is at stake. Shylock's life is at stake too, though he does not know it. He believes he is entirely justified by the civil law and the law of God, but he has unwittingly violated both. His immortal soul hangs in the balance. So the good Portia, in disguise as a lawyer, advises him. "The quality of mercy is not strained," she says. Mercy knows nothing of compulsion:

> Therefore, Jew,
> Though justice be thy plea, consider this:
> That in the course of justice, none of us
> Should see salvation. We do pray for mercy,
> And that same prayer doth teach us all to render
> The deeds of mercy.

Even to enemies? Especially to enemies.

– Anthony Esolen

JESUS TELLS OF A DEBTOR whose large debt is forgiven by the king, but who refuses to forgive someone who owes him so much less (Mt 18:21-35).

A longtime friend yelled at me because I had said something that touched a nerve and set him off. His reaction was over the top and unjustifiable.

The next day I expected a phone call of apology. Would I yell back? Would I offer a half-hearted forgiveness, the thin appearance of mercy wrapped around a chewy center of accusation? Would I feed on some juicy resentment?

There is a sick sweetness in hanging onto hurt; a feeling of superiority when you are owed an apology; a sense of power in thinking you can hold someone hostage to their sin; and it is all an empty lie!

How many times had I yelled or snapped or hurt people simply because they caught me at the wrong time in the wrong mood. Were I held bound to these sins, there is no way I could ever pay the debt.

I picked up the phone, called my friend, and said to him, "About last night, it was not a big deal." He thanked me and we spoke briefly.

After we hung up, I realized I had just thrown away my superiority, my power, my "right" to resentment.

And I walked out of prison, a free man!

I hope such a short sentence will become the rule in my life, rather than the exception.

– Father Richard Veras

To you, O God, Fountain of Mercy, I come, a sinner. May you wash away my impurity.

O Sun of Justice, give sight to the blind.
O Eternal Healer, cure the wounded.
O King of Kings, restore the despoiled.
O Mediator of God and man, reconcile the sinful.
O Good Shepherd, lead back the straying.

O God, have pity on the wretched, show leniency to the guilty, bestow life on the dead, reform the impious, and give the balm of grace to the hard of heart.

O most merciful God, call back the one who flees, draw back the one who resists, lift up the one who falls, support the one who stands, and accompany the one who walks.

Do not forget those who forget you.
Do not desert those who desert you.
Do not despise those who sin against you.

For in sinning, I have offended you, my God;
I have harmed my neighbor;
I have not even spared myself injury.

I abandoned you, Lord. I questioned your goodness by yielding to evil cravings and weakening myself with harmful fears. By such things, I preferred to lose you rather than abandon what I desired, to offend you rather than face what ought not to be feared.

Out of my weakness I beg you to pay heed not to my iniquity, but rather to your immense goodness. And I beg you mercifully to pardon what I have done, granting me sorrow for my past actions and precaution in the future.

– Saint Thomas Aquinas

Jesus the Nazarene (Lk 4:21-30)

We know him.
We know his family.
He is a member of our synagogue.
He lives down the street.
But we don't know him fully.
We don't know the half of him.
We have loved him,
but suddenly he incites us to rage.
He should have known better
than to say such things!
The one that we loved
we have driven from our sight.
He was one of us,
but he has crossed
the line—

the line
we all must cross.

We beg him
to come back to us.

– Rita A. Simmonds

LL SINS AGAINST HOPE, even if they do not reach the stage of open despair of salvation, strike at divine mercy. Herein lies their malice….

When a soul cannot satisfy its self-love, it yields to despondency and sadness. Slowly it becomes blind to the beauty of divine things. It forgets its supernatural destiny and the divine mercy which surrounds it on all sides. All those divine truths have become for it phrases devoid of all meaning. Any time it comes in contact with the things of God, it is seized with a sort of deep boredom or even bitterness. It begins to seek amusements in an attempt to stifle that boredom, and thus it withdraws from God more and more. These are the characteristic marks of the capital sin of laziness in the service of God in the soul of one entirely possessed by it.

How diligently we should watch *lest any root of bitterness springing up do hinder* (Heb 12:15*) the growth of hope which, like any living thing, should constantly develop and progress. As it has its foundation in faith, hope should be continually nourished with all that God revealed to us about his mercy, for it will find no other nourishment. Then, this life, burdensome and toilsome as it is, will give us a foretaste of heaven where we shall sing the mercy of the Lord forever.

– Servant of God Father Hyacinth Woroniecki, O.P.

---

* All quotations are from the Douay–Rheims Bible.

Saint Angela Merici

THE FAITH WAS COMMUNICATED early to Angela († 1540) through the tender love of her mother and father. She felt called to make a return, love for love. By her twenties, with her parents gone, she began to care for those in need as a lay Franciscan.

Moved by a vision, Angela went to Brescia, where brutal wars had left a wide gap between rich and poor. The desperate young women of the lower classes moved her heart. Angela wanted to shelter them, to teach them, to open their hearts to Christ. Her idea was to start a new way of life—a "company" of women. These women lived at home with their families and yet were consecrated to Christ. They pledged themselves to follow a superior and yet moved freely about the city, drawing in the most vulnerable girls. The women who followed Angela were on the front lines, right where the girls they were helping were.

In her last testament, Angela bade the women of her company to "live always on your living hope. How many are there among the rich, queens, noble ladies, who are unable to find peace amidst their superabundance and splendor…while the poor who give alms live abundantly in consolation and courage." Consolation and courage: this was the legacy of virginal love bequeathed by Angela to her daughters, the Ursulines.

– Lisa Lickona

Usually we bury only the dead who are connected to us by family or friendship or in the workplace. It is not common to attend the funeral of a complete stranger. Yet at unusual times the magnitude of this corporal work of mercy may strike us differently.

After the terrible earthquake in Haiti in 2010, when more than 200,000 people died within minutes from the collapsing buildings of Port-au-Prince, a new meaning penetrated this corporal work of mercy. Rubble and dust now filled a city punctuated by screams of terror. The desperate effort put forth to save the injured turned, by the third day, to another task: the need to bury the dead in that tropical climate.

For two long weeks this became the sacred task of survivors. Truckloads of the dead pulled out of crumbled concrete were loaded and taken to the nearby beaches. The burials were not unceremonious. On the contrary, ritual and respect remained honored and valuable in this Catholic country. The dead were placed in common graves dug in the sand, but always there were priests, taking shifts, to administer closing prayers. Holy water flowed abundantly as the waves churned nearby on the beaches. Most of the onlookers bowed in prayer were the volunteer workers who had helped to collect the bodies and place them in the graves. Now they joined in prayer, surgical masks still covering their faces, before returning to the city to continue the work.

The images are not our ordinary experience of a funeral service. Yet they remind us that a reverence for life requires as well a great respect for the conclusion of a human life. These demands and duties of love must include the poor in their lives and in their deaths.

In considering this corporal work of mercy, we harken back to Jesus' Passion and his own death on the cross. We are told that Joseph of Arimathea and Nicodemus wrapped Jesus in his burial shroud. What loving care must have been present in removing the nails from his hands and feet and in washing his blood-soaked body.

We should have an equal love for the bodies of the poor, living and dead. "Never forget that the poor man is our Lord himself," wrote Saint Jeanne Jugan, whose sisters sometimes bury the dead as part of their vocation. "Have great respect for the poor, always see God in them." The real mystery of love hidden in every corporal work of mercy is bound to this truth. We are brought into immediacy with the body of Christ. Every corporal work of mercy is in effect to touch the body of Christ in his Passion. Let us always honor this truth with a sacred conviction of faith.

– Father Donald Haggerty

FATHER ALFRED DELP (1907–1945), a German convert and a priest, fell into the hands of the Nazis during World War II. His crime, as he observed, consisted simply in being a Jesuit.

He was relegated to a solitary cell with both hands shackled. While awaiting trial, he somehow managed to work one hand free and to write, among other things, a stunning series of Advent meditations.

One incident speaks volumes about his humility and his capacity for mercy. The Nazis were beating him and calling him "Liar!" because he wouldn't give up the names of his friends. He wrote, "I prayed hard, asking God why he permitted me to be so brutally handled, and then I saw that there was in my nature a tendency to pretend and deceive."

Sentenced to death, awaiting execution, Father Delp didn't waste his time hating. He hoped, he wrestled with his conscience, he asked forgiveness, he apologized to all those to whom he had been unkind, unfair, and prideful. He wrote, "I will honestly and patiently await God's will. I will trust him till they come to fetch me. I will do my best to ensure that this blessing, too, shall not find me broken and in despair."

Father Delp was executed by hanging on February 2, 1945. The Nazis scattered his ashes over a manure field.

– Heather King

Mᴙ ꜰᴀᴛʜᴇʀ ʜᴀᴅ ꜱᴡᴏʀɴ that he would never reconcile with me, not even on his deathbed. Then when, at the
end of his life, he asked my mother to call everyone and
she asked "Everyone?" he did not answer. So she called
me. My father acknowledged me as his son, and we had a
calm chat before he passed. The fact is that in the extreme
moments of life very often the truest things come out. We
see this in our Lord.

In that extreme moment of racking pain, when the
tortures visited upon his person were ripping the life from
his unrecognizable body, out of the fog of that hellish torment, Jesus manages to speak: *"Father, forgive them, they
know not what they do"* (Lk 23:34). The unspeakable pres-
sure and pain engendered by the circumstances did not
darken his soul, but allowed us a last earthly glimpse of his
self, his identity, his mission. He pleads to the Father that
his mercy reach even those who are not aware of needing
to ask for it, those who have laid their hands upon him.

This is the core of his mission, and ours—we who
share his life: to offer our lives, especially our sufferings,
so that his mercy may reach all of us. This is what I saw in
my own father, whose last earthly act toward me was one
of reconciliation and mercy.

– Father Vincent Nagle, ꜰ.ꜱ.ᴄ.ʙ.

Everything, O my Lord, shall be dull and dim to me, after looking at you. There is nothing on earth, not even what is most naturally dear to me, that I can love in comparison of you. And I would lose everything whatever rather than lose you. For you, O my Lord, are my supreme and only Lord and love.

My God, you know infinitely better than I how little I love you. I should not love you at all, except for your grace. It is your grace which has opened the eyes of my mind, and enabled them to see your glory. It is your grace which has touched my heart, and brought upon it the influence of what is so wonderfully beautiful and fair.

How can I help loving you, O my Lord, except by some dreadful perversion which hinders me from looking at you? O my God, whatever is nearer to me than you, things of this earth, and things more naturally pleasing to me, will be sure to interrupt the sight of you, unless your grace interfere. Keep you my eyes, my ears, my heart, from any such miserable tyranny. Break my bonds—raise my heart. Keep my whole being fixed on you. Let me never lose sight of you; and, while I gaze on you, let my love of you grow more and more every day.

– Blessed John Henry Newman

Hungry for Mercy (1 Cor 15:10)

There is hysteria
behind my eyes
pressuring me
for release—
I refuse.
There is a mustard seed
of truth
in my heart.
I keep it enclosed
but I cannot stop
its growth.
People walk by.
Some are quick
to read my face.
I will speak
no other way.
The streets of my days
are lined with food
I cannot eat.
My hunger strikes God's mercy.
It is my greatest strength.

– Rita A. Simmonds

*T*HE SUPERIORITY OF MERCY over justice manifests itself in relation to rational beings, that is, to man. The reason for this is that man may address God not only as his Maker and Lord but also as his Father and friend. This is the very source of that infinite mercy we shall never cease to praise....

It was not required by divine justice that intelligent beings...be elevated to the supernatural state; that God should open to them the mystery of his intimate life, and should invite them to share therein as his adopted children. God could create man with the fullness of natural faculties and set up for him as his ultimate goal the acquisition of a state of natural happiness after his death.

If we consider the creation of the world and of man as an act of divine mercy in the broad sense, how much more can be said about the elevation of the human race to the dignity of children of God, about allowing them to partake of the very nature of God and of the eternal happiness enjoyed by the Blessed Trinity in its interior life. Here the preponderance of mercy over justice is striking. Divine justice gave man all that was necessary to attain the goal set up in his nature; divine mercy went much further and infinitely surpassed all desires of happiness that have ever entered into the heart of man (1 Cor 2:9).

– Servant of God Father Hyacinth Woroniecki, O.P.

Saint Josephine Bakhita

JOSEPHINE († 1947) WAS TEN when slave traders abducted her from her family farm in Sudan. The terrified girl forgot her name, so they called her Bakhita, "Fortunate One." She had a succession of owners, all cruel. One had Bakhita covered with tattoos. Designs were cut into her flesh, and salt was rubbed into the wounds. She thought she would die from the pain.

In 1882, an Italian purchased Bakhita, brought her to Italy, and gave her to his colleague, Augusto Michieli—a kind master, at last. While accompanying Michieli's daughters to the school run by the Canossian Sisters, Bakhita came to know the source of this kindness. "I am definitively loved and, whatever happens to me, I am awaited by this Love," she later wrote. "And so my life is good." In 1890, she was baptized as Josephine Margaret. Then Michieli's wife wanted to take her along on a trip back to Africa. Josephine refused. Instead, she won her status as a free woman, and, in freedom, she vowed herself to Christ.

For fifty years, Josephine tended the door at the Canossian convent. Her warm smile touched everyone. "If I were to meet the slave traders who kidnapped me and even those who tortured me," she once said, "I would kneel and kiss their hands, for if that did not happen, I would not be a Christian and a religious today."

– Lisa Lickona

THE FIRST IN TRADITIONAL LISTS of the spiritual works of mercy is the duty to admonish the sinner. It is not a coincidence that there are seven. That is part of a design evident even in the physical realm. What is sometimes called a "Unified Theory of the Universe" or a "General Theory of Everything" is the "Holy Grail" of physics. It is the long-hoped-for formula that would explain the behavior of all matter and how all the particular formulas for matter fit together in a design. One prominent physicist said that he did not know if it existed or would ever be found, but he speculated that if such a were discovered, its most astonishing quality would be its utter simplicity.

While not confusing physics with the moral explanation of reality, we do know that all things came into being by the will of God, and that there is a neat symmetry in all that God has set in motion for our moral well being. The obligation to admonish the sinner is for restoring a disordered soul to the harmony of God's design for it. This admonishment is merciful, for it offers eternal happiness: *"…there will be more joy in heaven over one sinner who repents than over ninety-nine righteous people who have no need of repentance"* (Lk 15:7). Those who are ordained do not weakly "deliver a homily." They lovingly preach the Good News to save souls from sin and to lead them to virtue. *How can they believe in him of whom they have not heard? And how can they hear without someone to preach?* (Rom 10:14). That is also an obligation of all Christians, for while there are those ordained to admonish, all the baptized help others examine their own consciences, by word and example.

Admonishment is not accusation. Our Lord did not accuse the adulterous woman, but his merciful look and consoling voice were a sufficient command for her correction. Jesus was bound and gagged when Peter denied knowing him, unable to move or speak, but his mere glance was more powerful than a soldier's lance, piercing Peter's soul so that he wept. What sometimes is called "tough love" is tough precisely because it is loving. When I was in the fifth grade, the school roof burst into flame. A classmate panicked, and was about to run into the smoke, but our teacher brought him to a better frame of mind by slapping him. Our Lord saves us from the fires of hell, not with a slap, but by touching with a hand that has a nail hole in it. *But he was pierced for our offenses,/ crushed for our sins,/ Upon him was the chastisement that makes us whole,/ by his stripes we were healed* (Is 53:5).

– Father George William Rutler

*N*EVER *G*IVE *U*P is not a book that I ever intended to write, but somehow it came into being in the midst of my most difficult professional and personal trials.

When my health collapsed in 2007–2008 and I had to retire from my beloved classroom work, I was devastated. I still hoped to do some writing but had no particular plans, as my whole life was spinning. I did have a folder of poems I had been working on, which I circulated among some friends until one of them recommended them to a publisher.

The publisher said they were interested in a book drawing on the Christian understanding of suffering that had inspired the poems. Though struggling with new setbacks in my health, I proposed the subject of human suffering and God's mercy. But when friends challenged me to write directly from my own experience, I changed my original plan and decided to write a very personal book. In particular, I saw the need to be open about my struggle with depression as well as my physical ailments.

This openness has been a great help to many people. The Lord used me as an instrument of his mercy during a time when I was exhausted, confused, and feeling myself a failure. He used my weakness and strengthened my confidence in his loving plan for me.

– John Janaro

WHAT WAS JESUS WRITING ON the ground (Jn 8:6)? There is, of course, no way to know. It is interesting, however, that whatever he writes, the Lord literally *engraves it with his finger*. After the mention in the preceding verse of the Law given to Moses, one recalls that God had engraved that Law with his finger on tablets of stone. Here, then, it as though Jesus were re-writing the Law upon the dust from which we were made. He overrules our hearts of stone, not with a letter that kills, but with a new Law of life.

Also interesting is that Jesus twice *bends down* to write. He stands tall when he says, let the sinless one cast the first stone: a lofty word condemning all who hear. It is this gesture of bending that best reveals Christ's forgiveness, however. Rather than stooping to pick up a stone—the stone he alone could cast—Jesus bends to address us mysteriously from the earth. The Word lowers himself to speak from within our mortal clay. Rather than standing aloft in his sinless divinity, Jesus touches our filth. He stoops not to condemn, but to address his word of mercy to our lowliness.

– Father Anthony Giambrone, o.p.

The Stations of the Cross

❨ *First Station: Jesus Is Condemned to Death*

Bear patiently those who do us ill: You accept injustice so that mercy can set me free.

❨ *Second Station: Jesus Takes Up His Cross*

Admonish sinners: Your acceptance of your cross moves me to reflect, convert, believe.

❨ *Third Station: Jesus Falls the First Time*

Counsel the doubtful: Your fall amends my doubt that humility is key to loving God.

❨ *Fourth Station: Jesus Meets His Mother*

Comfort the afflicted: When Mercy meets the Sorrowful Mother joy begins to be reborn.

❨ *Fifth Station: Simon Helps Carry the Cross*

Feed the hungry: In the heft of your cross Simon discovers that he hungers for you.

❨ *Sixth Station: Jesus Meets Veronica*

Give drink to the thirsty: You slake the thirst of one who helps you with the gift of your face.

❨ *Seventh Station: Jesus Falls a Second Time*

Instruct the ignorant: You model that wisdom comes from accepting what befalls us.

❨ *Eighth Station: Jesus Comforts the Women*

Welcome the stranger: Even in your Passion you are shelter for the afflicted and homeless.

❨ *Ninth Station: Jesus Falls a Third Time*

Visit the imprisoned: Your fall bespeaks your desire to reach those held captive, the ensnared.

◖ *Tenth Station: Jesus Is Stripped of His Garments*
Clothe the naked: The indignity you endure is the promise of my dignity to be restored.

◖ *Eleventh Station: Jesus Is Nailed to the Cross*
Heal the sick: These wounds are windows revealing the redemptive meaning of suffering.

◖ *Twelfth Station: Jesus Dies on the Cross*
Forgive offenses: No inflicted savagery can silence your undying desire—for our forgiveness.

◖ *Thirteenth Station: Jesus' Body Is Taken Down*
Pray for the living and the dead: Your mission of mercy proclaims life is changed not ended.

◖ *Fourteenth Station: Jesus Is Laid in the Tomb*
Bury the dead: Burial is an act of confiding—of looking to the future with hope.

– Father Peter John Cameron, O.P.

"Go before me with your grace;
follow me with your mercy.
Take from me whatever is not from you,
for I hate whatever is from me;
and still I hope in you."

– SAINT ANSELM

Temptation Is a Circus Act (Lk 4:1-13)

The devil
is a ringmaster
in topcoat and tails
inciting illusions
and dangerous feats:
"Turn bricks to bread,
plunge from a ledge
tumble and roll at my feet!"

Though we do it for show,
for the sake of applause
in the space of a tent
that will fold and move on,
Our Master is not our defeat.

– Rita A. Simmonds

*T*HIS IS THE OPPORTUNE MOMENT to change our lives! This is the time to allow our hearts to be touched! When faced with evil deeds, even in the face of serious crimes, it is the time to listen to the cry of innocent people who are deprived of their property, their dignity, their feelings, and even their very lives. To stick to the way of evil will only leave one deluded and sad. True life is something entirely different. God never tires of reaching out to us. He is always ready to listen…. All one needs to do is to accept the invitation to conversion and submit oneself to justice during this special time of mercy offered by the Church.

It would not be out of place…to recall the relationship between justice and mercy. These are not two contradictory realities, but two dimensions of a single reality that unfolds progressively until it culminates in the fullness of love….

Mercy is not opposed to justice but rather expresses God's way of reaching out to the sinner, offering him a new chance to look at himself, convert, and believe…. God does not deny justice. He rather envelops it and surpasses it with an even greater event in which we experience love as the foundation of true justice…. God's justice is his mercy given to everyone as a grace that flows from the Death and Resurrection of Jesus Christ.

– *Misericordiae Vultus* 19-21

Saint Claudine Thévenet

CLAUDINE'S († 1837) two brothers were captured as they fought for Lyons during the Reign of Terror. Before the young men were led away to their deaths, Claudine managed to get close to Louis. "Look, Glady," he said, addressing her by her nickname, "forgive, as we forgive." In a letter that was slipped to a servant the young men wrote: "We will be happier than you. In four or five hours, we will be before God…. We hope completely in his mercy."

The intensity of this shock brought on headaches that would trouble Claudine for the rest of her life. But her brothers' words of forgiveness freed her to act. Soon, she was working in her parish, serving those who were suffering the wounds of the Revolution. In 1815 she and a friend received two homeless waifs into the House of Providence, the beginnings of the Congregation of the Religious of Jesus and Mary.

At the end of her life, Claudine gently defended the charism of the order against a priest who was trying to assert control. This priest came to Claudine as she lay on her deathbed and denounced her in front of her sisters. Claudine admitted how much this hurt her, yet she offered her forgiveness. "Be disposed to suffer everything from others and not to make anyone suffer anything," she had told her young followers.

– Lisa Lickona

THE DUTY TO INSTRUCT THE IGNORANT is a work of mercy because there is something important that can be known and should be known to attain spiritual maturity. Cicero said, "To be ignorant of history is always to remain a child." That kind of ignorance is not the childlike innocence that leads to the Kingdom of heaven. It is the childishness of adults who do not know that there is much they do not know.

To thumb through a dictionary of the lives of saints is a delightful instruction in how many more saints there are than commonly appear on the calendars. When I once feigned surprise that an altar boy had never heard of Saint Frideswide, he said, "I suppose you think I'm pretty stupid." I told him that he was not stupid, just ignorant. He was not assured by that until I explained that stupidity has no cure, but ignorance can be solved simply by being informed. An intelligent wine merchant may be ignorant of the Third Law of Thermodynamics, while a learned physicist may be ignorant of the difference between a Burgundy and a Beaujolais.

Our Lord had something more to teach, of which the human race had previously been ignorant, despite the consolations of wisdom and the hints of prophets. It was the good news about himself, and no one anywhere should be deprived of it: *"Go into the whole world and proclaim the gospel to every creature"* (Mk 16:15).

Pope Francis, announcing his intention to canonize Father Junípero Serra, called him a "Founding Father" of the United States. Father Junípero was indeed a contemporary of those men who established the Republic, but his claim to the title was that, far away in California, he wore himself out instructing thousands of Native Americans in the mysteries of God. The Franciscan alluded to God's will that everyone be saved and come to a knowledge of the truth (1 Tm 2:4). "For that reason," wrote Saint Junípero, "he extends the golden bonds of his goodwill and love to entice us and unite us to himself."

When Christ rose from the dead, he continued to instruct his followers. The glory of Christ the King did not diminish his role as Christ the Teacher. Most of his instruction given during the forty days before his Ascension is not recorded, but we have an intimation of what he said when he mercifully rebuked the two men on the Emmaus road: *Oh, how foolish you are! How slow of heart to believe all that the prophets spoke!*" (Lk 24:25). Later the two men, radiant in such mercy, marveled at how their hearts were burning when he instructed them along the way.

– Father George William Rutler

Lord Angelo (in Shakespeare's *Measure for Measure*) stands before the Duke and the crowds. He's been exposed as a villain, morally guilty of raping a nun, Isabella (a rape he did not in fact accomplish) and of unjustly executing her brother Claudio for fornication. Claudio is alive, saved by the Duke, though nobody knows that yet. Isabella is Angelo's accuser. What to do with him now? The Duke cites the warnings of Jesus. Since Angelo condemned Claudio for the evil which he himself attempted to commit,

> The very mercy of the law cries out
> Most audible, even from his proper tongue,
> "An Angelo for Claudio, death for death!"
> Haste still pays haste, and leisure answers leisure;
> Like doth quit like, and Measure still for Measure.

Only one person pleads for Angelo's life: Mariana, whom he had jilted after her brother and her dowry were lost at sea. She knows he's been a bad man, but she loves him anyway, and she falls to her knees before the Duke. Who can forgive Angelo the death of Claudio? Mariana cries:

> Isabel,
> Sweet Isabel, do yet but kneel by me,
> Hold up your hands, say nothing, I'll speak all...
> O Isabel, will you not lend a knee?

"He dies for Claudio's death," says the Duke, looking straight at Isabel.

Shakespeare has a surprise in store. What would you do, reader?

– Anthony Esolen

In Jesus' surprising parable about the hired laborers (Mt 20:1-16), who would you rather be? The worker hired immediately who spends his whole day working? Or the worker not chosen until five PM, who suffers through hours of uncertainty and doubt wondering how he will support himself or his family?

Those who were given the great grace of being hired first, at the end of the day are grumbling. In their forgetfulness of the mercy they have received, they accuse the very one who has shown them this mercy. They seem to think they have done a favor for him.

I was once teaching a class about the liturgy of the hours, and while explaining how priests and religious are obligated to say morning, daytime, evening, and night prayers, I became uncomfortable, because I didn't want the students to get the impression that we who pray the hours are to be admired as heroes of holiness.

I reminded them, and myself, that these prayers are God's mercy toward us. We are so prone to forget God's mercy in calling us, so God gives us these liturgical prayers as merciful reminders.

We are at our most forgetful when we pat ourselves on the back for all the prayer and work we do for God, not understanding that these are all mercies that God in his goodness is giving to us, his wayward children.

– Father Richard Veras

In the bottomless depths of mercy, pardon, and love of the heart of Jesus, I drown sin, hatred, and godlessness.

Into his redeeming, sanctifying, and divine blood I plunge guilty, ungrateful, and blind souls.

I hide fearful, timid, and untrusting souls in his sacred wounds.

I submerge cold, obdurate, and rebellious hearts in the limitless ocean of his tenderness.

I thrust the entire world into his heart that is burning with love for all.

And finally, into this purifying, peace-giving, and sanctifying furnace, I cast, O my Father in Heaven, all your creatures, that they may be open to regeneration, perfection, and love; all those who have been led astray, who are doubtful, who are unbelieving; all the poor sinners; and I beg you to receive them, to guard them, to transform them, and to consume all of them in your immense love.

Eternally receive, without any interruption, relaxation, weakening, or omission, your Jesus Christ, the Eternal Infinite in whom I ceaselessly melt away under the guidance of the Holy Spirit, and with Mary my Mother, so that all of your plans of love in the Church and in the world may be perfectly accomplished.

– Venerable Marthe Robin

Our Transfiguration (Lk 9:28b-36)

This blinding light
that we read
on the mountain
is our teacher
transfigured
into eternity.
We are afraid
less of him
than of what we have done,
our hearts cracked
wide open
by the presence
of such a One.

Purified
by burning white
elevated above the earth
we promise
to never sleep again
in acceptance
of our sin.

– Rita A. Simmonds

THE SUPERIORITY OF MERCY over justice manifests itself even more in regard to our infidelities, failures, faults, and sins. Even in human relations it is generally accepted to soothe severity and justice with mercy. To surpass the measure in punishment is always considered as unjust, whereas reduction or suspension, or even pardon of the punishment to permit the guilty one to show by his life that he is not entirely corrupt, does not offend our sense of justice provided it is applied with due moderation.

As our Creator, our Lord, and the best of fathers, God avails himself of the right of mercy with the greatest bounty. He extends it to all our faults without exception; he is always ready to forgive and pardon them if we are sorry for them. Moreover, he knocks at the conscience of the sinner in order to call forth sorrow and contrition, the only condition to obtain his mercy. Grace stirs up his soul but does not violate his freedom; he alone remains entirely responsible for his decision. If he should refuse with full awareness to humble himself before God and to acknowledge with contrition and purpose of amendment his guilt, he would close the door on God's mercy. Grace will always be waiting for him. God will not cease to knock at his soul and arouse uneasiness therein.

– Servant of God Father Hyacinth Woroniecki, O.P.

Saint Adelaide of Burgundy

WHEN ADELAIDE WAS BORN IN 931, much of Europe was nominally Christian, yet politics was still carried on through manipulation, abduction, and murder. Adelaide lived all of it. At sixteen, she was married off to a young Italian prince, Lothair, to seal a peace treaty. Three years later she watched Lothair die, presumably poisoned by his political rival. The rival then imprisoned her, insisting that she marry his son. Adelaide escaped, and met and married the German king, Otto. And who is to say whether or not Otto married Adelaide simply to cash in on her immense popularity?

But Adelaide had her friends. First among them were the abbots of Cluny, Majolus and Odilo, and Bishop Adalbert of Magdeburg—all men who had staked everything on the cross, all someday to be revered as saints. Majolus helped Adelaide reunite with her son Otto II when his jealous wife Theophano had poisoned the relationship. A meeting was arranged, and Otto came, begging forgiveness on his knees. Adelaide's motherly heart leapt when she saw him.

Ten years later, Theophano threatened to turn Adelaide's grandson Otto III against her. Adelaide watched and prayed. After Theophano died, Adelaide ruled as regent for her grandson, with her dear friends as advisors. Gracious forgiveness was ever her rule.

– Lisa Lickona

COUNSELING THE DOUBTFUL assists others to follow Jesus as *the way and the truth and the life*. Such merciful counsel protects one from the merciless counsel of well-meaning busybodies who lead along wrong paths. "Counsel" means helping to make a decision. Counsel is needed only when doubt is a problem. That misunderstood word "doubt" comes from *dubium*, which is rooted in the word meaning "double." There are those who go through life unwilling to choose between two alternatives. The paradox dubiously attributed to the 14th-century priest and philosopher Buridan is that of a donkey that starves to death between two baskets of hay because it cannot decide which to eat. The godly will have none of that: *"Decide today whom you will serve…."* (Jos 24:15).

While unresolved doubt is the recipe for anxiety, doubt itself can be a blessing in a confused and confusing world. Had Saint Thomas not doubted the news of the Resurrection, our Lord might not have invited him to touch his wounds, as graphic evidence for us that the apparition was not a chimera or wishful thought. When this same Thomas frankly admitted that he did not know where to follow Jesus, he heard the earth-shattering declaration: *"I am the way and the truth and the life"* (Jn 14:6).

Any proud refusal to accept a truth on the grounds that it is not understood by limited reason is a moral defect, and the doubter can starve like Buridan's donkey. That is where faith comes in: not credulity, but trust in a reliable source. Nothing is more reliable than the voice of Jesus. Thus Saint Thomas Aquinas hymned the "faith that comes through hearing." That voice counseled doubting

Thomas: *"Blessed are those who have not seen and have believed"* (Jn 20:29).

Blessed John Henry Newman distinguished the rejection of sound counsel from those sensible questions we have about God: "A thousand difficulties do not make one doubt." But a decision must be made. Yogi Berra offered his unhelpful advice: "When you come to a fork in the road, take it." Robert Frost had his own counsel:

> Two roads diverged in a wood, and I—
> I took the one less traveled by,
> And that has made all the difference.

The way that is Christ is less traveled by in our world, but walking along it makes all the difference and resolves all doubt. And his name will be called *"Wonderful Counselor...."* (Is 9:5).

– **Father George William Rutler**

QUEEN ORUAL (in *Till We Have Faces*) has for years been penning her complaint against the gods. They gave her a face no man could love. They saddled her with a brutish father. They took away her beloved sister Psyche, leaving her as prey to some "holy" beast of the mountains, or as the consort of a god; Orual cannot tell which, nor even if there's any difference.

She's ruled her nation justly, never appearing before anyone except behind a veil, demanding much from her soldiers and counselors. She has, for the common good, devoured their lives. She hates the smell of holiness: the stench of burning or decaying blood, fat, and flesh. When her sister appeared to her as blessed, the bride of a divine Lover, Orual set about destroying it all, from one part unbelief and nine parts possessiveness and envy.

Now she's dying, and the gods have summoned her, to read her complaint. What she reads, to her surprise, is a drab childish litany of selfishness and petulance. The veil is torn from her eyes, so she can see herself as she has been. "Are you answered?" they say, in justice and mercy.

C. S. Lewis, the author, challenges us too.

"I saw well why the gods do not speak to us openly, nor let us answer. How can they meet us face to face till we have faces?"

– Anthony Esolen

Hᴏᴡ ᴍʏsᴛᴇʀɪᴏᴜs ᴀɴᴅ ᴀᴍᴀᴢɪɴɢ that, of all people, Jesus first reveals his identity as the Messiah to a serial divorcée. The great secret he hides throughout the Gospels, he rushes to spill out to this foreign woman he meets so seemingly by chance. Her life is more than a fivefold failure. She now no longer tries (*"the one you have now is not your husband,"* Jn 4:18). What shame and despair must cripple and plague her! How beyond the reach of mercy she feels: *"How can you dare to speak with me?"* she asks (cf. Jn 4:9).

Jesus indeed knows the depth of her wretchedness. Yes, *"the well is deep"* (cf. Jn 4:11)—the abyss of human suffering and sin. But the well of Living Water reaches deeper. Jesus, who explores the darkest places in our hearts, also plumbs the deepest heart of God. He not only reveals who *she* is, probing her dark secrets. He also reveals himself. As Jacob met Rachel here, disclosed his identity, and betrothed her and watered her flocks, so Jesus unveils himself as greater than Jacob. His Sacred Heart is the true well of God's infinite love, where Christ wills to show himself, wed sinful souls, and water them with his mercy.

– Father Anthony Giambrone, O.P.

Lord, in your highest love and your greatest and sweetest mercy—how they have ever flowed from your eternal Godhead, from heaven to earth—I ask you to preserve our souls in uprightness, our hearts in purity, our lives in true innocence, and all our desires and all our thoughts for our whole life in pure truth.

May your boundless mercy prepare us and may your perfect love draw us so that we live in the truth according to your dearest will. And I ask you, my Lord, by your holy sufferings that you forgive all the evil we have done in thought, word, and deed, and all the carelessness of our lives.

And may the power be given to us to overcome all human evil with ever increasing heartfelt love for you. I desire also that we be given the pure truth by the power of your five holy wounds. May truth be impressed upon us and may we be led by it so that it may live in us and we in it.

– Blessed Margaret Ebner, O.P.

The Fruit of Mercy (Lk 13:1-9)

I am a fruitless fig tree
three years barren
depleting the earth
of its resources,
giving nothing,
not even shade,
in return.

Who will plead the cause
of a fruitless tree?

One who looked like a gardener
came.
He bent to the ground,
wrote words I couldn't read
in the soil
around my feet.
He gave food to my roots
and asked me,

"Has no one condemned you?"

"No one, sir."

"Fig Tree!" he cried,
gazing up at me.

Figs sprouted from my limbs.
He rose and turned to go.
I could not cling,
but I will always carry fruit
for him.

– Rita A. Simmonds

*W*ATER QUENCHES A FLAMING FIRE *and alms resist sins. And God provides for him who shows favor: he remembers him afterwards, and in the time of his fall shall find a sure stay. Son, defraud not the poor of alms, and turn not away the eyes from the poor…. In judging be merciful to the fatherless as a father, and as a husband to their mother. And you shall be as the obedient son to the most High: and he will have mercy on you more than a mother* (Sir 3:33–4:1, 10-11*). Can any more beautiful promises be given us in human language than those in the last sentence?

For the multitude of mercies shown unto us God demands that we show mercy to others. It should be our response to God for what he has given us, and his pledge of such mercies as we wish yet to receive from him. We can lay up treasures of divine mercy for ourselves by practicing mercy to our neighbor no less than by practicing hope and fear of God. The practice of mercy will free us more and more from our faults and punishments.

– Servant of God Father Hyacinth Woroniecki, O.P.

---

* All quotations are from the Douay–Rheims Bible.

Saint Joseph Moscati

JOSEPH CAME FROM a large faith-filled family in Naples, Italy. The time spent in his youth caring for a brother who had suffered a serious head injury confirmed his call to medicine. Joseph advanced rapidly in his studies, excelling both in the laboratory and the examining room. At the age of thirty-one, he was made director of the Hospital of the Incurables.

Many of Joseph's colleagues were certain that science alone was the source of all truth. But Joseph lived his vocation from the depths of prayer. He was faithful to the rosary and Mass. He drew strength from the Blessed Sacrament and his dear Saint Thérèse. He was especially attentive to the poor and would go to great lengths to ensure their treatment.

On one occasion Joseph was visiting a patient and discovered that the medicine he had prescribed had not been ordered. He could see that the family was in dire straits. Joseph began to lecture them about the importance of following "doctor's orders." He then wrote out another prescription and hastily left. Afterward, the family found money stashed under the patient's pillow. Only then did they realize that Joseph had staged the incident to spare them the sting of having to accept his help. When Joseph died in 1927, the poor of Naples mourned him most.

– Lisa Lickona

GOOD CONFESSIONS ARE HONEST, clear, direct, and concise. Devout and regular penitents sometimes succumb to the temptation to do the work of both the priest and the penitent within the confessional. Occasionally regular penitents will confess a particular sin and then provide their own spiritual analysis of the action's sinfulness. At other times devout penitents will confess a sin and then proceed to offer an extended narrative or backstory about nonessential matters surrounding the sin. More often than not, neither of these two approaches is necessary.

While some details are essential to identifying a particular kind of sin, we need only recount those elements that pertain directly to the sins we are confessing. It is the job of the priest to understand and evaluate the nature and gravity of the sins we bring to the confessional. The penitent should trust that the priest will ask for clarification if anything remains unclear. We should always remember that it is Jesus who forgives our sins. The priest serves as the living instrument of Christ's healing (CCC 1465). Thus, we should approach the Sacrament of Reconciliation with an honest simplicity that fully trusts in God's loving mercy.

– **Father Cajetan Cuddy, O.P.**

GOD IN HIS HEALING MERCY often requires patience from us, but we creatures of time want our comfort right away. We would steal his lordship of time. The Father is wise, and knows not only what to give but when to give.

It's a common theme in Shakespeare, providential delay. The scene, in *Cymbeline*, is a jail in Britain. The prisoner is Posthumus Leonatus, "lion-born" after what seems his father's untimely death. He has fought on the British side against their Roman overlords. He believes himself responsible for the murder of his wife Imogen, whom he wrongly suspected of adultery. He is glad now to suffer:

> Most welcome, bondage, for thou art a way,
> I think, to liberty…. My conscience,
>   thou art fettered
> More than my shanks and wrists.
>   You good gods, give me
> The penitent instrument to pick that bolt,
> Then free forever. Is't enough I am sorry?
> So children temporal fathers do appease;
> Gods are more full of mercy.

He falls asleep, praying that the gods will take his life. But Jupiter—a literary figure for God the Father—appears to him in a dream. "Whom best I love I cross," he says, "to make my gift, the more delayed, delighted."

He knows what will bring us the most joy, in the fullness of his time.

– Anthony Esolen

WE WANT LIFE, but through our sins deserve death. Yet God is the God of life, who gave us life and desires that we live in his house with him for ever. But we have made ourselves unfit for his mansions. What to do? The answer is mercy.

But his mercy is a severe one, for we must be purified of our uncleanliness. Otherwise, if not made worthy of the promises of Christ of our own free will, we would not accept living in the Father's kingdom.

Imagine a girl all ready for the prom, with her expensive hairstyle, her dazzling gown, perfect shoes, and matching bag. As she descends the stairs of her house to meet her gorgeous date, her little brother, thinking she looks strange and funny, pours a bucket of water over her, ruining everything. Would she still go to the prom? No. She wouldn't fit in. She'd rather die. And so would we.

The Psalmist of Psalm 51 cries out with us, *Thoroughly wash away my guilt; and from my sin cleanse me!* We beg for this severe mercy, this cleansing, because it is not enough for us to be invited to the heavenly kingdom. We have to be made worthy of it, able to fit in and belong. Otherwise we will bar the door of hell from his entry. We'd rather die.

– **Father Vincent Nagle, F.S.C.B.**

Lord Jesus, I am struck dumb, immobile, inside
   and outside.
My heart is shrouded by this misery;
my eyes, which look upon your holy face,
are stricken, assaulted by the light,
aching red, longing to be shut beneath their lids.

   I have no voice except an inner cry,
a mute, distressed animal whimper
that cannot even summon itself to ask for mercy.
My fingers drift away from my hands,
and the tokens of your love are beyond their reach.

   How do I pray? O Lord, where is the longing of
my prayer?
Jesus, Mercy, hear the struggle of breath;
Jesus, Mercy, hear the scream inside the shaken
   contours of this skull, with brain pierced by
   some fiery blade.

   O God, Love! Hear the endless noise, the pound-
ing, the howling of skin and nerve, muscle and joint:
this cacophony of pain that groans all through the
place where I once felt that I had a body.

   Jesus, Mercy, forgive me.
   Jesus, Love.
   Jesus, I offer.

   In the end there is nothing but the hollowness
that holds a thing called me wanting you.

   I want you, Jesus.

                                        – John Janaro

Fatherhood (Lk 15:1-3, 11-32)

My heart is a distant country.
My fortune is a desert rock
that turns to sand
in my palm.
I grip to hold what I can.
There is no forgiveness
in an hourglass.
How long
before everything is gone?

I cry on the dunes
that have left me dry.
The hour has come
to die or remember
my father's love.

My cry is a scratch
in my throat
yet he has heard me
from a long way off!
Forgiveness
gushes like a stream—
desperate thoughts
no longer breathe.
My heart springs
to the top!
His arms surround me like the sea
yet carry me like a boat.
He is always and everything to me:
my journey and my home.

– Rita A. Simmonds

*S*IN DESTROYS THE PEACE AND JOY of a good conscience, takes away the soul's fervor, and leaves her an object abominable in the eyes of God and his saints.

The grace of justification delivers us from all these miseries. For God, in his infinite mercy, is not content with effacing our sins and restoring us to his favor; he delivers us from the evils sin has brought upon us, and renews the interior man in his former strength and beauty. Thus he heals our wounds, breaks our bonds, moderates the violence of our passions, restores with true liberty the supernatural beauty of the soul, re-establishes us in the peace and joy of a good conscience, reanimates our interior senses, inspires us with ardor for good and a salutary hatred of sin, makes us strong and constant in resisting evil, and thus enriches us with an abundance of good works....

This renewal of the inner man is so powerful, so true, that in baptism it is called regeneration, in penance resurrection; not only because it restores the soul from the death of sin to the life of grace, but because it is an anticipation of the last glorious resurrection.... Only the Holy Spirit...can tell the sweetness, loveliness, and strength with which he has enriched the soul. The beauty...of earth fades into insignificance before the unspeakable beauty of a soul in a state of grace.

– Venerable Louis of Granada

Saint Philip Howard

PHILIP HOWARD, the earl of Arundel (†1595), was one of Queen Elizabeth's favorite courtiers. While at court, he took in the "entertainment" of watching a tortured priest, Edmund Campion, defend his faith against the queen's theologians. Philip could not forget Edmund's testimony; the priest's arguments took root in his soul. Meanwhile, Philip's wife, Anne, who had stayed true to him through his many courtly affairs, entered the Catholic Church. Philip soon joined her. Anne, for her part, forgave her husband with all her heart.

Soon, Elizabeth's purges of Catholics intensified. Philip and Anne attempted to leave England, but the queen's ships intercepted them. Philip was taken to the Tower of London. As a nobleman, he was permitted all kinds of comforts, yet he chose to fast, pray, and do penance for his sins against his wife. Elizabeth would not let Philip see Anne or the son who was born after he was imprisoned. Philip grew more and more sickly, and, in 1595, he died, having spent six years in the Tower.

Not long before, Philip had written to Anne, begging her forgiveness once again and counseling total trust. "I beseech you for the love of God to comfort yourself whatever shall happen, and to be best pleased with that which shall please God best and be his will to send."

– Lisa Lickona

To COMFORT THE SORROWFUL is a spiritual work of mercy because it strengthens the human spirit in its weakest moral moment of sadness, just as the Holy Spirit strengthens the whole Church and all her members. To comfort is to fortify the soul: strengthening the intellect to understand the cause of sorrow and the means of its cure, and strengthening the will in order to keep faith in the face of discouragement. Man is made for happiness, and thus sorrow contradicts humanity. But ever since the first man and woman shed the world's first tears at the sight of enigmatic death and a lost paradise, sorrow has been the consequence of love, albeit love lost. The indifferent feel no sorrow. Saint John Vianney said to a man making a perfunctory confession with no real contrition: "I weep because you do not." In contrast, the hateful rejoice in the sorrow of others and are saddened only when they cannot inflict more sorrow.

The Man of Sorrows was Perfect Love, and in his perfection he was incapable only of indifference and hate. His sorrow was more intense than any the world has ever known. The liturgical "Reproaches" on Good Friday ask: "Is there any sorrow like unto my sorrow...?" So intense was that grief that the night before he was crucified, he sweat blood, a hemorrhage of all the world's agony. In those hours his human nature craved the comfort of friends. Peter and James and John were little comfort, as they were sleeping. *"Could you not watch with me one hour?"*

No sorrow is more revealing and expressive of the bond of love than the sorrow one has for the suffering of another. To comfort someone else strengthens the self as much as the other. This holy economy was visible between Christ on the cross and Mary at the foot of the cross, comforting each other in the world's most horrible scene. Empathy is stronger than sympathy. Jesus gave his Mother to mankind as he was dying so that she might be our paramount comforter in the tragic hours : "Pray for us sinners now and at the hour of our death." Saint Thérèse of Lisieux said, "I assure you that the good Lord is much kinder than you can imagine. He is satisfied with a glance. With a sigh of love." The greatest comfort is to be able to return that glance, as did his Mother. Then hear him say: *"Come to me, all you who labor and are burdened, and I will give you rest"* (Mt 11:28).

– Father George William Rutler

WE ARE AT THE END of Charles Dickens' novel *A Tale of Two Cities*.

Only one person among the prisoners and their keepers knows that an impostor has taken the place of the Marquis Saint-Evrémond. She's a little seamstress who cannot read and who doesn't know why she has been condemned to death. Sydney Carton, the false marquis, was not condemned to death. He visited the marquis in his cell, chloroformed him, dressed him in his own clothing, and had him smuggled out to safety. He's done this not because he wants to die, but because the marquis is a good young man, the beloved husband of a woman whom Carton himself loves, and whom he has vowed to help, even at the cost of his life.

"I think you were sent to me by heaven," says the seamstress, trembling. "Or you to me," says Carton. They hold one another by the hand, and he tells her not to be troubled, because the guillotine will be quick, and they will soon dwell in that land where there is no more pain, no anger, no sin, no tears. They are, as it were, married in the mercy they show to one another, she in admiration of his courage, he in consoling her innocence. Then their numbers are called.

I am the Resurrection and the life, says the Lord.

– Anthony Esolen

"*MASTER, are you going to wash my feet?*" (Jn 13:6). Peter asks Jesus, his voice full of unbearable shame. He couldn't understand it. To raise us out of our guilt, Jesus mercifully puts himself beneath the feet of his disciples. Peter finds it hard to accept: "*You will never wash my feet*" (Jn 13:8).

When I first went to live in the Middle East, one of the first things that I was told by those attempting to give me some cultural tips was never to put my feet up, either on a desk or a chair, in front of another person unless I intended to give grave insult. It is very offensive, since it suggests putting the other beneath oneself.

In his self-debasement, Jesus challenges Peter and us either to hold him in contempt or to accept that nothing less than this apparent degradation of the Son of God could convert us from our life of deadly sin to a life joined to and imitating the Son of God. I need Jesus to lower himself, for by my sin I have lowered myself beneath the dignity of the children of God.

Like Peter, we resist admitting the necessity of this. "Have I come so low?" we ask. But like Peter in front of this exceptional human presence, so full of passion for our fate, may we concede to this strange mercy, and cry, "*not only my feet, but my hands and head as well!*" (Jn 13:9).

– Father Vincent Nagle, F.S.C.B.

Veneration of a Crucifix

Beloved Jesus Crucified,
I offer you my heart.
I am sorry that it is broken.
It is the result, not of a soldier's lance,
  like yours,
but of my neglect of it—
not taking seriously my need for happiness,
  for true happiness.
I ignored my heart by my selfishness,
  my vanity,
  my resistance,
  my "knowing better,"
  my arrogance,
  my fear,
  my doubt,
  my distraction,
  my egoism,
  my presumption,
  my fascination with the ephemeral—
    pleasures that could never satisfy.
I let myself be infatuated with lesser things,
  compromises,
  false hopes,
  fantasies,
  my willful ideas,
  whims and imaginary worlds of my own making.
It broke when I broke from you and went astray.
And I am sorry.
I need to come back again.
Your outstretched arms are so much like
      the widespread welcome

of the forgiving father open to the repentant
  prodigal son.
I come before your crucifix just like him:
  starving,
  poor in my foolishness,
  laughable in my shame,
  a beggar,
  repugnant by every measure
    except yours.
Without your crucifix, where would I turn in
    my misery,
  so abject, the prey of despair?
Bereft, beaten down, lacerated by my self-seeking,
  I dare approach your ravaged image on the cross
    because
    it reminds me of me.
But you are sinless.
Your self-offering takes away my sin.
As I gaze upon you crucified
  may I see the love that moved you to sacrifice
    everything for me.
For my heart is made for you alone.
Your hands and your feet are held fast by nails
  to teach me how much I need pain and suffering
    in my life
  to be purified, set free, and saved from myself.
Your side—pierced, opened, and exposing your
    Sacred Heart—
  calls to me as the place where I am to dwell.
The gift of your cross separates me
  from everything that separates me from you.
O, let my heart be converted by looking upon you
  whom my sins have pierced.

– Father Peter John Cameron, O.P.

When Misery Meets Mercy (Jn 8:1-11)

"Let the one without sin
cast the first stone."

One by one
the men poised to throw
abandon their threats
drop their weapons
and go.

There is only one left:
"the one without sin"
the one with the right
to stone her to death.
He could crush her bowed head
and leave her to bleed
or condemn her to die
by Moses' decree.
He could plead righteousness,
let justice win!
She has sinned against God!
She has sinned against HIM!

Why doesn't he kill her
or condemn her to death?
He takes her transgressions
and lets her go free.
She will see them again
when he hangs on a tree.

– Rita A. Simmonds

[*H* OPE] ASSURES US THAT…divine mercy would not abandon us, but would come out to meet us and restore us to the dignity of a child of God, provided we offered no resistance to his mercy. Hope always has this certainty about itself, even in a soul which has turned away from God by mortal sin and has lost the virtue of love together with sanctifying grace.

This also is a proof of the great mercy of God that he often leaves in the soul of a sinner the seeds of spiritual regeneration in the form of faith and hope, which…do not cease to be God's priceless supernatural gifts. Under their influence man does not cease to pray. Since he is in the state of sin, he gains no merits by his prayer, but he can obtain by it the grace of conversion and forgiveness. The virtue of love is lost by any mortal sin, since every mortal sin is contrary to the very object of our love…. However, faith and hope are not lost by any mortal sin, but only by such sins as are opposed to…the revealed truths and to confidence in God's mercy.

Should one have the misfortune to turn away from God and to lose the virtue of love, he should take good care of that which remains of the spiritual life in himself. He should watch diligently to preserve faith and hope and with their help to storm heaven for the grace of conversion.

– Servant of God Father Hyacinth Woroniecki, O.P.

Saint Brigid of Kildare

IT IS BELIEVED THAT SAINT BRIGID was the daughter of a Christian slave and a pagan chieftain. After her mother's death, Brigid was left to toil in her father's house. But the young maiden had already heard the call of Christ. Slave though she was, she lived with the freedom of the daughter of a king: she was always giving away the goods of the household to the beggars at the door. Her exasperated father tried to marry her off, but Brigid struggled against these plans and won the right to consecrate herself to God.

She went to Kildare, where she became the abbess of one of Ireland's first convents. She wrote a reputedly strict rule and continued to witness to God's abundant love. Hers were the miracles of the multiplication of butter, beer, and bacon—always for the succor of the poor. She restored cows and sheep and blessed the marriage bed. Hers was the vision of heaven as endless feast, according to the ancient poem: "I should like a lake of ale for the King of Kings/ I should like the household of heaven to be there drinking it for eternity.../ I should like cheerfulness to be in their drinking/ I should like Jesus here also."

Saint Brigid, former slave, died at Kildare around the year 524. She is the patroness of Ireland.

– Lisa Lickona

To BEAR WRONGS PATIENTLY may well be the most difficult spiritual work of mercy, not because of the wrongs
but because of the patience. Physical injury and personal
insult may be tolerated as a strategy in order to get revenge
eventually, but patience requires a conviction that there is
something better than revenge. If you only get even, you
will not get ahead. Cardinal Nguyen van Thuan of Vietnam
spent thirteen torturous years in a Communist "reeduca-
tion camp" without complaint, and when he finally was
released, the warden who had supervised his suffering expressed amazement at how he had endured it. Not long
after, the man became a Catholic.

This is not always what happens. Often, and perhaps
more often that not, a wrongdoer persists in doing wrong.
Justice is as virtuous as patience, and in cases of calumny
and false accusation of crime, self-defense is both prudent
and proper. "Turning the other cheek" may mean an agile motion that preserves the assailant from slapping with
the palm of his hand the same way twice. What matters is
that one allows patience to polish dignity instead of letting grudges grind it down.

Jesus was patient with Judas, who was so impatient
with Jesus that he destroyed himself. Saint Catherine of
Siena believed that God the Father told her: "The despair
of Judas displeases me more and was a greater insult to
my Son than his betrayal had been."

The classical Stoics bore wrongs patiently because of a
narrow sense that the only satisfaction in life is tolerating
what is hurtful. That produces a masochist but not a saint.
The Christian has a farsighted view that what is wrong is

not just to be tolerated but can in fact be conquered by what is good. *"No one is good but God alone"* (Mk 10:18; Lk 18:19). Patience wins when wrongs are borne patiently for the love of God, who is patient with all the wrong we do. To *"bless those who curse you"* (Lk 6:28) is a lesson learned from the cross.

An anonymous letter, written probably toward the end of the 2nd century to a man called Diognetus, describes a new people called Christians who "display to us their wonderful and admittedly striking way of life" while not distinguishing themselves from others by any peculiarity of speech or dress or customs. They are singular in that they "share a common table, but not a common bed" and "do not destroy their offspring." Even more astonishing, "They are dishonored, and yet in their very dishonor they are glorified; they are spoken ill of and yet are justified; they are reviled but bless…."

– **Father George William Rutler**

A TERRIFIC MOMENT in C. S. Lewis' *Great Divorce*: A man stands before an angel who offers him mercy. The man isn't sure he wants it. On his shoulder sits a vile lizard, whispering lewd suggestions into his ear. That lizard has dominated his life. The man loathes it but cannot imagine living without it. Isn't there a way to shut the lizard's mouth?

There is. "I will kill him," says the angel, stepping forward.

Kill? The man writhes. Couldn't we try something gradual instead?

"The gradual process is of no use," says the angel. His fiery hands begin to close around the lizard, burning the man also. The pain is intolerable. The man is afraid to die, but the angel says he will survive. He says nothing about suffering.

The man protests. "Why didn't you kill the damned thing without asking me—before I knew?"

"I cannot kill it against your will. It is impossible. Have I your permission?"

The lizard starts to chatter. "Watch out! He can do what he says. He can kill me. One fatal word from you and he *will*! Then you'll be without me forever and ever. It's not natural. How could you live?" And on and on.

Finally the man cries, "Get it over. Do what you like," and whimpers, "God help me. God help me." And God does.

– Anthony Esolen

JESUS' MERCY IS nowhere more powerfully revealed than as he hangs upon his cross. On the cross Christ in every way proves himself. Throughout his ministry he had forgiven people's sins—but these were not injustices directed against his human nature. What had the adulterous woman ever done to the man from Nazareth? With the paralytic Jesus himself even noted, it is an easy thing to say, *"Your sins are forgiven"* (Mk 2:5, cf. 2:9).

On the cross, however, as the Lord bears the tortures due a crime he did not commit, the words become infinitely more impressive: *"Father, forgive them, they know not what they do"* (Lk 23:34). The high priest proclaims his solemn absolution at the price of his own blood.

Saint Dismas understands this. The good thief understands that Jesus innocently suffers a fate fit only for sinners. The Lord suffers *his* fate, Dismas' fate, on some order other than justice. That is what Jesus' mercy ultimately means. The Lord freely suffers with us, that we might reign with him. *"Today you will be with me in Paradise"* (Lk 23:43). The Lord makes the full burden of our sin his own, so that the full force of his merciful forgiveness might also be ours.

– Father Anthony Giambrone, O.P.

The Seven Last Words

◀ *"Father, forgive them."*

This last word before your death, Jesus, shows me why my life is such a misery. Let me live a healthy sense of sin. May I always beg forgiveness for myself even as you do for me.

◀ *"...with me in Paradise."*

The happiness I crave comes not by thieving, or conniving, or deceiving, but from receiving your gaze of mercy, Jesus—a look no brutality can mar. Your presence is paradise.

◀ *"Behold, your mother."*

To face the horror of my own evil, Jesus, you know I need the love of your Mother who, in beholding me, sees past my immorality, refuses to judge, and holds me close in compassion.

◀ *"My God, why have you forsaken me?"*

If your cry of forsakenness so moves my very callous heart, how can it not pierce the Father's? Your plea convinces me: I must pray when overwhelmed by trauma and anguish.

◀ *"I thirst."*

In your distress, Jesus, you ask something of me: a drink. You thirst for us to drink in the mercy pouring from your wounds. I give you what quenches by letting you give yourself to me.

◀ *"It is finished."*

With your death, Jesus, something new enlivens the world. Born is victory over doubt, defeatism, the scourge of cynicism. When despair strikes, come with your mercy: finish it off.

◀ *"...I commend my spirit."*

The grace to be able to hand myself over to God in total confidence, just the way I am, is the permanent mercy, Jesus, you purchase for me in your Passion.

– Father Peter John Cameron, O.P.

Saint Dismas (Lk 23:1-49)

At your right, above the din
your labored breath was like the wind.
When I drew breath, I took you in.
You changed my way of life.

The truth is not in earthly threats
nor in the taunts that can't accept
salvation from a failed step.
I see my faults and live.

I thought I heard a chorus cry
far above the dire sky.
Your Kingdom is another kind:
A different way to live.

I fall asleep; they break my legs.
It's not a dream yet there's no pain.
The sky is torn; it is today!
I turn to you and live.

– Rita A. Simmonds

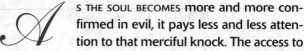

*A*S THE SOUL BECOMES more and more confirmed in evil, it pays less and less attention to that merciful knock. The access to God's mercy was not closed even for Judas as long as he had not breathed his last. Neither Judas nor those other unfortunates who have been or will be repulsed by God forever could ever complain that God was unmerciful to them.

On the contrary, when their intellects are no longer disturbed by the influence of the senses, considering their fate, they are forced to acknowledge that even in their damnation mercy surpasses justice because the punishment they suffer is far below what they have deserved by offending divine majesty, and in particular in having no regard for divine mercy and by persevering in sin until death.

– Servant of God Father Hyacinth Woroniecki, O.P.

Saint Dismas

Two thieves suffer alongside Jesus on Calvary (see Lk 23:39-43). Tradition names the one on the left "Gestas" and the one on the right "Dismas." In the Church's art, Dismas struggles behind Jesus, bearing his own cross with his hand clasped over his heart in a gesture of repentance. His name means simply "the dying one."

Even in the face of his impending death, Gestas joins the jeering crowd in their attacks against Jesus. But Dismas chides his fellow thief, exhorting him to the *"fear of God."* He acknowledges the justice of the thieves' punishment, *"for the sentence we received corresponds to our crimes."* Jesus, on the other hand, *"has done nothing criminal."* Dismas then turns to Jesus and begs for mercy from a man who is nailed to a cross. He professes belief in Jesus' true authority, an authority that is not of this world: *"Jesus, remember me when you come into your kingdom."*

The heart of the brutal thief is all at once totally conformed to that of our Lord. And Jesus says: *"Amen, I say to you, today you will be with me in Paradise."* Dismas asks simply to be "remembered." But Jesus replies with the gift of eternal communion: "You will be *with* me." In his commentary on this passage, Saint Ambrose remarked, "The Lord always grants more than one asks."

– Lisa Lickona

To forgive all injuries, like all the moral precepts that are not human in origin, is easier said than done. It requires the help of the Lord himself. "Who is this that he even forgives sins?" is a question often muttered about him, the answer to which unlocks the very secret of why Christ came into the world. The first thing he did when he rose from the dead and appeared to the Apostles was to give them the power to forgive sins. He made the world and he knows best what has gone wrong with what he made, and he alone can heal mankind's primeval injury, the Original Sin of selfish pride. Not one of his bones was broken on the cross, because his perfection makes straight what is fractured in man. Saint John the Baptist cried out at his coming that he would make a straight path to heaven through this world's moral wilderness. As orthopedics straightens bones, so orthodoxy, or true praise, straightens the intellect and the will.

With artful cynicism, Oscar Wilde said of Dickens' tragic heroine: "One must have a heart of stone to read the death of little Nell without laughing." Given the melodrama of the novel, one might excuse the remark, but the drama of salvation is not exploitive theatrics. The Sacred Heart was not of stone, and Jesus wept for the daughters of Jerusalem and their children, who were victims of a culture that rejected his mercy.

The mercy that forgives us would be like a stagnant stream if it did not run like a fast current through us, forgiving others. "Forgive us our trespasses as we forgive those who trespass against us." The first part, acknowledgment of the injuries that we ourselves have inflicted on others, prevents forgiveness from being manipulative. To say "I forgive you" can be an act of domination, asserting moral superiority, unless it is moved by recognition of one's own defects. Honest self-examination is the best cure for resentment. Just as a baby cannot nurse itself, a man cannot nurture himself by nursing his own grievances.

The purpose of forgiveness is reconciliation with God. Echoing the prophet Micaiah (1 Kgs 22:17), Jesus looked wistfully upon the sheep scattered on the hills, and wanted to bring them back to him. He does this through us. Faith rescues people from the indignity of grieving over past injuries and fearing present threats, by gladly, and not begrudgingly, showing how Christ can heal the injurer as well as the injury. Ralph Waldo Emerson said, "Sorrow looks back. Worry looks around. Faith looks up."

– Father George William Rutler

"BE YOUR TEARS WET?" asks the old King Lear, still vague in his mind. He is lying on a bed, surrounded by servants, a good physician, and his youngest daughter, the beloved Cordelia. He doesn't quite know whether they are dead or alive. But the tears are wet. "Weep not," he says, and then he pleads for mere justice:

> If you have poison for me, I will drink it.
> I know you do not love me; for your sisters
> Have, as I do remember, done me wrong.
> You have some cause, they have not.

Lear had banished Cordelia from the realm, when she would not flatter him in public with protestations of love, as did her treacherous elder sisters.

Do we know what we ask, when we call for justice? For the guilty Lear, it means a drink of poison, which he will take, because he deserves it. Cordelia has "cause," he says, to hate him. That's a legal word, "cause," and a philosophical one, too.

The mercy of God comes to us in love, and not as the result of a legal arrangement, or as something fixed into the universe. It is miraculous, always. So whenever we feel his merciful dew upon our souls, we can reply with Cordelia: "No cause, no cause."

– Anthony Esolen

IT HAPPENS OFTEN on singing competition shows. A would-be contestant steps onto the stage. Sometimes there is something odd about her appearance or what she says. She may seem too young or too ordinary to become a singing star. After some banter with the judge, everyone waits for the person to sing. The camera captures the looks of shock as the audience hears a beautiful voice coming from what seemed like an ordinary person.

The identity of the author of the Letter of Jude is uncertain; many think he was an obscure person in the early Church. His letter of only twenty-six verses is a warning against the false teachers of the day. The voice of this ordinary author soars in its beauty, reminding his listeners to live in the power of love and to *wait for the mercy of our Lord Jesus Christ* (Jude 21). He cautions us about listening to voices that say only what we want to hear. He encourages us to listen to the voices, often in unexpected people, that challenge us with the Good News of Jesus.

The mercy of God is found in the ordinary and odd moments of our life. And it must be found in us. Each of us stands on the stage of life. Someone is waiting in your life. Who might be surprised to hear the Good News from your voice?

– **Monsignor Gregory E. S. Malovetz**

Via Matris

◀ *First Sorrow: The Prophecy of Simeon*

Mother of Mercy, you allow your heart to be pierced by the sufferings of your Son so that mercy may pierce our hardened, doubtful, ignorant hearts and set them free.

◀ *Second Sorrow: The Flight into Egypt*

Mother of Mercy, the flight into Egypt is an act of your maternal mediation. You flee to preserve Salvation from the sword so that he can save us by the cross.

◀ *Third Sorrow: The Loss of Jesus in the Temple*

Mother of Mercy, your experience of the temporary loss of your Son makes your heart supremely tender to all those who suffer the loss of loved ones. Find me.

◀ *Fourth Sorrow: The Journey to Calvary and the Crucifixion*

Mother of Mercy, you always put yourself on the way of the cross, giving your maternal tenderness to anyone abandoned to the Father's will.

◀ *Fifth Sorrow: The Agony and Death of Jesus*

Mother of Mercy, the Passion of your Son impassions you to take up anew the announcement of the angel to be a Mother to those called to be God's children.

◀ *Sixth Sorrow: Jesus Is Taken Down from the Cross*

Mother of Mercy, in the Visitation the humanity of Jesus was hidden; in the deposition, his divinity. In both, you believe and bear his life to us.

◀ *Seventh Sorrow: The Burial of Jesus*

Mother of Mercy, as once you presented Jesus in the Temple, you escort him to the tomb. But entrustment is not the end. Your trust will see him alive, about his Father's business.

– Father Peter John Cameron, O.P.

The Race (Jn 20:1-9)

At times it seems
my life is racing
for the tomb.
I find the stone is rolled.
I wait to enter
the empty cold
that waits for me.
There is no stench,
just linen cloth
neatly placed
upon the floor
imprinted with a form:
It is the Lord!
And he is gone.
Even more
it is the Lord!
I touch the blood
that hemorrhaged from
the one who's disappeared.
It is the Lord!
Where has he gone?
His absence is my greatest fear.

No! My greatest hope!
My life is racing
for the One
who from within
can turn a stone.

– Rita A. Simmonds

*G*RACES FLOWING TODAY on mankind through Christ do not give us the strength that was given to our first parents through the grace of original justice. They do not suppress the discord introduced into our nature by the loss of original justice, and remaining in every one of us, even after the guilt of sin is forgiven. Due to it, suffering became a part of the whole of human life. Nevertheless, our present state is undoubtedly higher and more perfect than the original one, and manifesting the mystery of divine mercy with a much greater force and a much brighter light….

Every Christian…should see that no faint-hearted grudge takes hold of his soul against divine Providence for not having removed evil, sin, suffering, and the sight of our own misery from the world.

Suffering and our own misery are the main obstacles to our acknowledging the greatness and beauty of divine mercy in the plan of the redemption of the world by the Son of God. We shall never be deprived of God's help in overcoming that obstacle. Whoever lives in the fullness of faith, hope, and love, will not find it difficult to accept that plan of God, at first with surrender, and later on, with an ever-increasing joy, until he becomes enamored of it and sees in it his most precious possession in the world.

– Servant of God Father Hyacinth Woroniecki, O.P.

SAINTS   MARCH 29

Saint Philip Neri

In 1544, just before the feast of Pentecost, Philip Neri
(† 1595) was praying in the catacombs of Saint Sebastian
in Rome when the Holy Spirit entered his mouth in the
form of a great globe of fire. The swelling of his heart by
divine love was no metaphor; a doctor who later exam-
ined him testified to the enlargement of his heart. After
this, Philip Neri began to reach out to the desperate and
the indigent, the pilgrims and the prostitutes and, above
all, the youth. He became a priest, a sought-after confessor. He renewed the faith of people in all walks of life by
creating the Oratory, where they heard stirring talks and
beautiful music.

Philip's unique mixture of humility and humor was his
calling card. He loved jokes. He would do ridiculous things
like walking through town with half his beard shaved off
or doing a little whimsical dance. When one young man
came to ask him if he could wear a hair shirt, Philip said,
"Go ahead" and told him to wear it on the outside of his
clothes—probably a greater humiliation!

Those who went to Philip for confession felt a great
lightness afterwards. Those whom he pressed to his heart
experienced supernatural joy. Philip is the patron of those
who want to take themselves less seriously and those who
long for the gift of joy.

– Lisa Lickona

To PRAY FOR THE LIVING AND THE DEAD is a natural instinct with a supernatural inspiration. "Say a little prayer for me" is more than a cliché. Praying for the dead may seem a bit stranger, yet even in the most detached heart there is an urge to think of someone who has died. True religion is the antidote to superstitious attempts to contact the departed. With an intimation of life eternal, centuries before the Resurrection, Judas Maccabeus prayed that God might forgive his dead comrades whom he feared might have flirted with paganism: *...for if he were not expecting the fallen to rise again, it would have been useless and foolish to pray for them in death. But if he did this with a view to the splendid reward that awaits those who had gone to rest in godliness, it was a holy and pious thought* (2 Mc 12:44-45).

Saints do not think of themselves as saints. John Vianney tried to flee from his little parish in rural France three times to pray for his "poor soul." He was convinced that the priest who had trained him, Abbé Balley, was a saint and in this he may have been right, for the dying priest asked Vianney to hide any evidence of his pious practices for fear that people would think that after death he would not need their prayers. Vianney kept one relic of Balley: his shaving mirror. It reminded him to pray for the venerable priest each morning. *At present we see indistinctly, as in a mirror, but then face to face* (1 Cor 13:12). Saint Paul prayed for the soul of his dead friend Onesiphorus (2 Tm 1:18) and made no distinction between praying for the living and the dead.

The cry of Christ from the cross tore open the veil concealing the Holy of Holies in the Temple. Prayer for the dead "pierces through the veil" between earth and heaven, which is thinner than many think. Souls of the departed in purgatory are closer to bliss than we are. Their suffering is the opposite of the despair of the damned, who are beyond the influence of prayer. It is the ecstatic agony of a birthing mother at the end of her nine months, or the runner in the last seconds of a marathon. In the assurance of their approaching glory, their reciprocal prayers can pour out merciful graces on us who still are in the mercurial world of uncertainties. The words of Saint Monica helped her son Saint Augustine at least as much as he could help her: "Bury my body where you will; let not care of it cause you any concern. One thing only I ask of you: that you remember me at the altar of the Lord wherever you may be."

– **Father George William Rutler**

THE SCENE (in Manzoni's *The Betrothed*) is the *lazaretto* of Milan, where thousands of plague-ridden people lie, most of them dying, some recovering, and all of them tended, body and soul, by the tireless sons of Saint Francis.

One of the men lies unconscious. He is Don Rodrigo, a petty tyrant. He had thwarted the marriage of young Renzo and Lucia, lusting after the girl, wanting her for a mistress. The good Friar Cristoforo prevented him, and Renzo and Lucia had to flee in separate directions. Now the friar and Renzo stand above the sinner, who will never open his eyes again. And Renzo is glad, glad to see the man suffering his just deserts.

But someone else here is in danger of dying, eternally. It is Renzo, who refuses to pray for his enemy. The priest, himself dying of the plague, rebukes him sharply. "You, worm that you are, crawling on the face of the earth, *you* want to administer justice! *You* know what justice is!"

Renzo is ashamed.

He goes to the chapel, kneels on the lowest step, and sends up "a prayer, or rather a mixture of broken words, unfinished phrases, exclamations, laments, supplications, and promises. Such appeals," says Alessandro Manzoni, "are never addressed to men, for men lack the penetration to understand them and the patience to listen to them." But God hears.

– **Anthony Esolen**

It is an easy thing—far too easy—to object to those whom Jesus loves. For Jesus loves us all. When Jesus is criticized for consorting with tax collectors, like Matthew (Mt 9:9-13), the Pharisees are challenged to go and learn the meaning of Hosea 6:6: *"I desire mercy, not sacrifice."*

What was it exactly that Jesus' critics needed to learn? At one level, the challenge is obvious. *"I take no pleasure in the death of the wicked,"* the Lord says in Ezekiel (33:11). The Lord came to seek and save what was lost, and healthy hearts should be harmonized with this merciful mission of God.

There is also another meaning to this passage, however. At the time the Gospels were written, Hosea's text was understood as "I desire works of mercy, almsdeeds, not just sacrifice." As Jesus says elsewhere, the Pharisees are rightly concerned with tithes and religious observance. The problem is that they neglect justice and the love of God. One should be done as well as the other. It is not an either/or. Jesus intends his double love command. Love of God, through the cult, is effective only when loving mercy towards our neighbor gives it wings.

– Father Anthony Giambrone, o.p.

Via Lucis

◀ *First Station: Jesus Rises from the Dead*
At your rising, the peace, the forgiveness, the display of your wounds are healing mercy for me.

◀ *Second Station: The Disciples Find the Empty Tomb*
The emptiness inside me is a crushing sore. The mercy of your empty tomb frees me and fills me.

◀ *Third Station: Jesus Appears to Mary Magdalene*
To a frantic Mary who wants to carry away your body, you appear in Risen mercy to carry her away.

◀ *Fourth Station: Jesus Walks with the Disciples to Emmaus*
To the two discouraged disciples, your mercy appears as a sudden accompaniment. Walk with me!

◀ *Fifth Station: Jesus Reveals Himself in the Breaking of Bread*
All that our heart craves abides in the Last Supper bread breaking. Break through my forgetfulness!

◀ *Sixth Station: Jesus Appears to the Disciples*
You appear in your humanity: eating, consoling, ridding fear. By your mercy, help me be more human.

◀ *Seventh Station: Jesus Confers on His Disciples the Power to Forgive Sins*
You give, not the ability to live without sinning, but the power to forgive sin—the greatest mercy.

◀ *Eighth Station: Jesus Confirms Thomas in Faith*
In your mercy, doubt will not gain the upper hand. Touching the wound in your hand reclaims us.

◀ *Ninth Station: Jesus Appears to His Disciples on the Shore of Lake Galilee*
When we are adrift and dispirited, you come as a surprise, cooking us breakfast, calling us "children."

◀ *Tenth Station: Jesus Confers Primacy on Peter*
The unity the Church needs you provide in the Successor of Peter, its visible source and foundation.

◀ *Eleventh Station: Jesus Entrusts His Disciples with a Universal Mission*
I believe because of Christian witnesses who shared their faith. Make me a missionary of mercy!

◀ *Twelfth Station: Jesus Ascends into Heaven*
You ascend in your humanity to heaven to give us access to the Father's house and to God's life.

◀ *Thirteenth Station: Mary and the Disciples Await the Holy Spirit's Pentecost*
Thank you for the gift of the One who reminds us of all you said and who forms us in the life of prayer.

◀ *Fourteenth Station: Jesus Sends the Spirit Promised by the Father to His Disciples*
Lost though we are in a state of deformity, the Holy Spirit restores our original beauty and fills us with grace.

– Father Peter John Cameron, O.P.

The Risen Christ (Jn 20:19-31)

The first is the last is the One who lives.
He passes through locked doors.
Forgiveness is the breath he breathes.
His flesh is open sores.
He bids us touch the memory
we couldn't stay to make:
the severed side
the punctured palms—
He lets us now partake.

Redemption leaves a set of wounds
my Lord and God extends.
We cannot capture
yet receive
the Spirit that He sends.

– Rita A. Simmonds

*W*HAT A GREAT CONSOLATION is the conviction that hope as such has not changed even for a sinner, because there has been no change in its most precious element, the divine mercy, which hastens to every stray sheep with an infinite patience and long suffering.

Faith and hope are lost by such sins as are directly opposed to them: by rejecting the revealed truths and by taking no account of divine mercy. Sins of this type, if committed with full consciousness, are numbered among the sins against the Holy Spirit, the most grievous of which are directed against those attributes of God which form the very basis of our salvation.

Saint Augustine, who was the first to give more thought to the doctrine of sins against the Holy Spirit, found that of those sins two were especially directed against hope, namely, despairing of one's salvation and committing sins with hope of divine mercy, that is, in expectation of being forgiven by God's mercy.

– Servant of God Father Hyacinth Woroniecki, O.P.

Saint Katharine Drexel

KATHARINE DREXEL († 1955) was the daughter of a wealthy Philadelphia banker. Sacraments and prayer anchored the family's life. Emma, her stepmother, fed the poor from their country home three days a week—Katharine's own school of charity.

As a young woman, Katharine traveled to Europe. Praying at Saint Mark's Basilica in Venice, Italy, before a statue of the Virgin, she heard, *"Without cost you have received; without cost you are to give"* (Mt 10:8). At first, Katharine did not know what this meant. On her next trip, to the American West, Katharine saw the squalor of the Native Americans who had been exiled from their ancestral homes. She felt moved to pledge some of her immense fortune to create missions for them. When she went to Rome to ask Pope Leo XIII to send missionaries, he suggested that she become one herself. Another trip out West to visit Chief Red Cloud confirmed her calling. In 1891, she founded the Sisters of the Blessed Sacrament to serve Native Americans and the recently emancipated slaves.

Many schools and missions sprang up. Katharine founded Xavier University in New Orleans. Then, in 1935, she suffered a severe heart attack. For the last twenty years of her life, Katharine supported the work with her ardent prayer.

– Lisa Lickona

Saint Faustina and Divine Mercy

DID YOU KNOW that the Doctor of the Church known for the "Little Way" of merciful love, Saint Thérèse of Lisieux, once appeared to the Divine Mercy saint, Maria Faustina Kowalska? The subject of their encounter tells us a lot about Saint Faustina and her message.

It happened while Faustina was going through a particularly painful trial, the specifics of which she didn't disclose. Whatever it was, it caused the future "Secretary of Mercy" to wonder how she could go on living.

Though Faustina sought help from various saints, the situation had gotten worse. Then, the thought occurred to her to pray a novena to Saint Thérèse of Lisieux, to whom she'd had a devotion before entering the convent.

On the fifth day of the novena, Thérèse appeared to Faustina in a dream and comforted her. Faustina then asked the French sister if she, too, would become a saint. Thérèse replied, "Yes." But Faustina pressed further, "Shall I be a saint as you are, raised to the altar?" Thérèse replied, "Yes, you will be a saint just as I am, but you must...."

What do you think this Doctor of the Church said? Did she tell Faustina that she needed to spend more time in prayer or make more sacrifices? No. Amazingly, Thérèse told her simply, "you must trust in the Lord Jesus."

Trusting in Jesus gets to the heart of the Divine Mercy message and devotion that comes to us through Saint Faustina. It's why we find the prayer, "Jesus, I trust in you," at the bottom of every Divine Mercy image. It's also probably why Saint Thérèse appeared to Faustina. I say that because Faustina's message of mercy continues and develops Thérèse's "Little Way" of humble confidence in the Lord. In fact, both of their teachings bring us back to the fundamental spiritual attitude of Christians, which is trust—also described by Saint Faustina in her diary as "living faith."

When we turn away from sin and grow in a living faith (trust) in Jesus, our Lord is able to work miracles in our lives, even the miracle of forming us into great saints! For instance, Faustina tells us in her diary, "Let no soul, even the most miserable, fall prey to doubt; for, as long as one is alive, each one can become a great saint, so great is the power of God's grace. It remains only for us not to oppose God's action." How do we avoid opposing God's action? As Thérèse told Faustina, "You must trust in the Lord Jesus."

– Father Michael Gaitley, M.I.C.

In 1990, a drifter named Robert Knighton was convicted for murdering Richard Denney, sixty-two, and his wife, Virginia, sixty-four, in rural Oklahoma. Knighton made off with $61 and an old truck.

Richard Denney was the adoptive father of Sue Norton, a woman from Kansas. Virginia was Sue's stepmother.

When Knighton's trial began, Sue sat in the courtroom, confused.

"I should feel anger and want vengeance, but I was also taught I need to pray for him and forgive him."

During the trial, she learned of Knighton's childhood: a mother who had been married six times; reformatories and prisons starting at the age of twelve.

The day after the trial ended, she asked to meet with Knighton. He was six feet tall, shackled and angry. She took a deep breath and said, "If you are guilty, I forgive you." She offered her hand through the bars. He pulled back. She grabbed it and started praying.

"I learned that forgiveness is a gift to ourselves, not for the forgiven." She began to write to and visit him. "Executions just turn more families into victims," she insisted. She lost friends.

Knighton became a Christian on Oklahoma's death row.

Sue was present at his 2003 execution, his only friend among the witnesses.

– Heather King

Sometimes the Lord extends his mercy by asking us
to live in the presence of what he has already done. And
sometimes such mercy means rejecting our own hopes,
and living instead for others. After being freed from his
horrible bondage to the demonic Legion, the man from
Gerasa (Mk 5:1-20) begs to follow the Lord who healed
him: a holy aspiration one expects to be honored. Christ,
nevertheless, tells the poor man, *"Go home to your family and announce to them all that the Lord in his pity has
done for you"* (Mk 5:19). Somehow it is desirable for this
man to remain distant from the Lord.

It is like the case of Saint Paul, who wished to die and
be with the Lord—a thing in itself far better—but understood, still, that it was better for others if he remained in
the body. God's mercy to the sinner Paul is like his mercy to this rescued man in the Gospel. It is a mercy meant
to spill out upon others. The people of Gerasa sent Jesus
away. Now, only the healed man himself can bear them
witness and preserve the living presence of Christ's mercy among them.

– **Father Anthony Giambrone, O.P.**

I want to love you as no human soul has ever loved you before; and although I am utterly miserable and small, I have nevertheless cast the anchor of my trust deep down into the abyss of your mercy, O my God and Creator! In spite of my great misery I fear nothing, but hope to sing you a hymn of glory for ever. Let no soul, even the most miserable, fall prey to doubt; for, as long as one is alive, each one can become a great saint, so great is the power of God's grace. It remains only for us not to oppose God's action.

Jesus, when I look at the world and its indifference towards you, again and again it brings tears to my eyes.

Most merciful Jesus, I beseech you through the intercession of your saints, and especially the intercession of your dearest Mother who nurtured you from childhood, bless my native land. I beg you, Jesus, look not on our sins, but on the tears of little children, on the hunger and cold they suffer. Jesus, for the sake of these innocent ones, grant me the grace that I am asking of you, for my country.

At that moment, I saw the Lord Jesus, his eyes filled with tears, and he said to me, "You see, my daughter, what great compassion I have for them. Know that it is they who uphold the world."

– Saint Maria Faustina Kowalska

A Fisher of Hearts (Jn 21:1-19)

Fasting, praying, weeping,
and not sleeping,
I turn my mind to the sea;
I will solve my problem
with a line—
there are still so many mouths to feed.

At dawn you come with counsel:
"Cast, that I may fill."
Beyond all fathom,
such a weight!
I can't deny it's you.

I leave the catch to flip and gasp—
the net cannot be torn.
The greatest length is overcome
to feast with you on shore.

"Do you love me?"
is the line
that sounds and probes my heart.
It reels me in,
unhooks my skin
and measures not a mark.

– Rita A. Simmonds

*T*HE VICE IN SHARPEST CONTRAST with mercy is envy. Whereas mercy is sadness at another's misfortune, envy, on the contrary, is sadness at the success of another or joy at another's misfortune.... Often it penetrates our soul with a silent influence and produces in it continuous reactions of discontent at anything in others surpassing us. Surely, such an attitude cannot foster the development of Christian mercy.

As to the corporal works of mercy, their greatest adversary is avarice with its greediness and stinginess. An attachment to the goods of the world can uproot from the soul any compassion for human misery. He who has...yielded to it will always find an excuse to refuse help. As its symptoms become more acute he will feel dislike for all in want, and in his treatment of them he will often sin grievously against love of neighbor. The most common excuse in such cases is a doubt whether the poor person really needs help, or fear that he will deceive us or use our aid for evil ends.... Nevertheless, it is better to make ten mistakes in giving alms to the unworthy than to repel someone in need even once. We shall not be severely judged for our mistakes, but we know from the words of our Lord (Mt 25:31-46) what kind of a judgment is waiting for a refusal of mercy to those suffering from want.

– Servant of God Father Hyacinth Woroniecki, O.P.

Saint Leopold Bogdan Mandić

FROM HIS EARLY YEARS in his native Croatia, Bogdan († 1942) wanted to be a missionary. But he was unusually small of stature—just above four feet—and suffered from a severe speech defect. When he entered the Capuchins in Italy, his superiors confirmed what he already suspected: he would never be permitted to preach, and his delicate health would prevent him from rough mission assignments. Until the end of his life, Leopold remained in Italy, spending most of his time hearing confessions.

Leopold was a wonder in the confessional. The other priests thought that the little priest was too kind to sinners. But Leopold said, "I give my penitents only small penances because I do the rest myself." In summer's sweltering heat or winter's brutal cold, he sat in his little box—up to sixteen hours a day. Although Leopold's health grew progressively worse, his routines remained the same. He never took a vacation from the confessional. "A priest must die from apostolic hard work," he once said; "there is no other death worthy of a priest."

Leopold greatly desired the reunification of the East and West. He received the intimation in prayer that his work in the confessional was itself a means of reuniting estranged brothers and hence contributed directly to the end of schism.

– Lisa Lickona

On Indicating Species and Number of Sins in Confession

ONE GOAL OF THE YEAR OF MERCY proclaimed by Pope Francis is to occasion many good confessions. The Church reminds the Catholic faithful that, in order to make a good confession, it is necessary "to confess *in kind and number* all *grave sins* committed after baptism" (*Code of Canon Law* 988, emphasis added). This insistence requires some explanation.

One could have the wrong impression that this obligation arises merely from a rule of the Church, like the requirement to fast on particular days. The obligation to confess "in kind and number," however, is not the result of an extrinsic rule of the Church, but arises from the nature of the sacrament itself.

In the Sacrament of Penance, the penitent opens himself to God. In asking for God's mercy, one invites the Lord into every nook and cranny of the soul. To do so in an authentic way, one must ask the Lord to be Savior and Redeemer in every aspect of life.

Confessing in kind and number, then, expresses not so much a mathematical formula as a genuinely human interaction arising from the demands of interpersonal communion between God and a penitent sinner. For this reason, stating each sin in confession (which means its basic species—for example, adultery is a different kind of thing than fornication—and as best as one is able, the number of times each serious sin has been committed) expresses one's authentic desire for mercy.

For a penitent to confess merely "sins of unchastity" does not sufficiently open oneself up to God's merciful love. Instead, a penitent truly seeking God's mercy will ask forgiveness for precisely what sin has been committed, premarital sex, for example. Similarly, failure to attend Sunday Mass one time differs from missing Sunday Mass every Sunday for several months. Those seeking God's mercy for failure to worship him will ask his forgiveness for missing Sunday Mass "each Sunday for about six months."

Wise confessors are able to aid penitents in making an integral confession. The obligation to confess in kind and number has certain natural limits—the limitations of one's memory, for example. As well, the distinction in species or kind of sin is required only to the best of one's ability. Sound moral instruction outside the confessional equips the Catholic people to understand the difference between one sort of sin and another.

One hopes this Year of Mercy will bring about many good confessions—that is, those which open souls to God by the confession of sins in kind and number.

– Father Ryan Connors

April 15, 2007, was Divine Mercy Sunday. I especially prayed for my son Matthew, as he had become lukewarm in his faith. I left church filled with a profound peace, which continued into the next day, as the tragic events of April 16 unfolded at the Virginia Tech campus.

Matthew was a sophomore cadet in the Highty Tighties military band, had an Air Force ROTC scholarship, and was a political science major. By the end of the day, I knew Matthew was no longer in school but in his new home, embraced in our Lord's arms. I believed God's promise, "At the hour of their death, I defend as my own glory every soul that will say this [divine mercy] chaplet; or when others say it for a dying person…." God knew I wouldn't be beside my son, but he gave me the opportunity to pray for him.

As a mother, I needed to know what happened not only physically but also spiritually. We are made in the image and likeness of God. We are an integrated body and soul. How would I ever know what our Lord had witnessed that day?

Shortly after the funeral in Virginia, I met Senior State Trooper Gary Chafin. Gary had been a first responder in my son's classroom and felt compelled to tell us what he saw. He saw the unexpected. Part of his letter reads: "I never met Matthew in this life. I only saw him at peace, his spirit having flown away when I entered that room that day."

My son died with a smile on his face. What a precious gift Gary had given me. Matthew was at peace and full of joy. But what did he see? One night upon awakening from a deep sleep, the following thoughts came to me. Matthew was in his French class and his teacher was yelling "la porte!"—which means door in French. Matthew responded to hearing his name and instinctively ran to the secure door. What he saw coming through that door was the Divine Mercy. He was the cause of his smile, a smile that radiated out to Gary and from Gary to me and from me to others.

Matthew's legacy is one of love. Upon death he surrendered only his body. His soul and love are one and eternal. Now being boundless, his love desires to be given away. I can try to follow in his big footsteps and walk forward with him at my side. He will live on in my acts of mercy and kindness.

– Barbara Ann La Porte

"*A GOOD SHEPHERD LAYS DOWN his life for the sheep.... No one takes [my life] from me, but I lay it down on my own*" (Jn 10:11, 18).

What unimaginable mercy the Good Shepherd has! He will lay down his life not just for those who were hearing his voice in that place at that time, but for all who will hear his voice, for future sinners who will commit future sins.

Once, after I had visited a parishioner in a hospital, a nurse asked me to see another patient who had been asking all day for a priest. I will not forget the look on her face when she saw me walk into her room: such joy and gratitude and relief. She had been away from the Church, and she kept repeating her amazement at how much God must love her to send her a priest regardless of her falling away.

I was humbled by her appreciation of God's mercy. And I experienced a glimpse of the love of the Good Shepherd.

I didn't know this woman. I came to know her sins, but they were as nothing compared to the joy and desire that was bursting from her heart.

I wanted everything good for her at that moment. I rejoiced in assisting her toward the peace for which she longed. My heart was moved in a way that must have faintly echoed the heart of the Good Shepherd, who laid down his life for us in order to give us everything good.

– **Father Richard Veras**

Could you be made more happy by creating us? And how could we be happy but in obeying you? Yet we determined not to be happy as you would have us happy, but to find out a happiness of our own; and so we left you. O my God, what a return is it that we—that I—make you when we sin!

O my God, I confess that before now I have utterly forgotten this, and that I am continually forgetting it! I have acted many a time as if I were my own master, and turned from you rebelliously. I have acted according to my own pleasure, not according to yours. And so far have I hardened myself, as not to feel as I ought how evil this is. I do not understand how dreadful sin is—and I do not hate it, and fear it, as I ought. I have no horror of it, or loathing. I do not turn from it with indignation, as being an insult to you, but I trifle with it, and, even if I do not commit great sins, I have no great reluctance to do small ones. O my God, what a great and awful difference is there between what I am and what I ought to be!

– Blessed John Henry Newman

Heart Sense in Deep Water (Rv 7:9, 14b-17)

My heart leans heavy
on barren things
that can't support
the pain it sings.
Its arms must hug
the rocks
on shore,
while its feet
dance
the ocean floor.
Through salty water
swallowed at birth
its tongue must taste
the salt of earth.
Its ears,
submerged,
must hear the sigh
of sunken treasures'
daily try.
Its eyes must see
a final place
where running tears
can win the race.

– Rita A. Simmonds

HE MAIN PURPOSE OF THE INCARNATION is the complete satisfaction of divine justice. It is a testimony of how much God is concerned with justice, since it radiates so brightly in the Incarnation and the Redemption. But divine mercy shines therein even brighter than justice. We owe it to divine mercy that the manner of paying our debt has left us richer than before the fall of our first parents. The perfect reconciliation of justice with mercy in the Incarnation and the Redemption gives us a deep insight into the attributes of God's nature, and invites us to humble ourselves before God's wisdom, goodness, and omnipotence.

We have only to review briefly the elements of the work established by Christ to lead mankind uninterruptedly to salvation, to be struck still more with the riches of divine mercy in the Incarnation and the Redemption. In each particular element there is something more than was due, more than was necessary, and more than we could expect. Now, to give more than is due in order that any want might be averted is a clear sign of mercy. The abundance of supernatural life brought by Christ our Lord to his sheep (Jn 10:10) is the greatest testimony to the mercy with which his divine heart overflowed.

– Servant of God Father Hyacinth Woroniecki, O.P.

Saint Margaret of Scotland

MARGARET († 1093) was educated in Hungary and exiled from her native England as a young woman. Her ship blew off course and landed in Scotland, King Malcolm's land. Malcolm took Margaret and her family in and made her his queen.

And Margaret, in turn, brought culture and beauty to Scotland. She was most attentive to Malcolm, reading to her illiterate husband from the sacred books, leading him into prayer. She commissioned craftsmen to build sacred vessels and needlewomen to construct the most sublime vestments for the priests. She built monasteries and hostels to give refuge to pilgrims. And she instructed them about the proper use of Sunday. For the first time, under Margaret, the people of Scotland took their Sabbath rest.

Perhaps the most interesting detail given us by Margaret's biographer is that Margaret was the bringer of high fashion to the Scottish court. Margaret lived in a time when hairshirts were common and penitential fasts were long and hard. But such things did not, in her mind, preclude adornment and finery. Margaret lived the true rhythms of the Christian life. Without the fasts, no one could know the wondrous joy of the feasts. And Margaret was one who knew how to make the feast a thing of joy, an anticipation of our heavenly home.

– Lisa Lickona

What If I Have Been Away from Confession for More Than a Year?

SOMEONE WHO RETURNS TO CONFESSION after an extended absence is a source of great joy and celebration: for God and his angels (who know more joy in heaven over one sheep brought back to the fold than for ninety-nine who remained; Lk 15:7); for oneself; for the Church at large—and for the priest privileged to minister God's mercy.

Priests do not disclose the content or even that a person went to confession. Priests do occasionally confide that during a stretch of confessions, a "big fish" was caught in the net of God's loving forgiveness. The size of the "fish" may refer to the gravity of sin or the duration someone has been away from the sacrament.

Different factors may keep one away: a previous confessor who was more harsh than merciful; infrequent opportunities at a local parish; a tendency to procrastinate; a lukewarm belief that Jesus really intends confession to be a "house specialty" on the menu of his mercy; and the fear of being "outed" as someone who is unfamiliar with the sacramental ritual. More grave is the fear that if we submit ourselves to the unconditional love of God offered in radical forgiveness, we might want to let God take possession of our will, our heart, mind, and soul.

Saint John of Ávila describes one who balks at Christ's compassion. When invited into the current of God's mercy and reassured one would not drown, the person refuses because he or she might feel drawn to go out further and deeper, and might never want to come out at all. Yet the truth instilled in us is that we do not belong to ourselves, but to the Father of mercies who longs to save rather than condemn us.

Some practical steps to participate fully in the sacrament: technology can be a great asset, for one can readily access apps and websites that review how to go to confession, how to examine one's conscience, and how to make an act of contrition. It is fine to bring a handheld device into the confessional. Parish churches often stock similar resources in their pamphlet racks. To prepare and identify real sins we have committed, one could use Scripture such as the Ten Commandments (Ex 20:1-17), the Beatitudes (Mt 5:1-12), or a comparison of the works of the flesh versus the fruits of the Spirit (Gal 5:16-23).

Even if we have prepared well, we might still draw a blank when meeting the priest face-to-face. Be not afraid! God's grace has already drawn you to the well of mercy, and the priest will happily supply prompts that will dissolve anxiety and allow the Spirit to counsel us and absolve us of all sin, restoring us to full friendship with Jesus.

– Father William M. Joensen

As CATHOLICS, we believe God's greatest attribute is mercy. When my twenty-year-old brother was murdered in 2007 on the campus of Virginia Tech, I greatly struggled with this tenet of our faith. I felt abandoned by a God who lied to me about his goodness.

A year after Matthew died, my family received a letter from the mother of a student who had survived the ordeal. She thanked us for our son and brother's sacrifice, which she believed saved her daughter's life. Cadet Matthew La Porte had barred the classroom door with a desk. When the shooter forced his way in, Matthew charged him and sustained seven gunshot wounds.

I prayed for healing. God said, "Forgive the shooter. Tell your story." A giant leap of faith and trust in him enabled me to do the impossible—to forgive my brother's killer and share with others what I had experienced. It was then that my life changed a second time. Peace came to me when I put my energy into loving others rather than seeking revenge. Joy came when I saw how sharing my story helped others face their own personal struggles. Mercy does not allow those who wrong us to get away with injustice. Mercy repairs what is broken, restores hope, and molds us into holy souls who emulate more closely the heart of Jesus Christ. Mercy is everything.

– Priscilla La Porte

S HE WANTED TO KNOW her students better. That's what the news report said of a third-grade teacher of children from low-income families. She passed out paper, asking them to complete the statement, "I wish my teacher knew…." The results were touching and heartbreaking as some wished she knew they missed their deported father or that they had no friends. Once the teacher and children shared their fears and hopes, a stronger classroom emerged.

The ancient community of the Thessalonians faced a growing concern and worry: was the second coming of Jesus imminent? If given a piece of paper, they might have written, "I wish Jesus knew my fears and worry about when he will return."

It is Paul who takes out paper and writes his second letter assuring them Jesus does know. In his mercy he offers them *everlasting encouragement and good hope* (2 Thes 2:16).

Often the greatest mercy we can experience is realizing Jesus knows our doubts and worries. He never dismisses them. Instead he offers us mercy, showing us the reasons to have hope. We who have been shown this mercy create a stronger community of faith in listening to what others wish we knew.

– Monsignor Gregory E. S. Malovetz

It was in the Word's Passion
that souls came, by your light
to a perfect knowledge of your charity's affection.
For then the fire
hidden under our ashes
began to show itself
completely and generously
by splitting open his most holy body
one with wood of the cross.
And it was to draw the soul's affection
to high things,
and to bring the mind's eye
to gaze into the fire,
that your eternal Word
wanted to be lifted up high.
From there you have shown us love
in your blood,
and in your blood
you have shown us your mercy
and generosity.
In this blood
you have shown how our sin weighs you down.
In this blood
you have washed the face of your spouse, the soul,
with whom you are joined
by the union of the divine nature
with our human nature.
In this blood you clothed her
when she was naked,
and by your death
you restored her to life.

– Saint Catherine of Siena

"Behold, I make all things new"

(Rv 21:5a)

The new morning light
loves everything again:
the dangling leaves
kicking like children's feet
above the earth,
the clouds that captured darkness
like a spot on the lung
and gently wept
all night long,
the pink flowers
along the wall—
before un-adored,
chosen now
with a touch
that deepens blush,
fading the care of forgottenness.
And you—
still sleeping in your bed
though the sun through the skylight
brings a certain smile
to what's half sprung
from your pillow.
And me—
seeing you loved
in the new morning light,
stung with sorrow
for what I couldn't see
last night.

– Rita A. Simmonds

*W*E WILL BE ASKED if we have helped others to escape the doubt that causes them to fall into despair and which is often a source of loneliness; if we have helped to overcome the ignorance in which millions of people live, especially children deprived of the necessary means to free them from the bonds of poverty; if we have been close to the lonely and afflicted; if we have forgiven those who have offended us and have rejected all forms of anger and hate that lead to violence; if we have had the kind of patience God shows, who is so patient with us; and if we have commended our brothers and sisters to the Lord in prayer. In each of these "little ones," Christ himself is present. His flesh becomes visible in the flesh of the tortured, the crushed, the scourged, the malnourished, and the exiled…to be acknowledged, touched, and cared for by us….

This Holy Year will bring to the fore the richness of Jesus' mission echoed in the words of the prophet: to bring a word and gesture of consolation to the poor, to proclaim liberty to those bound by new forms of slavery in modern society, to restore sight to those who can see no more because they are caught up in themselves, to restore dignity to all those from whom it has been robbed. The preaching of Jesus is made visible once more in the response of faith which Christians are called to offer by their witness.

– *Misericordiae Vultus* 15, 16

Saint Catherine of Siena

THE TWENTY-FOURTH CHILD born to an Italian family, Catherine († 1380) was on intimate terms with Jesus from an early age. A vision led her to join the Dominican Third Order. In another vision, Christ offered Catherine an exquisite ring as a marriage gift. She could not refuse her "Sweet Jesus, Lord Jesus." And she could not help but recommend him to others. "Remember Christ crucified, God and man," she wrote to one friend. "Make your aim the Crucified Christ, hide in the wounds of the Crucified Christ and drown in the blood of the Crucified Christ."

Many sought Catherine's wisdom and hearkened to her preaching. She loved the poor with Jesus' own heart, the heart he had mystically placed within her. But the greatest beneficiary of Catherine's love was the pope, who was exiled from Rome. She called him "sweet Christ on earth" and offered him gentle correction, begging him to return—and he did. When the election of an antipope followed, throwing all of Europe into confusion, Catherine redoubled her prayers and intense penances. She fell gravely ill, choosing to offer her every pain for the suffering Church. As death drew near, Catherine declared, "In leaving my body, truly I have consumed and given my life in the Church and for the Holy Church, which is for me a most unique grace."

– Lisa Lickona

Why Should I Confess the Same Sins Over and Over Again?

SIN BORES US TO DEATH if we think that we are also boring God and so succumb to the lie that confession of habitual sins is an exercise in futility.

The Risen Jesus pulls Peter aside to pose the question three times: *"Do you love me?"* (Jn 21:15-19). Jesus is not rubbing Peter's face in his infidelity. His mercy repeatedly frees Peter to profess his love. Peter must radically depend on God if his words are to mean anything.

Every confession revives our capacity to love. We imitate Peter in a dynamic that correlates with three essential parts of the sacrament: contrition (love stirs remorse for sin); confession (actual naming and numbering of sins peels away my denial and lays bare my love); and penance (I remedy and restore love where it was forsaken).

The more we approach Jesus in the sacrament of confession, the more we share in the recreative power of the cross. As both penitent and confessor, I know very well how regular confession helps instill hope that God's grace, dripping like raindrops on a sometimes stony heart, softens habits of inertia so that, instead of a weary recitation of sins, we wonderfully recognize how this time, in this particular area of life, habit has been overcome, and—thanks be to God—we have truly heeded the call to *"go and sin no more."*

– Father William M. Joensen

"SOMETIMES A LANTERN moves along the night," says the poet Gerard Manley Hopkins, "that interests our eyes" (from "The Lantern Out of Doors"). And we wonder, who is he? Where is he going? The thought passes. After all, he is a stranger. But even those who leave their mark upon our minds, because of their beauty, their virtue, or their intelligence, fade from our memories with distance and time.

This forgetting is a sort of reverse-interest. The longer we leave the treasure in the bank of the soul, the less it is, until it dwindles to nothing. "Out of sight is out of mind," says the poet. It is all too easy for us to forget even our friends, let alone some sole wanderer of the night.

Mercy then is memory, and the memory of God does not fade. Christ is not only the king who expects profit from the golden talents he bestows upon us. He is himself the interest-maker, the merciful investor of his love in us. The profit he demands is friendship, and he is a dogged man of business indeed:

> Christ minds: Christ's interest,
>   what to avow or amend
> There, eyes them, heart wants,
>   care haunts, foot follows kind,
> Their ransom, their rescue, and first,
>   fast, last friend.

– Anthony Esolen

A MAN ONCE SAID TO ME that Catholic moral teaching was without pity for people, causing them to suffer. "It was therefore not Christian, for Jesus would never knowingly make anyone suffer," he said.

This made me think of Jesus' encounter with Peter over the breakfast on the shore of the Sea of Galilee, following the Resurrection (Jn 21:15-19). It is clear that, as enthusiastic as Peter is to see Jesus—to the point of leaping into the water to meet him—he still is not entirely comfortable in his presence; there is some unfinished, painful business to attend to.

As they finished breakfast, Jesus asked Peter three times, *"Do you love me…?"* And three times Peter was obliged to answer, *"Lord, you know that I love you."* The third time the Gospel tells us that *Peter was distressed.* This was because the third time made it clear to Peter that Jesus was referring to the three times that Peter had denied knowing him. It was very painful, but the mercy of Christ urged Peter to face the one he had betrayed in order to begin anew, without shadows, their path together. His questions made it clear that Peter had but to cling to the truth, that Peter *loved him*, in order to go on.

Mercy can be very painful, for mercy desires us to return to life, to reality. It is there that the Lord meets us.

– Father Vincent Nagle, F.S.C.B.

O Mary!
Mary!
Temple of the Trinity!
O Mary, bearer of the fire!
Mary, minister of mercy!
Mary, seedbed of the fruit!
The world was redeemed
when in the Word your own flesh suffered:
Christ
by his Passion redeemed us;
you,
by your grief of body and spirit.

O Mary, peaceful sea!
Mary, giver of peace!
Mary, fertile soil!
You, Mary, are the new-sprung plant
from whom we have the fragrant blossom,
the Word, God's only-begotten Son,
for in you, fertile soil,
was this word sown.
You are the soil
and you are the plant.
O Mary, chariot of fire,
you bore the fire,
hidden and veiled
under the ashes of your humanness.

– Saint Catherine of Siena

A Greater Crash (Jn 14:23-29)

"I am going away
and I will come back to you."

The waves come in
whitewash the shore
texture it with wind
and deposit gifts
of clear creatures,
strands of emerald weed,
shells, smooth stones.

The ocean retreats
leaving a trace of itself
that glistens the grains
that look like billions of tiny eyes
beneath glass
surveying the sun
that does not blind
but beholds their gaze:
A dazzling exchange—
the sun and the shore
awaiting the crash
of a greater force.

— Rita A. Simmonds

*W*E CANNOT OMIT one more gift complementing the work of the Incarnation and the Redemption, namely, the participation of the Mother of the Savior in the work of her Son. This gift was not so necessary a one because, according to…Saint Thomas, one drop of Christ's blood would suffice to redeem the whole world from all its crimes. But how wonderfully did it correspond to the most profound needs of the human heart, longing to cling close to the heart of a mother.

Therefore, in giving to us from the height of the cross as our spiritual Mother her whose heart he knew better than anyone else, Jesus showed us one more proof of his mercy, which proof we should value next to the gift of himself in the Church and in the Eucharist.

Also the gift of his Mother as Co-redemptrix and Mediatrix of all graces was neither due to nor expected by us. This is also an outcome of the infinite goodness of our heavenly Father who was pleased to give the Mother of his Son the great dignity of the spiritual Mother of all people, for, as Saint Bernard expressed it centuries ago, "it pleased God that we would have everything through Mary." It is not surprising, therefore, that we see the closest bond uniting Mary with divine mercy and that we greet her every day as our Queen and Mother of Mercy.

– Servant of God Father Hyacinth Woroniecki, O.P.

Saint Gianna Beretta Molla

GIANNA (†1962) was two months pregnant with her fourth child when doctors discovered a tumor on her uterus. A physician herself, Gianna understood her options: either remove the uterus with the tumor, ending the child's life, or remove the tumor and leave the child, risking a severe injury to her uterus, a threat to her own life.

Gianna told them to remove the tumor. For seven months she watched and prayed. "I have entrusted myself to the Lord in faith and hope, against the terrible advice of medical science, 'Either mother or child'.... I renew the offer of my life to the Lord. I am ready for anything provided the life of my child is saved." On April 21, 1962, a healthy baby girl was born to Gianna. Gianna, however, contracted a grave infection. Those around her testified to her agony leading up to death. Again and again she kissed the crucifix, cleaving to Christ.

Gianna, Saint John Paul II taught, lived in a world that has declared the values of the Christian mother to be "obsolete." "As a result, a woman who is determined to be consistent with her principles often feels deeply alone, alone in her love which she cannot betray, and to which she must remain faithful. Her guiding principle is Christ, who has revealed the love which the Father bestows on us."

– Lisa Lickona

Why Do We Need to Tell Our Sins to a Priest?

IF CHRIST HAD NOT DIED FOR OUR SINS, we would not have to confess our sins to a priest in order to find reconciliation with God. Before Christ, it was enough to acknowledge one's sins before God by bringing an animal for a sin-offering. But there was no such thing as telling the priest what you were sorry for—it wasn't any of his business. And before the Law of Moses, every man was on his own before God.

But in the New Law, if we want reconciliation with God, we must confess to the priest. For if we want reconciliation with God, we must find reconciliation with Christ. He bought this reconciliation by laying down his life. And he did this quite knowingly for every person who ever would sin and seek reconciliation, for every generation down to the end of time.

As Saint Paul said, "he died for me"; so must every Christian say the same. He died not for the race; not for man in general; not for a better humanity in the future. For me. So, seeking reconciliation with Christ for my sin, I seek reconciliation with the one who died for this, precisely this sin that I, and no one else, committed.

If Christ here embarrasses us with his knowledge of our sin, he also offers us a surer reconciliation. And in this light, it seems strange to ask forgiveness without mentioning our sin to the one who grants forgiveness at the price

of his blood. This would be like the Prodigal Son slipping back onto the estate without confessing his sin to his father.

But then, why confession to a priest? Why can I not just turn to Jesus in my heart? No, the cross was public and visible; reconciliation is visible and sacramental. Just so, the priest is the ambassador of Christ, the minister of Christ exercising Christ's power to forgive sin.

So the Risen Lord says to the Apostles: *"Receive the Holy Spirit. Whose sins you forgive they are forgiven."* And: *"Whose sins you retain, they are retained"* (Jn 20:22-23). Evidently, the Apostle knows what he is forgiving or retaining. So we really and truly confess our own sin to Christ in confessing it to his minister.

And this relieves us of the burden and pride of judging ourselves before God. Which we do, willy nilly, if we do not confess to the minister of Christ. The message we need to deliver is then delivered to the true Judge. Confession is what follows from the transaction of the cross. It's the way incarnate mercy works.

– Father Guy Mansini, o.s.b.

Vigil to Dry Tears
Litany of Consolation

◀ When my life lacks any purpose or direction—Lord Jesus, you say:
Come to me, all you who are weary and find life burdensome.

◀ When the harshness and ruthlessness of life assail me—Lord Jesus, you say:
I am gentle and humble of heart; your souls will find rest.

◀ When I am full of doubt, with no one to depend on—Lord Jesus, you say:
Everything is possible to one who trusts.

◀ When bitterness and resentment poison my heart—Lord Jesus, you say:
If the Son frees you, you will truly be free.

◀ When I see nothing but my wrongdoing and failures—Lord Jesus, you say:
Do not let your heart be troubled; have faith in me.

◀ When I am done in by the hatred and violence of the world—Lord Jesus, you say:
Take courage; I have overcome the world.

◀ When I think that happiness is nothing but a delusion—Lord Jesus, you ask me:
"Do you love me?"

◀ When my life reaches a dead end and I lack all desire—Lord Jesus, you ask me:
"Do you love me?"

◀ When it seems that life has no meaning—Lord Jesus, you ask me:
"Do you love me?"

◀ Yes, Lord Jesus, I do!—Lord Jesus, you say:
Live on in my love.

– Father Peter John Cameron, O.P

MANY PEOPLE HAVE EXPERIENCED an extension on their life and have used their added years—after surviving a grave illness or accident, for example—to live with new and godlier priorities. King Hezekiah experienced this mercy in the Book of Isaiah (38:1-20). Such moments of being rescued from death are certainly a gift and grace from the hand of the Lord. It may then be, in accordance with this pattern, that the young man raised by Jesus in Nain (Lk 7:11-17) stood to profit from his new lease on life. The tragedy of a young life cut short inevitably makes all good hearts ache.

The way the Gospel goes, however, the Lord's merciful compassion is pointed in another direction, toward the *mother*, rather than the son. Indeed, the son's life is almost an incidental consideration. Jesus' single gesture after the miracle is to give the boy to his mother—as he will give John to Mary from the cross. In every similar experience of loneliness and loss we can stand alongside this abandoned and vulnerable widow, beneath the cross by the Mother of God, to hear Jesus' words, *"Do not weep"* (Lk 23:28), and receive from his hand the mercy of a presence stronger than death.

– Father Anthony Giambrone, O.P.

Mother of silence, who watches over the mystery of God, save us from the idolatry of the present time, to which those who forget are condemned. Purify the eyes of pastors with the eye-wash of memory: Take us back to the freshness of the origins, for a prayerful, penitent Church.

Mother of the beauty that blossoms from faithfulness to daily work, lift us from the torpor of laziness, pettiness, and defeatism. Clothe pastors in the compassion that unifies, that makes whole; let us discover the joy of a humble, brotherly, serving Church.

Mother of tenderness who envelops us in patience and mercy, help us burn away the sadness, impatience, and rigidity of those who do not know what it means to belong. Intercede with your Son to obtain that our hands, our feet, our hearts be agile: let us build the Church with the Truth of love.

Mother, we shall be the People of God, pilgrims bound for the Kingdom. Amen.

– Pope Francis

Martyrdom (Acts 7:55-60)

We live in a pained world
with hearts full of pain.
We remember Stephen
on the ground
converting his killers,
accepting stones
for an ignorant age.

"Do not hold their offenses
against them."

Our hearts keep burning
as the world keeps offending
and turning.

Is there no end to this ending?
Does anyone know what he does?
Do I even know what I do?
what I've done?

Yet the ink still bleeds on the page
and every word
(My God!)
is saved.

– Rita A. Simmonds

*T*HE DIVINE HEART OF JESUS…gives us his own dearly beloved Mother, Mary, as our Mother and protector. She is the saintly creature among all saints and angels, to whom he refuses nothing, since she is the worthiest and most loved of all mothers. Besides, he has given her a very large heart, which enables her to notice even the smallest of tears and work for the salvation and sanctification of every single human being.

She is the bridge that leads us to the most Holy Heart of Jesus.

Should we then despair if we happen to fall in sin and sink into a vicious life, despising the divine graces if we no longer pay attention to the good example shown by other people, if we are deaf to every wholesome inspiration and become unworthy of new graces? No, not any more!

In fact, we now have a Mother who has been given to us by God, a Mother who tenderly watches over every action, every word, every thought of ours.

She does not ask herself whether we are worthy or unworthy of the grace of her tenderness. She is only the Mother of Mercy; therefore, she rushes to our help even when we do not invoke her name, even when the poverty of our soul is so clearly evident. In fact, the more our soul is disfigured by sin, the more shall divine mercy show itself to us, that mercy which the Immaculate embodies.

– Saint Maximilian Mary Kolbe

Saint Damien de Veuster

WHEN DAMIEN DE VEUSTER SUCCUMBED to Hansen's disease on the Hawaiian island of Molokai in 1889, he had been fifteen years among the lepers. Only a few years later, Scottish man of letters Robert Louis Stevenson visited the colony and interviewed those who had known him. Shortly after this, C. M. Hyde, a Presbyterian minister, vilified Damien's memory in print, calling the priest a "coarse, dirty man, headstrong and bigoted." Stevenson, himself a Presbyterian, came to Damien's defense.

Stevenson admitted that Damien was neither sophisticated nor cultured. He was no teacher of hygiene. But he had come from Belgium to Molokai to stay with people who had no hope of cure or comfort; he endured to the end where others, horrified by disease and deformity, feared even to set foot. Stevenson gives us the real Damien, who, "crowned with glories and horrors, toiled and rotted in that pigsty of his under the cliffs of Kalawao," the "plain, uncouth peasant" who "steps into the battle, under the eyes of God, and succors the afflicted, and consoles the dying, and is himself afflicted in his turn, and dies upon the field of honor."

Stevenson predicted that this "plain, noble human brother and father of ours" would someday become a saint. Indeed, Damien de Veuster was canonized in 2009.

– Lisa Lickona

The Difference between Contrition and Attrition

ONE OF THE KEY MOMENTS IN CONFESSION occurs when the priest asks the penitent to say an "act of contrition." Catholics commonly memorize a form of this prayer. But we might ask: *What exactly is contrition?* The Church gives us a definition: "sorrow of the soul and detestation for the sins committed, together with the resolution not to sin again" (CCC 1451). Contrition is a gift from God that enables us to recognize the true horror of sin.

Authentic contrition takes various forms. One is "perfect" and the other "imperfect." The reality that characterizes *perfect contrition* is the presence of the supernatural virtue of charity—the love of God above all else, and the hatred for sin because it is contrary to our common life and friendship with God. Because charity is present, perfect contrition forgives all sins (even grave sins). Moreover, it always includes the firm resolution to go to confession as soon as possible (CCC 1452).

Imperfect contrition (also known as "attrition") is sorrow for sin "born of the consideration of sin's ugliness or the fear of eternal damnation and other penalties threatening the sinner" (CCC 1453). Because it lacks the divine friendship of charity, however, imperfect contrition does not obtain the forgiveness of grave sins.

Penitents may be tempted to self-diagnose the type of contrition they bring to the confessional: *Am I sorry for my sins because I feel a profound love of God, or merely because I am afraid of the punishments that follow upon the sins I have committed? Do I have perfect contrition or only imperfect contrition?* However, an overemphasis on this line of questioning does not benefit the penitent. It fosters a harmful preoccupation with one's own psychological disposition (which is often uncertain) rather than the saving power of God's love (which is always certain).

In his mercy, our Lord has given us an infallible means of ensuring the presence of perfect contrition in our soul. He has given us the gift of confession. In the Sacrament of Reconciliation, Jesus always imparts the grace of charity that makes contrition perfect. He actually forgives our sins when we go to confession. Even if a sinner only has imperfect contrition when he or she approaches the confessional, perfect contrition and the forgiveness of sins is truly caused within the sacrament. Our Savior always perfects what is imperfect in the sorrow of those who draw near to the sacrament of his mercy.

– Father Cajetan Cuddy, O.P.

THE INDULGENCE OF THE WORLD is indifference, with a bland and fading smile. But there's nothing bland about the mercy of God.

A young man, a failure, apparently dying, has returned ("The Enduring Chill") to a shambles of a southern village, his home. His ambition was to be a great writer, mingling with intellectuals in New York. He believes in nothing. All his works were stillborn. He has destroyed them, except for a letter intended for his mother after his death. That letter takes up two notebooks. In it he is merciless: "I have no talent. I can't create. I have nothing but the desire for these things. Why didn't you kill that too? Woman, why did you pinion me?"

But the author, Flannery O'Connor, never leaves those she loves in peace. Asbury longs to die. He wants his icy words to give his mother an "enduring chill," but the chill will be his, colder and cleaner than he can imagine. It turns out he has "undulant fever," not deadly, but incurable. So from his bed he stares at an old water-stain on the ceiling, in the form of a bird of prey carrying an icicle, and he knows he will be the victim of God's mercy: "The Holy Ghost, emblazoned in ice instead of fire continued, implacable, to descend."

– Anthony Esolen

A MAN SPEAKING ABOUT his recovery from addiction told of how he had been counseled, "You have to hug the cactus." That is, you have to embrace your real circumstances, own up to the truth about your life. This is because mercy can come to us only on that narrow path of reality as it is, instead of reality as we might like it to be. Truth is the high cost of receiving Jesus' freely offered mercy.

We see this in the encounter between the Canaanite woman and the Lord (Mt 15:21-28). She is a pagan coming from outside of salvation history. Thus the Lord does not receive her entreaties, but calls her a dog: *"It is not right to take the food of the children and throw it to the dogs."*

In Middle Eastern culture, calling someone a dog is liable to result in lethal combat. Jesus has made perfectly clear to the Canaanite woman the gulf between them. Yet she embraces his painful words in order to draw closer to the Savior: *"Please, Lord, for even the dogs eat the scraps that fall from the table of their masters."*

She accepts her status as lowly outsider and recognizes Jesus the Jew as Master. The Lord says to her, *"O woman, great is your faith!"* And he heals her sick daughter. The truth may be objectionable to us, but it is the only place where mercy can be found.

– Father Vincent Nagle, F.S.C.B.

Spirit of truth, you who search the depths of God,
memory and prophecy in the Church,
lead mankind to recognize in Jesus of Nazareth
the Lord of glory, the Savior of the world,
the supreme fulfillment of history.

Come, Spirit of love and peace!

Creator Spirit, hidden builder of the Kingdom,
by the power of your holy gifts guide the Church
to carry to the coming generations
the light of the Word who brings salvation.

Spirit of holiness,
      divine breath which moves the universe,
come and renew the face of the earth.
Awaken in Christians a desire for full unity,
that they may be for the world an effective sign
      and instrument
of intimate union with God and of the unity
      of the whole human race.

Spirit of consolation,
      unfailing source of joy and peace,
inspire solidarity with the poor,
grant the sick the strength they need,
pour out trust and hope upon
      those experiencing trials,
awaken in all hearts a commitment to a better future.

Spirit of wisdom, inspiration of minds and hearts,
direct science and technology
to the service of life, justice, and peace.

Spirit of life, by whose power the Word was made flesh
in the womb of the Virgin Mary,
    the woman of attentive silence,
make us docile to the promptings of your love
and ever ready to accept the signs of the times
which you place along the paths of history.

– Saint John Paul II

What Is a Jubilee?

I HAVE PROCLAIMED an *Extraordinary Jubilee of Mercy* as a special time for the Church, a time when the witness of believers might grow stronger and more effective…. We want to live this Jubilee Year in light of the Lord's words: *Merciful like the Father*…. I present, therefore, this Extraordinary Jubilee Year dedicated to living out in our daily lives the mercy which the Father constantly extends to all of us…. In this Jubilee Year, may the Church echo the Word of God that resounds strong and clear as a message and a sign of pardon, strength, aid, and love.

– Misericordiae Vultus 3, 13, 25

IN THE ROMAN CATHOLIC TRADITION, a Holy Year, or Jubilee, is a great religious event. It is a year of forgiveness of sins, of reconciliation between adversaries, of conversion and receiving the Sacrament of Reconciliation, and consequently of solidarity, hope, justice, commitment to serve God with joy, in peace with our brothers and sisters. A Jubilee year is above all a year of Christ, who brings life and grace to humanity.

The origin of the Christian Jubilee goes back to the Old Testament. The Law of Moses prescribed a special year for the Jewish people: *You shall hallow the fiftieth year and proclaim the liberty throughout the land, to all its inhabitants; it shall be a jubilee for you when each of you shall return to his property and each of you shall return to his family.*

This fiftieth year is to be a jubilee year for you: you will not sow, you will not harvest the un-gathered corn, you will not gather the untrimmed vine. The jubilee is to be a holy thing to you, you will eat what comes from the fields (Lv 25:10-12). This year was announced with a goat's-horn trumpet, called *Yobel* in Hebrew—the origin of the word "jubilee". The celebration of this year also included the restitution of land to the original owners, the remission of debts, the liberation of slaves, and the land being left fallow. In the New Testament, Jesus presents himself as the One who brings the old Jubilee to completion, because he has come to *preach the year of the Lord's favor* (Is 61:2).

The Jubilee is called Holy Year, not only because it begins, is marked, and ends with solemn holy acts, but also because its purpose is to encourage holiness of life. It is convoked to strengthen faith, to encourage works of charity and brotherly communion within the Church and in society, and to call Christians to be more sincere and coherent in their faith in Christ.

A Jubilee can be "ordinary" if it falls after the set period of years, and "extraordinary" when it is proclaimed for some outstanding event. There have been twenty-six "ordinary" Holy Years so far. "Extraordinary" Jubilees began in the 16th century, and they can vary in length from a few days to a year. There were two extraordinary Jubilees last century: 1933, proclaimed by Pope Pius XI to mark the 1,900th anniversary of Redemption, and 1983, proclaimed by Pope John Paul II to mark 1,950 years since the Redemption carried out by Christ through his Death and Resurrection in the year 33.

The History of the Jubilee

The first ordinary Jubilee was proclaimed in 1300 by Pope Boniface VII. Throughout the world, there was great suffering, caused by wars and diseases; the people had a great desire to return to a more holy way of living. So Christians determined to walk to Rome, to pray at the tombs of the Apostles Peter and Paul, and to receive the pope's blessing, in order to obtain the grace and strength to carry on. They came in their thousands at Christmas in 1299. Because of their great number, the pope, full of admiration for their faith, proclaimed a "year of forgiveness of all sins." A similar year was to be held in the future, every hundred years.

During the Avignon Papacy (1305–1377), there were many requests for the second Jubilee to be held in 1350 instead of 1400. Clement VI gave his consent and set a period of fifty years between Jubilees.

Later, Pope Urban VI decided to reduce the period to thirty-three years, in memory of the earthly life of Jesus. But it was in 1425, and not in 1433, that Pope Martin V proclaimed the Holy Year 1425 with two novelties: a special commemorative Jubilee Medal and the opening of a Holy Door in the Cathedral of Saint John Lateran.

In 1470, Pope Paul II fixed the Jubilee for every twenty-five years. The next Holy Year, 1475, was proclaimed by Sixtus IV, who for the occasion ordered the building of the Sistine Chapel and the Sixtus Bridge over the Tiber (both named after him).

In 1500, Pope Alexander VI announced that the Doors in the four major basilicas would be opened, and that he himself would open the Holy Door of Saint Peter's.

During the Jubilee 1750, proclaimed by Pope Benedict XIV, Saint Leonardo da Porto Maurizio set up fourteen stations of the cross inside the ruins of the Coliseum.

In 1950, just a few years after World War II, Pope Pius XII called the Holy Year. It was during this year—on November 1, 1950—that the pope defined the Assumption into heaven of Mary, the Mother of Jesus, as a dogma of the Catholic faith. The Jubilee was called in 1975 by Pope Paul VI with two main themes for reflection and action: renewal and reconciliation. For the Jubilee Year 2000, Pope John Paul II called Christians to create a new culture of international solidarity and cooperation.

– **From the Vatican website**

The Gift of the Indulgence

A JUBILEE ALSO ENTAILS the granting of *indulgences*. This practice will acquire an even more important meaning in the Holy Year of Mercy. God's forgiveness knows no bounds…. The mercy of God…becomes *indulgence* on the part of the Father who, through…his Church, reaches the pardoned sinner and frees him from every residue left by the consequences of sin…. Let us live this Jubilee intensely, begging the Father to forgive our sins and to bathe us in his merciful "indulgence."

– *Misericordiae Vultus* 22

THE CELEBRATION OF THE JUBILEE YEAR is not only an extraordinary occasion for benefiting from the great gift of indulgences which the Lord gives us through the Church, but it is also a fitting opportunity to call the catechesis on indulgences to the attention of the faithful. The Apostolic Penitentiary is therefore publishing this sacred notice for the benefit of all who will be making Jubilee visits[1].

General Remarks on Indulgences

1. This is how an indulgence is defined in the *Code of Canon Law* (can. 992) and in the *Catechism of the Catholic Church* (n. 1471): "An indulgence is a remission before God of the temporal punishment due to sins whose guilt has

---

1. These guidelines were published by the Vatican for the Great Jubilee of 2000.

already been forgiven, which the faithful Christian who is duly disposed gains under certain prescribed conditions through the action of the Church which, as the minister of redemption, dispenses and applies with authority the treasury of the satisfactions of Christ and the saints."

2. In general, the gaining of indulgences requires certain prescribed *conditions* (below, nn. 3, 4), and the performance of certain prescribed *works* (nn. 8, 9, 10 indicate those specific to the Holy Year).

3. To gain indulgences, whether plenary or partial, it is necessary that the faithful be in the *state of grace* at least at the time the indulgenced work is completed.

4. A *plenary indulgence* can be gained only *once a day*. In order to obtain it, the faithful must, in addition to being in the state of grace:

— have the interior disposition of *complete detachment from sin, even venial sin*;

— *have sacramentally confessed* their sins;

— *receive the Holy Eucharist* (it is certainly better to receive it while participating in Holy Mass, but for the indulgence only Holy Communion is required);

— *pray for the intentions of the Supreme Pontiff*.

5. It is appropriate, but not necessary, that the sacramental confession and especially Holy Communion and the prayer for the Pope's intentions take place on the same day that the indulgenced work is performed; but it is sufficient that these sacred rites and prayers be carried out within several days (about twenty) before or after the indulgenced act. Prayer for the Pope's intentions is left to the choice of the faithful, but an "Our Father" and a "Hail Mary" are suggested. One sacramental confession suffices for several

plenary indulgences, but a separate Holy Communion and a separate prayer for the Holy Father's intentions are required for each plenary indulgence.

6. For the sake of those legitimately impeded, *confessors* can commute both the work prescribed and the conditions required (except, obviously, detachment from even venial sin).

7. Indulgences *can* always *be applied either to oneself or to the souls of the deceased*, but they cannot be applied to other persons living on earth.

Specific Aspects of the Jubilee Year

Having fulfilled the necessary *conditions* in nn. 3-4, the faithful may gain the Jubilee indulgence by performing one of the following *works*, listed here below in three categories:

8. *Works of piety or religion*

— Either make a *pious pilgrimage* to a Jubilee shrine or place—in Rome, to one of the four Patriarchal Basilicas (Saint Peter, Saint John Lateran, Saint Mary Major, or Saint Paul), or to the Basilica of the Holy Cross in Jerusalem, the Basilica of Saint Laurence in Campo Verano, the Shrine of Our Lady of Divine Love, or one of the Christian Catacombs—and participate there in Holy Mass or another liturgical celebration (Lauds or Vespers) or some pious exercise (the stations of the cross, the rosary, the recitation of the *Akathistos* hymn, etc.);

— or make a *pious visit*, as a group or individually, to one of these same Jubilee places, and there spend some time in Eucharistic adoration and pious meditations, ending with the Our Father, the profession of faith in any approved form, and prayer to the Blessed Virgin Mary.

9. *Works of mercy or charity*

— Either visit for a suitable time *their brothers or sisters in need or in difficulty* (the sick, the imprisoned, the elderly living alone, the handicapped, etc.), as if making a pilgrimage to Christ present in them;

— or *support* by a significant contribution *works of a religious or social nature* (for the benefit of abandoned children, young people in trouble, the elderly in need, foreigners in various countries seeking better living conditions);

— or *devote* a suitable part of *personal free time to activities benefiting the community* or other similar forms of personal sacrifice.

10. *Acts of penance*

For at least one whole day

— Either *abstain from unnecessary consumption* (smoking, alcohol, etc.);

— or *fast*,

— or *abstain from meat* (or other food according to the specific norms of the Bishops' Conferences), and *donate a proportionate sum of money to the poor*.

– **From the Vatican website**

Jubilee Pilgrimage

*T*HE PRACTICE OF *PILGRIMAGE* has a special place in the Holy Year, because it represents the journey each of us makes in this life. Life itself is a pilgrimage, and the human being is a *viator*, a pilgrim travelling along the road, making his way to the desired destination. Similarly, to reach the Holy Door in Rome or in any other place in the world, everyone, each according to his or her ability, will have to make a pilgrimage. This will be a sign that mercy is also a goal to reach and requires dedication and sacrifice. May pilgrimage be an impetus to conversion: by crossing the threshold of the Holy Door, we will find the strength to embrace God's mercy and dedicate ourselves to being merciful with others as the Father has been with us.

– *Misericordiae Vultus* 14

"THE WHOLE OF THE CHRISTIAN LIFE is like a great *pilgrimage to the house of the Father*...." The apostolic letter continues: "This pilgrimage takes place in the heart of each person, extends to the believing community and then reaches to the whole of humanity" (*Tertio Millennio Adveniente*, 49). This awareness makes each of us pilgrims, wayfarers on a common journey. By putting ourselves in continuity with the holy men and women who have gone before us, we enact the archetypal pattern devised for us *from the foundation of the world* (Mt 13:35). Moreover, when we remember that the Acts of the Apostles refers to the early Christian communities as members of *the Way* (Acts

18:26) and followers of *the Way* (Acts 24:14), we learn that the earliest name for the Church was *the Way* (Acts 9:2).

Despite our different backgrounds and personalities, despite our different interests and desires, can we discern any commonalities as we make our Way? Three come to mind: our processional life, the place of the old dispensation, and our transition to the new.

Our Processional Life

First of all, we are brought to the Church. Somebody carries us as an infant, or leads us as an adult, in order to receive the Sacrament of Baptism. This small procession, made up of parents and godparents, the priest and server, friends and relatives, symbolizes the direction of our life. For after having received the Sacrament of Initiation, we are free to enter the church and face the sanctuary. Over the years, we will have entered many churches and many sanctuaries, but the gaze remains primordial. As the Psalmist sings, *Your face, Lord, do I seek!/ Do not hide your face from me* (Ps 27:8-9). Presumably, when we are carried for the last time, again in a processional, from the church to our burial place, this prayer and its sentiments will be accomplished. *One thing I ask of the Lord;/ this I seek:/ To dwell in the Lord's house/ all the days of my life,/ To gaze on the Lord's beauty,/ to visit his temple* (Ps 27:4).

The Old Dispensation

Between these two moments of rebirth and birth, we live our various lives. Like the chosen people of Israel, we too must make our way from Egypt to Jerusalem by way of the desert. That is, we grow up generally under the sign of the Old Testament. All too quickly we learn "the dos" and "the don'ts." Parental authority confirms divine revelation

202

so that we cultivate a moral sense. Often enough, this superego exaggerates or minimizes our sense of responsibility, thereby revealing the liability behind the Yahweh of the Old Testament. Fear and vengeance do not bring out our healthier instincts. Nevertheless, the Ten Commandments, however believed and practiced, remain normative. Like every law, however, they are imposed; they come from without. So Saint Thomas Aquinas, for example, observes that however beneficial the old law was, it was also imperfect (*Summa theologiae* I-II, q. 94, a. 1). Like the Jews of old, we too must get beyond our desert experience and move to the more fertile plains associated with the Jordan. Otherwise, we risk becoming a wanderer, instead of a pilgrim.

Christ the Way

At some point in our life, the grace of Christ really moves us. It transforms us from children of the wrath to children at the gate. Saint Thomas refers to this transition as "the new law" or "the law of the gospel" (*Summa theologiae* I-II, q. 108, a. 2). The encounter with Christ proves so decisive that it moves us from exterior preoccupations to inner coherence. We approach the Lord in much the same way that we meet one another. At first, somewhat tentatively, formally, even distantly. But as the relationship develops, we find much to share. And while the Lord gradually takes possession of mind and heart, he discloses an ultimate value. At the heart of his personality lies an absolute love. Once we apprehend this fact, we are overcome, stunned, and bewildered. Like the burden that we call "the cross," he carries this absolute wherever he goes. Caught up in this personal finality, we too become increasingly solicitous. The love of Christ has a way of relativizing all other concerns and interests. At this point we recognize that he really is *the way* (Jn 14:6).

The interior life discloses something of the authentic Christian personality. Animated by the beatitudes, instead of the commandments, it confirms the Christian program appropriate for personal growth and for public outreach. So we are not talking about any static ideal. En route, the pilgrim extends the Christological form to every human event. In this way, he fulfills the Apostle's injunction to *redeem the time* (cf. Eph 5:16). To the extent that the pilgrim advances the Kingdom of God, paths seem to converge: the rural byway and the city highway, the mountain trail and the desert road meet, auguring something like another processional: *You have approached Mount Zion and the city of the living God, the heavenly Jerusalem, and countless angels in festal gathering* (Heb 12:22). The pilgrim has arrived!

Christians travel with Mary along the roads of love and join Elizabeth, who typifies the sisters and brothers in the world with whom a bond of faith and praise is to be established (see Lk 1:39-56). The *Magnificat* then becomes the song par excellence, not only of the *peregrinatio Mariae* but also of our pilgrimage in hope. Christians travel with Mary along the roads of the world to ascend right up to Calvary and be beside her like the Beloved Disciple, so that Christ may hand her over to them as their Mother (see Jn 19:26-27). Christians travel with Mary along the roads of faith so as to reach the Cenacle in the end and there, together with her, receive the gift of the Holy Spirit from her risen Son (see Acts 1:14; 2:1-4).

– **Father John P. McIntyre, s.j.**

Jubilee Holy Doors

I WILL HAVE THE JOY OF OPENING the Holy Door on the Solemnity of the Immaculate Conception. On that day, the Holy Door will become a *Door of Mercy* through which anyone who enters will experience the love of God who consoles, pardons, and instills hope. On the following Sunday, the Third Sunday of Advent, the Holy Door of…the Basilica of Saint John Lateran will be opened. In the following weeks, the Holy Doors of the other Papal Basilicas will be opened. On the same Sunday, I will announce that in every local church, at the cathedral…or, alternatively, at the co-cathedral or another church of special significance, a Door of Mercy will be opened for the duration of the Holy Year. At the discretion of the local ordinary, a similar door may be opened at any shrine frequented by large groups of pilgrims…. In this Jubilee Year, let us allow God to surprise us. He never tires of casting open the doors of his heart.

– *Misericordiae Vultus* 3, 25

PREPARATION TO ENTER A JUBILEE DOOR

I am the door of life.
I entreat all "Enter!"
Whoever seeks the joys of heaven
will cross through me.
He who was born of the Virgin

but not created by the Father—
he himself will save those who enter
and guide those who go out.

The Doors of Our Lives

Each day we enter and leave by so many doors without ever noticing…. It is good to stop and give thanks for all the doors God opens for us…. We reflect on Christ, the door to the Father, who knocks at the doors of our hearts, our homes, and our churches.

The Door to Our Hearts

We live in an age which longs for the presence of God. Our hearts search endlessly for meaning and purpose, never at rest until the grace of God enables us to answer his call.

Christ stands at our hearts and knocks. He calls tenderly to us, and as in that upper room where the disciples huddled in fear, he calls out to us: *"Do not fear! It is I!"*

And so the first Jubilee door I am called to prepare is the door to my heart. I am called to open my heart to Christ. Like Mary, who bore him deep within her body, Christ gives us the grace to open our hearts to the conversion, unity, and justice of the Kingdom of God.

The Door to Our Homes

We all remember the stories of the days of our grandparents when "no one locked their doors." We now live in an age of deadbolts and alarm systems….

Gone are the days we once knew, when the doors of our homes would open regularly to grandma and grandpa and all the aunts, uncles, and cousins. The doors of our homes don't seem to swing open quite so easily or as often as they used to.

Thus, a second challenge...is to find a way to open the doors of our homes to our families, our friends, and all who need us.

The Door to the Church

The third door of our lives is the door to the Church, the *ianua ecclesiae*. The Church door is the silent witness to all the moments of our lives. It is at this door that the priest or deacon first welcomes the parents of the newborn child and reminds them of the joy that embraced them when first they held that child in their arms. The same Church door looks down years later when that child arrives to be married as the priest receives the couple and greets them in a warm and friendly manner, showing that the Church shares their joy. Finally that door stands witness at the end of life as the body of the deceased Christian is received into the Church at the beginning of the funeral liturgy.

The Church door is the door to salvation, the portal of the Kingdom of God. Thus at the dedication of a church the bishop invites the people to enter through these doors for the first time with the words: "Go within his gates giving thanks, enter his courts with songs of praise."

Christ the Good Shepherd
Is the Door to the Kingdom

It is interesting to note that the antiphon that is sung as the dedication procession passes through these doors for the first time indicates that Christ himself is present in the procession: "Lift high the ancient portals! The King of

Glory enters." Christ himself is the door to life, and each of the casements of wood or metal which mark our churches or homes are but a reminder of him through whom we enter eternal life.

Christ himself told us that he is the door to the Kingdom of Heaven.

So Jesus said again, "Amen, amen, I say to you, I am the gate for the sheep. All who came [before me] are thieves and robbers, but the sheep did not listen to them. I am the gate. Whoever enters through me will be saved, and will come in and go out and find pasture. A thief comes only to steal and slaughter and destroy; I came so that they might have life and have it more abundantly" (Jn 10:7-10).

Jesus is using the images of two types of sheepfolds here. In the first two verses he describes the kind of "communal sheepfold" which each village would maintain and to which the shepherds might return their flocks each night. The pen was protected by a strong door which could be opened only by the chief shepherd's key.

The second type of sheepfold is described in subsequent verses. Such a containment was provided for those nights when the sheep were to be kept in the fields (as on the night of Jesus' birth). Such temporary sheepfolds usually consisted of a circle of rocks, with an opening at one end. The shepherd himself would serve as the gate to such sheepfolds, lying across its entrance to sleep.

Whether a sheep tried to leave a wolf tried to enter, they would have to do so by way of the shepherd himself!

In ancient Israel, the doors of Zion symbolized the very idea of entrance into God's presence. When Isaiah speaks of the day of universal peace he describes it as a time when God's *gates shall stand open constantly;/ day and night they shall not be closed* (Is 60:11). Likewise, the altar of holocausts was placed not within the tabernacle, but *in front of the entrance of the Dwelling of the meeting tent* (Ex 40:6). Christ is the fulfillment of all these expectations; he is the door through which we have *access…to the Father* (Eph 2:18). He is the *new and living way* (Heb 10:20). We might join our prayer to the Psalmist:

> Lift up your heads, O gates;
> rise up, you ancient portals,
> that the king of glory may enter.
> Who is this king of glory?
> The LORD, a mighty warrior,
> the LORD, mighty in battle.
> Lift up your heads, O gates;
> rise up, you ancient portals,
> that the king of glory may enter.
> Who is this king of glory?
> The LORD of hosts is the king of glory.
>
> (Ps 24:7-10)

Christ, then, is not only the door; he is the king who enters and the temple to whom the door leads! In days gone by, the *door to heaven* was the sky from which God gave us manna (see Ps 78:23), but now Christ is the true bread come down from heaven (cf. Jn 5:51). Jacob saw *the gateway to heaven* (Gn 28:17) in the earthly shrine at Bethel, but when the martyr, Saint Stephen, gazes at the door to heaven he sees the *glory of God and Jesus* (Acts 7:55).

Christ not only invites us to enter the Kingdom of Heaven through him, he even leaves the keys to his Apostles, assuring them that *whatever you bind on earth shall be bound in heaven; and whatever you loose on earth shall be loosed in heaven* (Mt 16:19). Unlike the foolish virgins whose lamps were not trimmed in time for the wedding banquet, those who repent of their sins and receive Christ's forgiveness through the Church will not find the door barred when the bridegroom returns (see Mt 25:10).

The Return of the Prodigal Son, Rembrandt (1606–1669)

– **Adapted from a blessing prepared by the Secretariat for the Liturgy of the National Conference of Catholic Bishops**

Hymn of the Jubilee of Mercy

Misericordes sicut Pater! [cf. Lk 6:36]
Misericordes sicut Pater! [motto of the Jubilee]

1. **Give thanks to the Father, for He is good**
in aeternum misericordia eius [cf. Ps 135:6]
He created the world with wisdom
in aeternum misericordia eius
He leads His people throughout history
in aeternum misericordia eius
He pardons and welcomes His children [cf. Lk 15]
in aeternum misericordia eius

2. **Give thanks to the Son, Light of the Nations**
in aeternum misericordia eius
He loved us with a heart of flesh [cf. Jn 15:12]
in aeternum misericordia eius
As we receive from Him, let us also give to Him
in aeternum misericordia eius
Hearts open to those who hunger and thirst [cf. Mt 25:31 ff.]
in aeternum misericordia eius

Misericordes sicut Pater!
Misericordes sicut Pater!

3. **Let us ask the Spirit for the seven holy gifts**
in aeternum misericordia eius
Fount of all goodness and the sweetest relief
in aeternum misericordia eius

Comforted by Him, let us offer comfort [cf. Jn 15:26-27]
in aeternum misericordia eius
Love hopes and bears all things [cf. 1 Cor 13:7]
in aeternum misericordia eius

4. Let us ask for peace from the God of all peace
in aeternum misericordia eius
The earth waits for the Good News
    of the Kingdom [cf. Mt 24:14]
in aeternum misericordia eius
Joy and pardon in the hearts of the little ones
in aeternum misericordia eius
The heavens and the earth will be renewed [cf. Ap 21:1]
in aeternum misericordia eius

Misericordes sicut Pater!
Misericordes sicut Pater!

The Official Jubilee Calendar of Events

> **DECEMBER 2015**

Tuesday, December 8, 2015
Solemnity of the Immaculate Conception
Opening of the Holy Door of Saint Peter's Basilica

Sunday, December 13, 2015
Third Sunday of Advent
Opening of the Holy Door of the Basilica of
Saint John Lateran and in the Cathedrals of the world

> **JANUARY 2016**

Friday, January 1, 2016
Solemnity of Mary, the Holy Mother of God
World Day for Peace
Opening of the Holy Door
of the Basilica of Saint Mary Major

Tuesday, January 19–Thursday, January 21, 2016
Jubilee for those engaged in pilgrimage work

Monday, January 25, 2016
Feast of the Conversion of Saint Paul
Opening of the Holy Door of the Basilica of
Saint Paul Outside the Walls
Jubilee sign of the Holy Father:
witness of the works of mercy

Tuesday, February 2, 2016
Feast of the Presentation of the Lord
Day for Consecrated Life
Jubilee for Consecrated Life and the closing of
the Year for Consecrated Life

Wednesday, February 10, 2016
Ash Wednesday
Sending forth of the Missionaries of Mercy,
Saint Peter's Basilica

Monday, February 22, 2016
Feast of the Chair of Saint Peter
Jubilee for the Roman Curia
Jubilee sign of the Holy Father:
witness of the works of mercy

› MARCH 2016

Friday, March 4 and Saturday, March 5, 2016
"24 Hours for the Lord" with a penitential liturgy
in Saint Peter's Basilica
on the afternoon of Friday, March 4
"Vigil to Dry Tears" on Saturday, March 5

Sunday, March 20, 2016
Palm Sunday
The diocesan day for youth in Rome
Jubilee sign of the Holy Father:
witness of the works of mercy

> ## April 2016

Sunday, April 3, 2016
Divine Mercy Sunday
Jubilee for those who are devoted to
the spirituality of Divine Mercy

Sunday, April 24, 2016
Fifth Sunday of Easter
Jubilee for young boys and girls (ages 13 to 16)
To profess the faith and construct a culture of mercy
Jubilee sign of the Holy Father:
witness of the works of mercy

> ## May 2016

Sunday, May 29, 2016
The Solemnity of Corpus Christi in Italy
Jubilee for deacons

> ## June 2016

Friday, June 3, 2016
Solemnity of the Most Sacred Heart of Jesus
Jubilee for priests
160 years since the introduction of the Feast
by Pius IX in 1856

Sunday, June 12, 2016
11th Sunday in Ordinary Time
Jubilee for those who are ill and
for persons with disabilities
Jubilee sign of the Holy Father:
witness of the works of mercy

Tuesday, July 26–Sunday, July 31, 2016
To conclude on the 18th Sunday in Ordinary Time
Jubilee for young people
World Youth Day in Kraków, Poland

> SEPTEMBER 2016

Sunday, September 4, 2016
23rd Sunday in Ordinary Time
Memorial of Blessed Teresa of Calcutta—September 5
Jubilee for workers and volunteers of mercy

Sunday, September 25, 2016
26th Sunday in Ordinary Time
Jubilee for catechists

> OCTOBER 2016

Saturday, October 8 and Sunday, October 9, 2016
Saturday and Sunday after
the Memorial of Our Lady of the Rosary
Marian Jubilee

> NOVEMBER 2016

Tuesday, November 1, 2016
Solemnity of All Saints
Holy Mass celebrated by the Holy Father
in memory of the faithful departed

Sunday, November 6, 2016

32nd Sunday in Ordinary Time

In Saint Peters Basilica, the Jubilee for prisoners

Sunday, November 13, 2016

33rd Sunday in Ordinary Time

Closing of the Holy Doors in the Basilicas of Rome and in the dioceses of the world

Sunday, November 20, 2016

Solemnity of Our Lord Jesus Christ,
King of the Universe

Closing of the Holy Door of Saint Peter's Basilica and the conclusion of the Jubilee of Mercy

Little Office of Divine Mercy

God's mercy is from age to age to those who fear him!

*Glory to the Father, and to the Son,
and to the Holy Spirit, as it was in the beginning,
is now, and will be for ever. Amen. (Alleluia!)*

HYMN

There's a wideness in God's mercy
like the wideness of the sea;
there's a kindness in his justice,
which is more than liberty.
There is welcome for the sinner,
and more graces for the good;
there is mercy with the Savior;
there is healing in his blood.

There is no place where earth's sorrows
are more felt than up in heaven;
there is no place where earth's failings
have such kindly judgment given.
There is plentiful redemption
in the blood that has been shed;
there is joy for all the members
in the sorrows of the Head.

PSALM   cf. Ps 118:4, 13-15, 22-24

Antiphon: By the help of the Lord's mercy may we be always free
from sin.

Let those who fear the Lord say,
  "His mercy endures forever."

I was hard pressed and was falling,
  but the Lord helped me.

My strength and my courage is the Lord,
   and he has been my savior.

The joyful shout of victory
   in the tents of the just.

The stone which the builders rejected
   has become the cornerstone.

By the Lord has this been done;
   it is wonderful in our eyes.

This is the day the Lord has made;
   let us be glad and rejoice in it.

Glory to the Father....

Antiphon: By the help of the Lord's mercy may we be always free from sin.

CANTICLE   Colossians 1:12-20

Antiphon: When we were justly condemned, in mercy God redeemed us.

Let us give thanks to the Father
for having made you worthy
to share the lot of the saints
in light.

He rescued us
from the power of darkness
and brought us
into the kingdom of his beloved Son.
Through him we have redemption,
the forgiveness of our sins.

He is the image of the invisible God,
the first-born of all creatures.
In him everything in heaven and on earth was created,
things visible and invisible.

All were created through him;
all were created for him.
He is before all else that is.
In him everything continues in being.

It is he who is head of the body, the church!
he who is the beginning,
the first-born of the dead,
so that primacy may be his in everything.

It pleased God to make absolute fullness reside in him
and, by means of him, to reconcile everything
   in his person,
both on earth and in the heavens,
making peace through the blood of his cross.

Antiphon: When we were justly condemned, in mercy God
redeemed us.

Word of God
1 Peter 1:3-5; 2:10

BLESSED BE THE GOD and Father of our Lord Jesus Christ, who in his great mercy gave us a new birth to a living hope through the resurrection of Jesus Christ from the dead, to an inheritance that is imperishable, undefiled, and unfading.

Once you were "no people"/ but now you are God's people;/ you "had not received mercy"/ but now you have received mercy.

Have mercy on us, O Lord.
℟ For we have sinned against you.
Show us, O Lord, your mercy.
℟ And grant us your salvation.

INTERCESSIONS

Trusting in the mercy of Jesus, our divine Savior and Redeemer, we pray:

℟   Lord, rich in mercy, have mercy on us!

Bless us with the grace to live with a healthy
sense of sin:
– may we always live longing for your mercy,
thankful for this gift.

Make us generous in showing to others the corporal
works of mercy:
– feeding the hungry, giving drink to the thirsty,
clothing the naked, sheltering the homeless,
visiting the imprisoned, comforting the sick,
and burying the dead.

Let our lives be radiant with the spiritual works
of mercy:
– instructing the ignorant, counseling the doubtful,
admonishing sinners, bearing wrongs patiently,
forgiving offenses, comforting the afflicted,
and praying for the living and the dead.

Personal intentions

Our Father....

CLOSING PRAYER

Most merciful Father, you overlook people's sins to bring them to repentance. Be merciful to your people and absolve them from all sins, so that what we deserve by our offenses may be avoided by your pardon. Grant that, in the gift of the forgiveness of sins, we may be able by your grace to avoid sinning, and to be constant and generous in showing your mercy to others. Through Christ our Lord.

Penance Service
for the Year of Mercy

Father Richard Veras

OPENING PRAYER

God the Father of Mercies, you invite us to come to know your salvation through the forgiveness of our sins. We come before you, sorrowful for our sins, and hopeful for your compassion.

For your Fatherhood is from all eternity, and your Father's heart beats in the Sacred Heart of your Son, and your Spirit has been received by your priests so that they may incarnate your forgiving love. Come and embrace us, your wayward sons and daughters, who have come to you that our redemption may bear witness that your mercy endures for ever.

We ask this through our Lord Jesus Christ, who lives and reigns with you in the unity of the Holy Spirit, one God for ever and ever.

WORD OF GOD

A reading from the Book of Genesis 3:19, 21

[The LORD said,]

"BY THE SWEAT of your face/ shall you get bread to eat,/ Until you return to the ground,/ from which you were taken;/ For you are dirt,/ and to dirt you shall return."

[…] For the man and his wife the LORD God made leather garments, with which he clothed them.

[Jesus said to the woman caught in adultery,] "**W**OMAN, where are they? Has no one condemned you?" She replied, "No one, sir." Then Jesus said, "Neither do I condemn you. Go, [and] from now on do not sin any more."

From the Gospel of Luke   19:5-7

JESUS LOOKED UP and said to him, "Zacchaeus, come down quickly, for today I must stay at your house." And he came down quickly and received him with joy. [...] they began to grumble, saying, "He has gone to stay at the house of a sinner."

REFLECTION

How tender is God's mercy!

Adam and Eve were given Paradise itself, and rejected it. Devoid of gratitude, devoid of love, but full of empty pride and false suspicion, they rejected God's love.

They separated themselves from God and, for the first time, they experienced nakedness. They tried to cover this nakedness with fig leaves.... It would be laughable if it weren't so sad.

What does God do? He clothes them himself with leather garments. It isn't enough for him to make their clothes, he clothes them himself, like a father who has pity on his poor children.

He takes no pleasure in the sad consequences of their sin. His heart is full of love for them, as it always was, and his love is mysteriously magnified when he is moved by their nakedness. This movement of the Father's heart is the pouring forth of mercy.

The last thing Jesus wants to do is to condemn the woman caught in adultery. He wants to give her all the love her heart has pined for and more. He aches when he sees her wounded by the violence of lust. And his healing love is magnified when he is moved by her shame. This movement of Jesus' heart is the pouring forth of mercy.

How Jesus must have loved Zacchaeus, who had extorted so many, but who desired to be loved and taken back like a lost child who has run away from home. Zacchaeus compromised his dignity by climbing that tree. His desire to be brought back to the fold trumped all other ambitions. Whose house would Jesus want to enter more than his? By inviting himself to Zacchaeus' house, it was Jesus who was welcoming Zacchaeus, like a friend, like a father. Jesus' loving desire to welcome the sinner is magnified when he sees the sinner hoping to be welcomed back. This movement of Jesus' heart is the pouring forth of mercy.

Examination of Conscience

Lord, that I may look with honesty and contrition at the times that I have ignored you, or taken you for granted, or arrogantly accused you, come and clothe me with your mercy.

Lord, that I may look with honesty and contrition at the times that I have done violence to another or myself through envy, resentment, or lust, come and heal me with your mercy.

Lord, that I may look with honesty and contrition at the times when I have reduced a person made in your image through gossip, greed, or mockery, welcome me by inviting your merciful presence into my life.

After a period of silence....

(to be prayed antiphonally)

Have mercy on me, God, in your kindness.
In your compassion blot out my offense.
O wash me more and more from my guilt
and cleanse me from my sin.

My offenses truly I know them;
my sin is always before me.
Against you, you alone, have I sinned;
what is evil in your sight I have done.

That you may be justified when you give sentence
and be without reproach when you judge,
O see, in guilt I was born,
a sinner was I conceived.

Indeed you love truth in the heart;
then in the secret of my heart teach me wisdom.
O purify me, then I shall be clean;
O wash me, I shall be whiter than snow.

Make me hear rejoicing and gladness,
that the bones you have crushed may revive.
From my sins turn away your face
and blot out all my guilt.

A pure heart create for me, O God,
put a steadfast spirit within me.
Do not cast me away from your presence,
nor deprive me of your holy spirit.

Give me again the joy of your help;
with a spirit of fervor sustain me,
that I may teach transgressors your ways
and sinners may return to you.

O rescue me, God, my helper,
and my tongue shall ring out your goodness.
O Lord, open my lips
and my mouth shall declare your praise.

For in sacrifice you take no delight,
burnt offering from me you would refuse,
my sacrifice, a contrite spirit,
a humbled, contrite heart you will not spurn.

CLOSING PRAYER

Lord, remember your promise of mercy.
Hear the cries of your people,
as each of us cries for ourself
and as all of us cry for each other.
Have pity on us poor sinners.

Lord, have mercy (℟)
Christ, have mercy (℟)
Lord, have mercy (℟)

May almighty God have mercy on us,
forgive us our sins,
and bring us to everlasting life.

SACRAMENT OF PENANCE

Tongues of Flame (Acts 2:1-11)

Today I went to a Pentecost Party
the birthday of the Church
full of seven gifts
specified and explained
to the several children
sitting in small chairs
waiting to light
a candle red—each gift
a candle white—their wish.
Carefully supervised
they placed their tiny flame
near the gift they wanted most:
Many wanted Knowledge.
I was given Fear.
We sang songs
and ate velvet cupcakes,
each with a fiery tongue.
The children got excited.
They jumped and ran around.
At the birthday of the Bride
the candle's lit but not blown out.

– Rita A. Simmonds

*L*ET WORKS OF MERCY BE OUR DELIGHT, and let us be filled with those foods which nourish us even to eternity. Let us rejoice in refreshing the poor, whom our gifts have made content. Let us be happy in clothing those whose nakedness we have covered with the needed garments. Let our human kindness touch the sick in their confinement, the feeble in their weakness, exiles in their suffering, orphans in their destitution, and widows in the sorrow of their loneliness.

In aiding them, there is no one who can fail to receive some portion of this kindness. No wealth is small if love is great, nor is the measure of mercy or devotion dependent on property. The riches of goodwill are rightly never lacking even with property which is insignificant. Donations of the rich are greater and of the less endowed smaller; but the fruit of their work is no different where there is the same goodwill in the workers.

In this very opportunity of exercising virtue…there are occasions for other rewards which we receive… if only license is withstood, if the love of drink is renounced, and carnal lust is controlled by the laws of chastity, if hate passes into love, if hostility turns into peace, if serenity puts out wrath, if mildness cancels injury…. With this observation, dearly beloved, we will obtain God's mercy.

– Saint Leo the Great

Saint Monica

ALMOST EVERYTHING WE KNOW about Monica († 387) comes from her son Augustine, convert to the faith and bishop and Doctor of the Church. He told of his mother's virtues, but also her faults and her struggles. We learn, for instance, that Monica had a drinking problem as a girl, one that she conquered only after she was shamed by a slave. Moreover, Monica did not always make the best decisions for her children: her concern for her son's education prevented her from seeking an early marriage for him, a choice that would have saved him many missteps. And Monica's zeal was sometimes over the top, as when she brought cakes and wine as offerings to the shrines of the saints. The bishop, Saint Ambrose, ordered her to stop this practice, a throwback to pagan times and a sure way to encourage wanton drinking around the sacred shrines.

But Monica did not seem to have spent much time thinking about her missteps. She flew forward at every moment toward Christ. And so, time and again, her love was purified—her love of wine, her love for the saints, her love for her son. Augustine's own converted heart, God's answer to her prayers and pleading, became her great maternal treasure. Once she saw him safely in the Church's bosom, she longed only for death.

– Lisa Lickona

Mercy and the Unforgivable Sin

GOD OFFERS US LIMITLESS MERCY. There is no offense, no wound, no darkness that God's mercy cannot forgive, heal, and illumine. As the Psalmist says, *He does not deal with us according to our sins, nor requite us according to our iniquities. For as the heavens are high above the earth, so great is his steadfast love toward those who fear him; as far as the east is from the west, so far does he remove our transgressions from us* (Ps 103:10-12). The divine mercy is never exhausted by those who seek it.

Even though God's mercy is boundless, Jesus nevertheless refers to an unforgivable sin (Mt 12:31-32). This sin is unforgivable not because God is lacking in mercy but because, in his love for us, God gave us the freedom to refuse his love and reject his mercy. Jesus refers to this as sinning *"against the Holy Spirit."* Commenting on Jesus' words, the *Catechism* teaches, "There are no limits to the mercy of God, but anyone who deliberately refuses to accept his mercy by repenting, rejects the forgiveness of his sins and the salvation offered by the Holy Spirit (cf. John Paul II, *Dominum et vivificantem* 46). Such hardness of heart can lead to final impenitence and eternal loss" (CCC 1864).

Thus, the only thing that can be said to "limit" the mercy of God is a stony heart. When a person refuses to ask for God's mercy or avail himself of the sacraments instituted to effect forgiveness and reconciliation, he cuts himself off from the infinite stream of divine mercy flowing from the heart of Jesus. God will not force the proud heart to submit to the order of his wisdom and love.

In other words, as Pope Francis has said many times since his first Angelus address: "God never tires of forgiving us! The problem is that we ourselves tire, we do not want to ask, we grow weary of asking for forgiveness." We become hard-hearted and lose confidence in God's mercy.

The remedies to hardness in the human heart are lively faith and hope in the goodness of God. Christians must cling to the truth that the grace of Christ promised them in the Church and her sacraments is sufficient to heal them from every sin and renew them from within.

No bad habit or vicious activity, no moral flaw or sinful choice, can exhaust the love and mercy of the crucified and risen Christ. However, we must open the door to his mercy by avoiding hardness of heart, cultivating instead hearts of humble faith and confident hope.

– **Father Christopher Seiler**

THE YOUNG CURATE—Georges Bernanos' country priest—
is dying.

He's tried his best to bring the mercy of God to the
hardhearted men and women of his parish. They are people such as one finds everywhere, rebellious, indifferent,
mocking, longing, loving much, hating some, fearing death,
and fleeing the mercy they need above all.

He does not blame them.

A few days before his death, he writes these words:

"Even from the cross, when our Lord in his agony
found the perfection of his saintly humanity—even then
he did not own himself a victim of injustice. *They know not
what they do.*' Words that have meaning for the youngest
child, words some would like to call childish, but the spirits of evil must have been muttering them ever since without understanding, and with ever-growing terror. Instead
of the thunderbolts they awaited, it is as though a hand of
innocence closed over the chasm of their dwelling."

What do we suppose the damned find harder to bear—
the justice of God, or the sheer childlike innocence of his
mercy? Old and hardened sinners can talk about debts and
payment and vengeance. But before the clear brow of the
child they must retreat in shame. Be advised, fellow sinners. Our God is younger than we.

– **Anthony Esolen**

CELEBRATING MASS in a rehabilitation center, I would look at the people gathered for the Mass, so many of them lame, bent, and suffering, and ask myself what they thought when they heard me read from the Gospels about Jesus' power of healing. Did they ask themselves, "If Jesus is so merciful, why has he left me in this broken, humiliated body?"

"What does Christ's mercy consist of? Does it have to do primarily with making our bodies whole, or is it something else?" I would ask. Jesus' power of healing was a sign of his mercy but not the fulfillment of his mercy. Salvation is the fulfillment of his mercy.

For example, there was a sick woman who approached Jesus (Mk 5:25-34). *"If I but touch his clothes, I shall be cured,"* she said. She was cured even without Jesus intentionally healing her. When he asked who it was who touched him, she threw herself at his feet and confessed.

But Jesus said to her, *"Your faith has saved you. Go in peace and be cured of your affliction."* She was healed, but afterwards didn't she eventually get sick and die all the same? The salvation remains; the healing doesn't, for it is but a sign of that mercy, his offer of salvation. If we have his merciful salvation, we already have the promise of eternal life and can freely offer our suffering to share more deeply with him.

– Father Vincent Nagle, F.S.C.B.

May Devotions to Our Lady

◖ *On Sundays:* O Mary, the Immaculate Conception, your immaculate creation cries escape to a world mired in misery. The remedy that saves us from repeating Eden's disobedience we call "Mother."

◖ *On Mondays*: We celebrate your nativity, O Blessed Virgin, to reclaim for ourselves the Mercy that becomes flesh once your flesh appears in the world and is offered to the Spirit as his Spouse.

◖ *On Tuesdays*: All that is darkness and annihilation ends at the Annunciation, O Blessed Virgin, when—in the face of heaven's might—you live by faith, speaking your *Fiat*.

◖ *On Wednesdays*: Mary, with child you go in Visitation so that all may be with your child. You bring close the One you are expecting, who is our expectation. You visit us with the Mercy who has visited you.

◖ *On Thursdays*: Merciful Mother of God, in you all who belong to Jesus are made alive. By your unique maternal mediation, make me more and more human in the likeness of your Son.

◖ *On Fridays*: Our Lady of Sorrows, you are the Mother of Mercy. The tribulation you endured equips you to reach all those who, on the verge of giving up, will accept an irresistible offer: the merciful love of a Mother.

◖ *On Saturdays*: O Blessed Lady assumed into heaven, you, who have the deepest knowledge of the mystery of God's mercy, live for ever in its heart. May your merciful presence in heaven carry me away with hopefulness.

– Father Peter John Cameron, O.P.

A Gaze I Can't Remember
but Won't Forget (Ps 8:4)

Always before me,
you look after me.
You set the sky over my head
and the land under my feet.
You keep me straight
as you rotate the earth.

I can think back
to the time
when I was known
by you alone,
for you were there
fixing the growth
of my beating heart
my paddle limbs
my black bulb eyes.
I remember nothing—
not warmth,
nor water,
nor maternal sighs,
but your gaze
never left me.
Thriving in silence,
I held your look
in the tiny ball of my being—
a swimming seed
attached at the stomach
by a string.

Who am I that you should be mindful of me?

– Rita A. Simmonds

*I*N THIS JUBILEE YEAR, let us allow God to surprise us. He never tires of casting open the doors of his heart and of repeating that he loves us and wants to share his love with us. The Church… knows that her primary task, especially at a moment full of great hopes and signs of contradiction, is to introduce everyone to the great mystery of God's mercy by contemplating the face of Christ. The Church is called above all to be a credible witness to mercy, professing it and living it as the core of the revelation of Jesus Christ.

From the heart of the Trinity, from the depths of the mystery of God, the great river of mercy wells up and overflows unceasingly. It is a spring that will never run dry…. Every time someone is in need, he or she can approach it, because the mercy of God never ends. The profundity of the mystery surrounding it is as inexhaustible as the richness which springs up from it.

In this Jubilee Year, may the Church echo the Word of God that resounds strong and clear as a message and a sign of pardon, strength, aid, and love. May she never tire of extending mercy, and be ever patient in offering compassion and comfort. May the Church… repeat confidently without end: *Be mindful of your mercy, O Lord, and your steadfast love, for they have been from of old* (Ps 25:6).

– *Misericordiae Vultus* 25

Saint Rita

DESPITE HER PROTESTS that she was destined for religious life, Rita's († 1447) parents married her to Paolo di Fernando when she was twelve. For fifteen years Rita bore her husband's violent temper with patience. Then, Paolo was suddenly, brutally murdered. Rita begged for, and received, the grace to forgive her husband's murderers. But she could see that her sons did not, and she prayed that they would not renew the vendetta. A few months later, both sons took ill and died. Neither had struck against their father's assailants. The mother's prayers had prevailed.

Soon Rita entered the Augustinian convent in Cascia. She gave herself over to contemplating the perfect love of the Crucified One. During one Lenten retreat she asked Jesus to be permitted to share in the smallest part of his suffering—the stab of the tip of one of the thorns on his crown. In 1432 a wound appeared on Rita's forehead. The constantly festering wound, a source of pain and isolation, remained until Rita's death. When Rita's tomb was opened in the twentieth century, a forensic examination confirmed the damage to her skull.

According to Saint John Paul II, Rita of Cascia, wife, mother, and mystic, "learned to understand the sorrows of the human heart." She is the refuge of those in hopeless situations.

– Lisa Lickona

Mary, the Mother of Mercy

READING THE SHORT COMMENTARY that the *Catechism of the Catholic Church* provides on the "Hail Mary," we learn that Catholics approach the Blessed Virgin Mary as the "Mother of Mercy" (CCC 2677). In order to understand why we ask Mary to "pray for us sinners," let us recall the message that the angel delivered to Saint Joseph: Mary *"will bear a son and you are to name him Jesus, because he will save his people from their sins"* (Mt 1:21). These words express the motive for the Incarnation of the Son of God. A gospel without redemption from sins creates an illusion. It offers no good news.

There is more. Personal sins cause those who commit them more difficulties than many people suspect. Sins can blackmail the sinner. Sins produce self-absolving rationalizations. Sins, in the final analysis, corrupt the good of the human person. Those who succumb to blackmail, who court rationalizations, or who become corrupted shy away from worshiping God. They instead suffer alienation.

Mary finds her place in the life of the Christian for one reason only. God put her there. It is not a question whether or not we need a maternal mediator. The saving fact is we have one. So to whom may sinners turn if not to a Mother of Mercy? The suavity of God appears in the choice of Sweet Mary to play this role.

– Father Romanus Cessario, O.P.

ONE SUMMER I TOOK some youth to a Christian festival. Among them was Isaiah—a true light. But he and his friends made bad choices, stealing. I grounded them for the night.

It didn't work. I saw Isaiah and his friend, walking toward the local arcade. "Where are you going?" I called. "I told you stay in your room." He said, "I will do what I want."

I told them that if they wanted to continue to be part of the weekend they needed to get back to their room. Isaiah said, "I'm not afraid of you."

He pulled out a knife and said, "I will kill you." I got closer. He put the knife to my throat. I said, "Kill me right now, and I will still love you." Isaiah yelled, "You don't love me!" I said, "I might not love you but God loves you. He loves you." Isaiah began telling me that I didn't know him or his life. I just said, "But I know God does."

Crowds came. The police came. They started questioning Isaiah. They said they needed to take him to the police station. I told them not to. I said I knew the rules, but that I believed God desired mercy, not sacrifice, for Isaiah.

Four years later, I drove into a car wash…and there was Isaiah, working! He came over right away and said, "I really want to wash your van." And he did, with all his heart and soul.

He handed me three different air fresheners, telling me my van would probably need them. We laughed and I gave him a hug.

Mercy gave Isaiah the chance to turn things around, and he did.

– Justin Fatica

I GREW UP IN FRONT OF AN OCEAN that is cold and has strong currents. The waves are unpredictable, the ocean occasionally throwing up what we called "sneaker waves" that flow powerfully up the sand of the beach far beyond the previous waves. We loved the sea, yet the first lesson we learned was never to take our eyes off of her. After all, she is so very, very powerful, and we are so small. Our fear of her is part of our love for her.

This helps me understand a line in Mary's song of God's mercy, the *Magnificat* (Lk 1:46-55), *"His mercy is from age to age/ to those who fear him."* What does fear have to do with mercy? A preceding line gives us a clue: *"[God] has looked upon his handmaid's lowliness."* Mary recognizes her lowliness, and thus her need of the One on High. Mercy, in fact, is the compassionate gaze of the one who has upon the one who has not, who is in need.

The one in need depends upon the sympathy of the other. Thus the one in need keeps his eye on the greater one, like my family and me on the beach always facing the ocean. This is the fear that Mary refers to. She hopes for the Most High to look down upon her. This inequality, this "fear" is part of the mercy. Our first lesson, with Mary, is to keep our eye on him, for we depend always on him.

– Father Vincent Nagle, F.S.C.B.

I adore, O God, all-powerful Father, the infinite love that caused you to give your Son, the most beloved of your eternal goodnesses, your unique One, to the world, lost through Original Sin and through the numberless sins of the present day. I adore this same divine charity, manifested in the choice of the means employed by the Incarnation.

You did not wish to have recourse to your limitless power, but you called upon your divine wisdom, your goodness, your mercy, your love. Could you have drawn so near to us by any other means? Who could have had an inkling otherwise of how dear and precious the Virgin Mary is to you? You have created and enriched her with the greatest gifts of grace so that she could be the honored Mother of your most Beloved Son.

Your Incarnation, O Divine and Eternal Word, is the focal point of the world, prepared from all eternity, and its consequences extend beyond time and encompass all eternity.

I adore you, accepting and receiving from your Father the supreme mission of redeeming us, saving us, delivering us from the slavery of sin, reinstating us, giving back to us the life of grace that was lost by that same sin, placing us at your disposal, incorporating us into the eternal life of glory.

I adore you, O Jesus, making ready to lay aside the splendors of your glory to become one of us!

– Venerable Marthe Robin

How to Feed Five Thousand (Lk 9:11b-17)

Offer your morning catch,
meager as it is,
and watch the fish swarm
the dry land.

Let the grain of wheat fall
to its death
and sprout bread
in the sand.

Five loaves
and two fish
is the gift in our hands.
Our guests number thousands.
The Host is One Man.

And the spread is stupendous
for "God grants the growth"
of the fish and the bread
and the flesh
of the Host.

— Rita A. Simmonds

*T*HE GIFT OF THE EUCHARIST contains three blessings which step by step enhance ever more the mercy of the Savior....

[Christ] concealed himself under the appearance of very ordinary food in order that we might receive him into our bodies and he might strengthen the life of grace in our souls time and again. This also might have been sufficient, for surely it would infinitely surpass all we could expect from the mercy of our Savior.

But he went still further, and forever united the Eucharistic transubstantiation with his bloody sacrifice on the cross, thus giving it the character of sacrifice equal in value to that of the cross. He commanded his Church to offer that sacrifice with the participation of the faithful. In so doing he made it possible for every one of us to offer God something of infinite value that God cannot reject and that can obtain from him everything for us.

At the same time, Christ made the Eucharist the center of the whole life of his Mystical Body. He surrounded it with other sacraments which all serve it and draw from it their strength and their value. Christ's presence in the tabernacle should be a continual reminder of our Savior's mercy for us;...every Holy Communion, and...the Eucharistic sacrifice of the Mass should strike us as evidence of his mercy.

– Servant of God Father Hyacinth Woroniecki, O.P.

Saint John Paul II

ON MAY 13, 1981, Pope John Paul II (✝ 2005) was shot by the Turk Mehmet Ali Ağca as he toured Saint Peter's Square. He was rushed to the hospital. In his agony, John Paul was heard to repeat, "Mary, my Mother! Mary, my Mother!" Doctors operated to remove the bullets that had penetrated his abdomen, and four days later he spoke to the faithful from his hospital bed: "I pray for the brother who wounded me, whom I have sincerely forgiven." From the first, John Paul was certain that Mary had thwarted the assassination attempt, which had happened on her feast, the commemoration of her first appearance to the three children at Fatima. And it seems his Mother had helped him to forgive.

Six months earlier, the pontiff had written of Mary's role as Mother of Mercy. No one, John Paul II taught, has experienced mercy like Mary, in whom the Son of God became incarnate. And, because of her perfect share in Christ's sacrifice on the cross, Mary has a unique role in "revealing" God's merciful love. This work of Mary "is based upon…her particular fitness to reach all those who most easily accept the merciful love of a Mother" (*Dives in Misericordia* 9).

John Paul II readily accepted Mary's love, and, in turn, he showed mercy. Mary's Motherhood, he said, is "one of the great life-giving mysteries of Christianity."

– Lisa Lickona

What Is the Sacramental Grace
of Penance?

WHEN WE SIN, we cannot fix things up with God on our own. We know we have to be forgiven. But once we sin, we do not have it in us even to be sorry, and to ask rightly, humbly, reverently for forgiveness. Why not?

When we sin, we fall from charity; that is to say, we fall out of friendship with God. This friendship is purely God's gift to us in Christ. It puts us above ourselves. To sin is to step down, or fall down from charity. And then we can't reach high enough on our own to get back where we were. In an ordinary friendship, there is still something in common between us, even if only our humanity, if I offend my friend. I can say I am sorry and do my part to put things back together. But when we lose charity, we don't have anything in common with God anymore. With charity, God is the very "commonality" of the relation—its beginning in Christ, its course in the Spirit, and its term in the vision of heaven.

Paradoxically, to ask for forgiveness from God rightly and fittingly, I have to ask from charity—the only thing there ever was in common between us. But I threw that away. And now I need it more than ever in order to be rightly sorry for having thrown it away. I may be regretful that I sinned and was so stupid. Feeling stupid is not an exercise of friendship. I may fear the justice of God because I sinned. Such fear is not from charity. I may dread the loss of heaven and fear the pains of hell. These things are self-regarding. The sorrow of heart, the contrition I now need is being sorry I have offended my Friend. Who is my friend only with charity. Which sin destroys.

What the sacrament is for is to jump-start things. I come to the sacrament self-wounded, self-centered, self-bound, but still with enough wit to know what I lost, longing once again to have the freedom of the house of God as a son, and not as a servant or slave. I confess my sins. I hear again the Gospel truth I scorned. I submit to judgment. I express my sorrow as best I can, aware of what real contrition before God would be. I hear the words of absolution. And these acts of penitent and priest God uses to produce in me some true breath of contrition, animated then and there by charity. That's the promise, the surety, of the sacrament: it permits me to speak in the sacramental moment as friend to Friend. The risen Lord could have asked Peter, "Are you sorry?" But what he asked in fact was "Do you love me?"

– **Father Guy Mansini, O.S.B.**

JESUS IS SO GENEROUS with his mercy in my life. I am learning to be *attentive*, because his love often touches our lives within the most ordinary circumstances. One of the enduring sources of his mercy for me is my wife and family. After nearly twenty years of marriage—and more than half of those years struggling together with my complicated and frustrating illnesses—I have come to recognize the mercy of God in my wife's persistence in accompanying me, suffering with me, and taking care of me in so many simple things. Of course, she's not perfect: that's not the point. The mercy is in the dedication, the willingness to *be there* day after day. Jesus gives so much grace through the sacramental bond of marriage, and it is good for the spouses to depend on that grace, to ask for it, and to allow it to shape their lives.

I have also learned never to underestimate the kids. They have had all the usual problems in growing up, but they have been resilient in many surprising ways. They rise to the challenge of making sacrifices and investing themselves in a family where the father has disabilities, when they see that the radical security of family life—the certainty that they are loved and protected—is founded on their parents' trust in God's mercy.

– **John Janaro**

IN PORTRAYING FOR US a Pharisee and a tax collector (Lk 18:9-14), Jesus tells us that the Pharisee prayed his prayer *"to himself."* His tirade of self-aggrandizement was a prayer he prayed to himself. He is in a closed system, a vicious cycle. He does not know mercy, and so does not know God. His god is a false god who wields a merciless measure.

If he does not know mercy, what can he do but profess his impeccable holiness?

The tax collector is so aware of the reality of God, so in awe of God's otherness and holiness, that he stands at a distance, not even raising his eyes.

Once, while I was hearing confessions at the high school where I taught, a student apologized to me for his nervousness but, he said, confession was scary. I asked him if he thought anyone in the school, including himself, was afraid of me. "No, Father," was his answer. If he wasn't afraid of me, then there was Someone Else present whom he feared.

That boy was before the very real Mystery of God. And why was he there, facing his fear? Because he wanted mercy.

The truest thing to do before God, who is real and who is beyond my measure, is to beg for mercy.

The god that I try to impress is no god at all, but an idol of my petty imagination.

– **Father Richard Veras**

Immaculate Heart! Help us to conquer the menace of evil, which so easily takes root in the hearts of the people of today, and whose immeasurable effects already weigh down upon our modern world and seem to block the paths towards the future!

From famine and war, *deliver us.*

From nuclear war, from incalculable self-destruction, from every kind of war, *deliver us.*

From sins against the life of man from its very beginning, *deliver us.*

From hatred and from the demeaning of the dignity of the children of God, *deliver us.*

From every kind of injustice in the life of society, both national and international, *deliver us.*

From readiness to trample on the Commandments of God, *deliver us.*

From attempts to stifle in human hearts the very truth of God, *deliver us.*

From the loss of awareness of good and evil, *deliver us.*

From sins against the Holy Spirit, *deliver us.*

Accept, O Mother of Christ, this cry laden with the sufferings of all individual human beings, laden with the sufferings of whole societies.

Help us with the power of the Holy Spirit to conquer all sin: individual sin and the "sin of the world," sin in all its manifestations.

Let there be revealed, once more, in the history of the world the infinite saving power of the Redemption: the power of *merciful Love!*

– Saint John Paul II

The Widow's Cry (Lk 7:11-17)

The widow's cry
is magnified—
she's lost her only son.
The Heart of Christ
cannot deny
the plea of such a one.
"Do not weep,"
His voice replies
to sorrow He will bear—
His Virgin Mother
near the cross—
He sees her standing there.
She takes His Body
in her arms
and folds Him in her dress.
The thorny wreath
that rounds His head
she presses to her breast.
"Do not weep,"
He will not say;
No breath to form a word.
And she must cry and beg for souls
her stricken heart will serve.

– Rita A. Simmonds

LTHOUGH DISTRUST OF DIVINE MERCY is a serious offense against God, and deeply wounds the Heart of the Savior, so full of pity for us, a lighthearted reliance on it without keeping the Commandments is also sinful, and…can become a grave sin against the Holy Spirit….

Such an attitude of the soul which, under the pretext of trust in God's mercy, is oblivious of God's justice and does not take into account the wisdom of God's rule over the world, is also gravely sinful and, like despair of salvation, dangerous to the soul because it deprives it of fear of the consequences of sin. There is no question here of any excess of hope, for we cannot trust too much in divine mercy; nay, we might even say that true hope is lacking here, and its place is taken over by light-minded self-confidence which, as Saint Thomas points out, has its source in pride and vanity.

To prevent a serious deformation of the spiritual life, it is necessary for the fear of God to strike deep roots in the soul. Together with hope, fear of God will prevent the soul from being deprived of the mercies of the Lord; what is more, it will help the soul to profit by them.

– Servant of God Father Hyacinth Woroniecki, O.P.

Saint Teresa Benedicta

EDITH STEIN WAS BORN OF A JEWISH FAMILY in Breslau, Germany, now part of Poland. At the age of fourteen, she left off prayer, determined to be her own master. Yet, she continued to long for truth to guide her. Her passion led her to the study of philosophy and the companionship of Christian friends. While on a visit with them, she happened upon the memoir of Saint Teresa of Ávila. Her immediate response: "This is the truth!"

Edith was baptized, and eventually decided to enter Teresa's own order, the Carmelites, as Teresa Benedicta of the Cross. Meanwhile, the Nazi threat was beginning to grow, and Teresa was moved from Germany to a convent in Holland to protect her from the pogroms aimed at anyone of Jewish blood. When Holland was invaded, Teresa took her stand, resolutely embracing the cross with one arm and her Jewish brethren with the other. When offered the chance to escape the Carmel in Holland, she protested: "Why should I be spared? Is it not right that I should gain no advantage from my baptism? If I cannot share the lot of my brothers and sisters, my life, in a certain sense, is destroyed."

On August 2, 1942, Teresa was taken from the convent to the crowded truck that bore her to Auschwitz and the gas chamber. She died, Saint John Paul II said, as a "martyr for love."

– Lisa Lickona

Go to Confession—the Priest Is Jesus

IF GOD IS TRULY MERCIFUL why do we need to go to confession? After all, the *Catechism of the Catholic Church* teaches that God reveals his infinite mercy "by freely forgiving sins" (CCC 270). The Sacrament of Penance appears to render God's mercy conditional and less than freely given. Why can't Christians just confess their sins to God in the privacy of their own hearts and homes? Why do we need priests?

We need confession because the infinite mercy of God is not lifeless or inert. His mercy produces definite, saving effects within the Christian person. After the Resurrection, Jesus gave his chosen disciples a remarkable power: the power to be living instruments of his own divine mercy. *"As the Father has sent me, so I send you.... Whose sins you forgive are forgiven them, and whose sins you retain are retained"* (Jn 20:21-23). Just as the eternal Father sent the eternal Son to save the world from its sin and misery, so the eternal Son sends his priests into the world to extend his saving mercy to all peoples (CCC 1441-1442).

Jesus really takes away the sins of the world. He does freely forgive. And it is in confession that we truly encounter the merciful Savior in his living instruments of mercy—the priests of his Church.

– Father Cajetan Cuddy, O.P.

And There Was Light is the strange and beautiful autobiography of Jacques Lusseyran, blind hero of the French Resistance. Born in Paris in 1924, Lusseyran lost his sight at the age of eight in a schoolroom incident.

In 1940, the Germans invaded France. Jacques, seventeen, continued studying for the entrance exams to the École Normale Supérieure. From the back bedroom of his parents' apartment, he also mobilized fifty-two of his friends into an underground youth resistance movement known as Les Volontaires de la Liberté.

He was betrayed by a member to the Gestapo. Jacques' dearest childhood friend, Jean, died under torture. Lusseyran himself was interrogated, imprisoned for six months, and sent to the concentration camp at Buchenwald.

Of his fifteen months there, he observed: "This is what you had to do…be engaged…. The self-centered life has no place in the world of the deported." When the U.S. Army liberated the camp in April 1945, he was one of only thirty survivors of the original shipment.

In spite of everything, he viewed existence as pure mercy, pure gift.

"When you said to me: 'Tell me the story of your life,' I was not eager to begin," he later wrote. "But when you added, 'What I care most about is learning your reasons for loving life,' then I became eager, for that was a real subject."

– Heather King

Jesus' insight into human suffering is penetrating. Confronted with the scene described in Mark 2:1-12, whose heart would not be moved with pity by the determined helplessness on display? On the one hand, we see a paralyzed man: his body his prison, in which his spirit is sentenced to standing frustration with every whisper of his will to try to move. On the other hand, we meet the undeterred force of his bearers' will, mounting him over the top of the unbudging crowd until he reaches the Lord.

Altogether, the spectacle expresses a desperate desire to be freed from this horrible burden. Rather than responding to this pitiable physical suffering, however, Jesus' impulse is immediately to free the man from his sins. Indeed, the Lord seems almost to ignore the man's manifest malady, as though his weight of suffering lay entirely elsewhere. And it does!

Who knows (except the Lord) what anger or despair festered in this poor man's heart? It is his inner illness that defines the man's true suffering. Bedridden saints, like Anna Schäffer, however, show that the penetrating mercy of God's grace might fortify the spirit with profound faith, hope, and love, while leaving the body mortally infirm.

– **Father Anthony Giambrone, O.P.**

Oh eternal Godhead,
how well mercy suits you!
How well it suits you
that your servants should arouse your mercy
against the judgment the world deserves
because of its sins!
Your mercy created us,
and the same mercy redeemed us from eternal death.
Your mercy rules over us
and holds back your justice,
keeping the earth from opening up to swallow us,
keeping the animals from devouring us.
All this your mercy does.
Your mercy preserves us
and prolongs our life,
giving us time to return and be reconciled with you.
In mercy you grant us consolation to coax us to love,
for the human heart
is attracted by love.
The same mercy gives and permits sufferings
    and hardships
so that we may learn to know ourselves
and acquire the little virtue of true humility—
and even to give yourself a reason
to reward those who fight bravely,
suffering with true patience.
In mercy you preserved the scars in your Son's body
so that he might with these scars
beg for mercy for us before your majesty.

– Saint Catherine of Siena

Forgiven Woman's Sonnet (Lk 7:36-50)

If you but knew the shyness that you strike—
a piece of heart untapped and yet untamed,
that cannot show its face without a fight
with booming beats so rash and unashamed.

If you but knew the knowing of your eyes
that catch the soul that's feasted while you turned,
who swallows smooth to suffocate surprise,
though in a gaze her adoration's learned.

If you but knew the beauty of your ways
that lead my heart to tread in endless bloom,
would you rejoice to concretize these days
that pass within my mind? Oh perfect groom!

Accept aloud the ripeness of my cheek!
It's no mere rogue that waits for you to speak.

– Rita A. Simmonds

*G*OING TO CONFESSION REGULARLY has given me a new appreciation for this sacrament. I often ask why people don't go to confession today more than they do. It can't be that we're sinning less. Can we have lost our appreciation for the Sacrament of Reconciliation because we no longer realize how terrible sin is? Is it that we no longer appreciate the suffering and death of Jesus, that he died for us? Do we no longer realize that all we have to do, to claim the benefits of his suffering, is to confess our sins and to rely on his mercy?

It is much easier to strive for holiness when you can go to Jesus in this sacrament regularly. It is a great spiritual consolation, and a reminder of Jesus' great love, to be able to come to the priest and to hear those great words, "Your sins are forgiven." As long as we are making an effort to avoid sin, we know that in the Sacrament of Reconciliation we are cleansed and we can start afresh....

The Sacrament of Reconciliation is not just for wiping away the sins already committed; the grace of the sacrament enables people to eradicate the sinful habit in their lives.

I realized that the more I went to the sacrament, the less I fell into my own sins. The sacrament gave me hope in the Lord's mercy and strength in the face of temptation.

– Sister Briege M. McKenna, o.s.c.

Saint Tarcisius

TWELVE-YEAR-OLD TARCISIUS († 257) lived in Rome during the persecutions of the Emperor Valerian. He went often to the catacombs for Mass. One day when the priest was making ready to bring the Eucharist to the sick—at the risk of his own life—Tarcisius offered to go in his place. When the priest objected that this was no task for one so young, Tarcisius replied, "My youth will be the best shield for the Eucharist."

Tarcisius set out, the Host wrapped in linen cloth and pressed tightly to his chest. Soon he met some other boys who were curious about his package. When he refused to show it to them, they began to tease him. His calm refusals provoked the boys: was this one of the hated Christians? The attack turned violent, and the boys began to pelt Tarcisius with stones. Still Tarcisius clung to Christ's Body and suffered the onslaught—until at last a mortal blow was struck. An onlooker carried his lifeless body back to the catacombs.

In a 2010 address, Pope Benedict recounted the tradition that no Host was found on Tarcisius. The Body of Christ had become one with the body of the boy, forming "a single immaculate Host to God." Tarcisius, the martyr of Eucharistic charity, is the protector of all youth, but especially those who serve at the altar of the Lord.

– Lisa Lickona

The Role of Mercy in Each of the Sacraments

IN *MISERICORDIAE VULTUS*, the papal document declaring a Year of Mercy, the Holy Father explains that mercy is "the ultimate and supreme act by which God comes to meet us" (2). Since the *Catechism* tells us that a sacrament is "a meeting of God's children with their Father," it is most especially in the sacraments that we find God's great act of mercy (CCC 1153).

Each of the seven sacraments instituted by Christ enacts the merciful healing of God. The mercy of Christ's sacrifice on the cross flows over us in the seven sacraments as each heals a disorder present in the human community.

Baptism, for example, cleanses the wounds of Original Sin. God's mercy heals the sin of Adam by means of adoption into the Trinity. Far from simply a community initiation, in baptism the mercy of God flows from his pierced side to his newly adopted children.

In confirmation, God's mercy heals the fear that often accompanies being a public witness to the faith. How needed in our age is the merciful grace of confirmation to restore the Church's public witness, especially about the truth of the moral law.

God's mercy is enfleshed in the Holy Eucharist. Jesus, the merciful face of the Father, heals venial sins in Holy Communion. The mercy of God, which brings us the Eucharist, means we are never alone. God's mercy waits for us in the sacrament of love.

The Sacrament of Penance is the sacrament of mercy par excellence. Sin, more than any other wound, requires God's healing. And being drawn to his mercy—even more than revulsion against sin—should bring us to confession.

The Sacrament of the Anointing of the Sick heals the effects of sin. In holy anointing, God's mercy ensures that the doubt and despair that often accompany sickness and death are healed in a soul already restored to his friendship in confession.

The Sacrament of Holy Orders ushers a man into the role of instrument of mercy. As Pope Francis so often reminds his priests, they are to be, perhaps more than anything else, messengers of mercy. This sacrament heals the division that arises when God's people lack sound pastoral care.

And finally, the Sacrament of Matrimony applies God's mercy to human love. Sacramental marriage can heal the disordered appetites so evident in our culture. The community flourishes when spousal love is raised to the dignity of a sacrament.

God in his goodness comes to meet us with his mercy. And he does so most of all in the sacraments.

– Father Ryan Connors

A SCENE, courtesy of our beloved Karol Wojtyła (in his play *The Jeweler's Shop*).

Anna approaches the jeweler's shop where she and her husband Stefan had bought their wedding rings. She wants to sell her ring. "Whether he was unfaithful to me I do not know," says Anna, "since I took no interest in his life either."

They have grown apart over the years. Would it be mercy, a sort of euthanasia, to kill the marriage once and for all? She hands the ring to the jeweler, who puts it on his scales, to see what its gold is worth. But the scales do not budge.

"Your husband must be alive," he says, "in which case neither of your rings, taken separately, will weigh anything—only both together will register." That is because the scales weigh not metal, "but man's entire being and fate."

A mysterious stranger named Adam tells Anna that she must not give up on love. The Bridegroom is coming soon, the Bridegroom who will take her as his bride, and bring to her the love for which she longs. Anna runs toward him, "full of hope," but she is stunned by his face. It is Stefan's.

"Why must he have that face for me?" she cries. "Why? Why?"

Mercy never absolves us from the fearful adventure of love.

– Anthony Esolen

T HEY WERE BRIGHT YELLOW, and you couldn't miss them. Years ago, members of our youth ministry program designed t-shirts they would wear while attending a national convention. The front proclaimed the name of our diocese, while the back spoke a unique New Jersey fact: *We don't pump our own gas.*

It is not known for certain who was the author of the Letter to the Hebrews, and the letter's intended audience is also uncertain. What is certain is that the recipients were Christians losing faith. Their struggle was not with outside persecution but with the weariness that comes from the demands of living the Christian life. As their spiritual life was near empty, the author reminds them they cannot find the strength to renew their spirits on their own. He invites them to *approach the throne of grace to receive mercy* (Heb 4:16).

Like those ancient Christians, we too lose heart and hope when following Jesus is a struggle. We may try to fuel ourselves by choosing what is convenient or costs little. But this produces only temporary results. The moment of faith is when we admit we cannot do this alone. We need to be fueled by love and grace. We must come to Jesus.

– **Monsignor Gregory E. S. Malovetz**

A Meditation for
Eucharistic Adoration

The manna in the desert was the gift of God's mercy. Loving Savior, Bread of Life, your mercy is always manna. And your mercy is from age to age. You fill the hungry with good things. For you are the Giver of multiplied loaves for famished masses. You are the Master who seats his servants at table and waits on them himself with himself.

Increase our trust in your mercy. What father would hand us a stone when we ask for a loaf? The birds in the sky do not sow or reap. Yet our heavenly Father feeds them. That feeding is mercy.

The seed of your Word, set in rich soil, yields hundredfold mercies. When we fast, we do so to grow in our hunger for mercy. Give us this day our daily bread so that we can forgive others as we have been forgiven. You call us to be the salt of the earth so that the food of the world will taste of enticing Gospel grace.

Help me to respond to the Lazarus at my door who longs for scraps from an overladen table. May the leaven of our corporal and spiritual works of mercy cause the dough of God's Kingdom everywhere to rise. In planning a dinner, we are to invite beggars, the crippled, the lame, the blind—those who cannot repay and, thus, will see our meal as mercy. You, Jesus, are the King who has invited us first to your wedding feast: *See, I have my dinner prepared! Come to the banquet.* Blessed are they who hunger and thirst for this mercy.

– Father Peter John Cameron, O.P.

Parched and Drenched (Ps 63)

I thought I should not walk
in the onslaught of rain
to Monday morning Mass.
No obligation or high celebration
just hungry and thirsting
for God knows what
and eager to break my fast.

With umbrella, a poor and sudden shield,
I pass the rushing drains.
My feet move fast
and slap the path
for such a sodden strain.

Oh solemn, dark, day-broken sky,
how long have you held back this cry?

Parched and soaked, I keep my course
knowing there's a sacred space,
a great indoors, a pace away.

With greater weight, I pull the door.
Silence, like a cloak, welcomes me back home.
The rain drops to my feet.
Unworthily drenched, I wait,
not to be dry,
but to raise my famished I
and eat.

– Rita A. Simmonds

O UR FEAR OF GOD is not limited to the fear of punishment by him…. We should cultivate in our souls the fear of guilt in offending God's majesty and disrespecting his mercy. This fear… is called…filial fear, whereas the other is called servile fear. These very names point out just how much they differ from each other. Although there is room for both of them in our spiritual life, filial fear should play the leading part…. Filial fear should relegate servile fear more and more to a secondary place….

As long as he lives on earth, man cannot exclude the fear of punishment altogether, first, because he can never be sure of his changing will, yielding as it does so easily to temptations, and secondly, because he may have to pay to divine justice many a debt contracted by his former faults…. It follows that in the life of a Christian it is always necessary to have the virtue of contrition, consisting of sorrow for past sins and a firm purpose of amendment or vigilance lest our will turn away from God, and also of a desire to render satisfaction to God for our offenses by penance. As our spiritual life progresses and our love learns to forget self, we become more and more free from the fear of punishment, and at the same time become more penetrated with filial fear for God's honor.

– Servant of God Father Hyacinth Woroniecki, O.P.

Saint Germaine Cousin

GERMAINE († 1601) WAS BORN IN PIBRAC, France, to poor farm workers. From birth she had a deformed hand and disfiguring lesions on her neck. Germaine's mother died young, and her father's new wife decided that she could not abide the sight of the malformed girl. She sent Germaine to tend the sheep and gave her a wooden plank under the stairs for a bed. A mess of vines served as Germaine's pillow.

Germaine accepted her stepmother's animosity with extraordinary patience. The rosary and daily Mass were her consolations. Little children liked to visit with Germaine, and she taught them of the good God. When the poor came begging, Germaine willingly shared her meager crusts.

As time passed, the villagers began to notice that, when Germaine went to Mass, she left her sheep alone in the fields, yet no marauding wolf ever attacked the flock. Once she was seen to pass through a raging river to attend church. The tales about the little shepherdess came at last to Germaine's father and stepmother, who began to see her in a different light. They invited her back into their home. But Germaine preferred to remain poor. She died soon after, at the age of twenty-two.

When Germaine was beatified, more than 400 miracles were attributed to her. She is the friend of the abandoned and the abused.

– Lisa Lickona

Mercy and Justification

I WAS SEATED ON A PLANE next to a woman wearing a neck brace. She tersely indicated that she was traveling to be with her dying father, but she "didn't want to get into it," because of the messy sibling relations she would soon confront. I let her be, though when I saw her pull out a booklet with Scripture passages in it, I ventured, "Will there be spiritual support for you when you arrive?" She confided, "Yes, I'm Catholic." "And I'm a Catholic priest." Tears flowed as she said, "It's been so long with this brace since I've turned my head to see who's sitting next to me."

The rigidity of sin ratified for so long made humans unable to turn to God, let alone to one another, as relationships were stiffened by our willing offenses. Only the Word made flesh, conformed to the cross, fixing his gaze upon us, makes it possible for us to turn and behold mercy face to face. Kathleen Berken relates, "Forgiveness is abandoning all hope of ever having had a better past." Christ's Passion and Death takes up our past with all its spiritual and actual deaths and folds it into a future full of hope. All our relationships, starting with God himself, can be salvaged, "justified" in God's sight. "Justification," then, is solely by the merit of Christ offering himself as an innocent victim on our behalf to the heavenly Father. Jesus unleashes the grace that transforms us interiorly; "our new life is solely due to the forgiving and renewing mercy that God imparts as a gift and we receive in faith," which "in the Holy Spirit becomes effective in active love"

(Lutheran–Catholic Joint Declaration on the Doctrine of Justification, nn. 17, 24).

Rather than exact justice in the strict sense, God rewrites and extends his "adoption clause" to include all persons who by baptism affiliate with his Son in his Spirit. Nature and grace are organically sealed in souls who participate in the Paschal Mystery of Christ's dying and rising. With the Spirit drawing us into Jesus' own relation with his Father, we love God for himself, and all others as God first loves us. We are fixed no longer by the flesh and the fear that accompanies it, but by the Spirit who saves, by a friendship God ardently desires. Christ's death does not eat glory or destroy it, for God's merciful love engulfs death. Made holy and righteous in God's sight, the "most excellent work of God's mercy" in us tends toward the "glory of God and of Christ, and the gift of eternal life" (CCC 2020).

– Father William M. Joensen

MY FAVORITE PHILOSOPHER in the works of Charles Dickens may be the amiable half-mad Mr. Dick, who can't finish writing his history of England but always gets mixed up at the beheading of Charles I. At which point he takes the papers and makes a kite of them; an expedient I recommend to many a scholar of our time.

"What shall I do with him, Mr. Dick?" demands Aunt Betsy Trotwood. The boy David Copperfield has run away from his horrible work at a bottle company in London. He's half starved and black with grime. His clothes are in tatters. "Come! I want some very sound advice."

Mr. Dick doesn't speculate on profit and loss, or whether Miss Trotwood's charity might be better expended elsewhere. He doesn't have the brains to be that stupid. David tells the story:

> "Why, if I was you," said Mr. Dick, considering, and looking vacantly at me, "I should—" The contemplation of me seemed to inspire him with a sudden idea, and he added briskly, "I should wash him!"

"Mr. Dick sets us all right," says the aunt to the maid. "Heat the bath!" Out of the mouths of babes and odd fellows comes wisdom. "No one knows that man's mind as I do," says Betsy Trotwood.

– Anthony Esolen

"*IF THEY WILL NOT LISTEN TO MOSES and the prophets, neither will they be persuaded if someone should rise from the dead*" (Lk 16:31).

At the conclusion of the parable of the rich man and Lazarus, Jesus' prophetic reference to his own Resurrection offers an amazing revelation: the Death and Resurrection of Jesus is not enough to save or persuade even one single soul, without that soul's free assent. We are free to accept or reject Jesus' offer of mercy.

Mercy is not a response to sin; mercy comes before sin. Mercy is God's initiative. Jesus will suffer and die and rise so that we have the possibility of being saved. But he will not force his mercy upon us.

Christ puts himself in the humiliating position of giving everything to us, like a suitor wooing his beloved, and then waiting, with heart exposed, for us to accept him or reject him.

This primacy of mercy is heard from Jesus' cross: "*Father, forgive them, they know not what they do*" (Lk 23:34). Jesus begs for mercy for his persecutors before they ask for it...without any guarantees that they ultimately will ask for it.

Mercy is infinitely greater than sin. Mercy proceeds from Eternity, from the heart of the Father. Sin began in time.

May freedom choose well!

May freedom be persuaded by the One who is Risen from the dead.

– **Father Richard Veras**

Take away, then, Creator,
    take away so much evil from your creature;
    if he is to give thanks that you made him;
Lord, snatch your servant away from so much evil,
    if he is to rejoice to have you as his Lord.
Spare, God, spare your sinner,
    if he is not to despair of your goodness.
For even if I have sinned more than the first sinner
I do not hate you as he does, nor detest your goodness.
Then, by the great merit of your Baptizer,
    renew in me the grace of your baptizing.
Go before me with your grace;
    follow me with your mercy.
Give me back through the sorrow of penitence
what you had given through the Sacrament
    of Baptism.
Give to me who asks,
    what you gave to him who knew you not.
Refashion the face that I have spoiled,
    restore the innocence that I have violated.
You, Lord, were not involved in that sin
    which you were born to bear.
Lord, take away the sin that I have contracted
    in living.
Take away, you who take away the sin of the world,
    these which are sins of the world,
    which I carry from living in the world.
Take away, you who take away the sin of the world,
by the merits of him who with that same word
    of witness
    pointed you out to world,
take away the sins that I have contracted in the world;
    take from me whatever is not from you,
for I hate whatever is from me; and still I hope in you.

                            – Saint Anselm

Abounding Mercy (Lk 9:60)

Death cannot raise the dead.
Evil deeds cannot spark
the mustard seed's growth.
In the horror of our day,
mass graves gain ground
but cannot create new earth
to cover shocking holes.

Where sin abounds

the cloth will tear,
the wineskin burst,
the dead will bury their dead,

but the living
thirst!

Grace abounds

from the blindness of the grave
where the seed of freedom sounds:
"Lord, have mercy on our age!"

– Rita A. Simmonds

*T*HE PURPOSE OF THE FEAR OF GOD IS…to prevent people not only from turning completely away from God by mortal sin, but also from loitering on the way to God through venial sins. The fear of God should maintain in us a certain delicacy of conscience which does not allow any willful offense against divine mercy, and watches with diligence to see that the number of sins of frailty constantly diminishes.

Could we consider as truly filial a fear of God which restrained us from mortal sins but allowed all kinds of venial sin without the least concern? How great a disrespect of the mercy of God it would be! How naturally it would gradually numb our conscience in all matters related to God's honor and glory! Soon, one violent temptation would be sufficient to turn us from God and deprive us of the state of grace by mortal sin.

In return for the countless proofs of mercy towards us, God wills that we have an unlimited trust in him, and that we honor his mercy and never consciously contradict it by our acts, indicating thereby our lack of appreciation of this greatest of our treasures. This two-fold response to divine mercy is briefly expressed in Psalm 147: *The Lord taketh pleasure in them that fear him, and in them that hope in his mercy* (Ps 147:11).

– Servant of God Father Hyacinth Woroniecki, O.P.

Saint Martin of Tours

MARTIN OF TOURS († 397) is almost always pictured in the act of removing his military cloak, cutting it in two with his sword, and handing half to a starving beggar. This Martin did do, outside the gate of Amiens, France. That night, Christ appeared to him, wearing the beggar's cloak: "Martin, still a catechumen, has covered me with his garment," he said. And Martin, his biographer tells us, "flew to be baptized."

Another, less common, image has Martin with a goose. When Martin was asked to be bishop of Tours, he flew again, this time into hiding. Supposedly, a goose, or a flock of geese, gave him cover. In the second half of the 4th century, there was nothing attractive about the job of bishop. The Roman Empire was beginning to crumble, leaving rough pagan pockets, genuine mission territory. And the Arian heretics threatened good, faithful bishops with exile—or worse. Martin was the not the first would-be bishop to go into hiding. But he came out, for his charity got the best of him. When he heard that a sick friend was calling for him, he came back to Tours. The people hastily elected him.

During his episcopate, Martin traveled much, bringing Christ to the poor country folk. He razed the pagan temples and wrought many miracles. Martin is still much revered in France.

– Lisa Lickona

WHEN MY BEST FRIEND and his wife got married, I realized our relationship would never be the same. He had been my Friday night "Let's go grab a beer" buddy, but a lot more. When their son was born, we drifted apart even more, though we lived minutes away from one another. The demands of his job, a newborn, and a wife working on her master's degree came to compete with *my* work, *my* deadlines, *my* responsibilities. Weeks of not seeing each other turned into months and then years.

One day I was working in the yard when his wife and little boy pulled up. I felt like we needed an introduction, since he was almost two years old and she was clearly pregnant with their second child. "My husband misses you," she said. "I miss you. We all miss you." While their son played in the grass, she and I talked about all that had happened since we had last seen each other—a lot, it seemed; and, then again, not all that much. Not so much, it turned out, that when my friend called me later that day to invite me over for a beer, I didn't hesitate…didn't look back.

The return to communion with God after having lost it through sin begins with the grace he extends to us (CCC 1489). He invites—sometimes simply, sometimes dramatically—and we need to seize it, hold on, and never look back.

– Father Tim S. Hickey

CHARLES DICKENS UNDERSTOOD the difference between mercy and what he called "telescopic philanthropy." Mercy brings together flesh and blood. Telescopic philanthropy keeps them conveniently far apart. Mercy costs us in sweat and time. Mercy demands that we listen even to the rambles of a bad or sick man. Telescopic philanthropy pretends to pay a human debt by a sort of business exchange, a clean deal.

In *Bleak House*, he illustrates the difference by showing us the household of Mrs. Jellyby. She spends all her day shaking people down for "subscriptions" for the natives of far-off Borrioboola-Gha, all while neglecting her own children nearby. When the heroine Esther Summerson, a quiet wonder of feminine charity and mercy, first visits the Jellybys, she finds a little boy with his head stuck through the area railings, beneath the level of the street, crying for help among a crowd of children.

Esther extricates the poor lad, thinking that his mother must not be home. But Mrs. Jellyby is busy with her subscriptions, in a grimy room "strewn with papers and nearly filled by a great writing-table covered with similar litter," assisted by her eldest daughter, "jaded and unhealthy looking" and "biting the feather of her pen."

Saint Paul tells us that now is the acceptable time. We might add that here is the acceptable place.

– Anthony Esolen

It is fortunate for Saint Francis (and Catherine of Siena, Damien de Veuster, and others) that homilies transforming biblical leprosy from a grotesque deformation into a case of eczema are quite new. Christian spirituality and the radical discipleship of the saints are marked by the assumption that Christ the Lord touched not only an outcast, but a man rotting and repulsive to every sense (Mk 1:40-45).

If Jesus' healing of the paralyzed man moved straight and swiftly to the spirit, the healing of the leper makes immediate contact with the body, for the Word *Incarnate* heals not just with his words, but with his hands. The image of salvation is stark.

The leper is Adam, ourselves, the human race, godly creatures, now deteriorating and doomed to death, banished from the only society that saves. Just as the first man was exiled from God's presence in the Garden, so were lepers excluded from worship in the Temple. When Jesus abhors not to touch our sinful flesh, he himself becomes the baptism that cleanses, that fits us to go sacrifice at the altar. *"Be made clean!"* By Christ's mercy our putrid nature is remade, clean once more, and sent to stand before the Lord.

– **Father Anthony Giambrone, O.P.**

O my Lord Jesus, whose love for me has been so great as to bring you down from heaven to save me, teach me, dear Lord, my sin—teach me its heinousness—teach me truly to repent of it—and pardon it in your great mercy!

I beg you, O my dear Savior, to recover me! Your grace alone can do it. I cannot save myself. I cannot recover my lost ground. I cannot turn to you, I cannot please you, or save my soul without you. I shall go from bad to worse, I shall fall from you entirely, I shall quite harden myself against my neglect of duty, if I rely on my own strength. I shall make myself my center instead of making you. I shall worship some idol of my own framing instead of you, the only true God and my Maker, unless you hinder it by your grace. O my dear Lord, hear me! I have lived long enough in this undecided, wavering, unsatisfactory state. I wish to be your good servant. I wish to sin no more. Be gracious to me, and enable me to be what I know I ought to be.

– Blessed John Henry Newman

The Harvest Is Plenty (Lk 10:1-12)

Though we are highly employable,
much in demand,
we apply everywhere
and petition without ceasing.
Our only qualification
is acceptance of the job.
We are trained while we work.
Our Boss is always present—
moving us along.
There is always more than enough to do.
Sometimes undercover
we stalk ruined fields.
Sometimes, in the spotlight
our heads are handed to us.
Our pay is God's Grace in abundance
and souls stolen from foxes' lairs.
We are rich in demand.

Lord, in Your mercy
grant us steady supply
of You!

– Rita A. Simmonds

*T*HE PRESENT-DAY MENTALITY...seems opposed to a God of mercy.... Humanity and the modern world need so much. And they need mercy even though they often do not realize it....

Making the Father present as love and mercy is, in Christ's own consciousness, the fundamental touch-stone of his mission as the Messiah....

Christ proclaims by his actions even more than by his words that call to mercy which is one of the essen-tial elements of the Gospel ethos. In this instance it is not just a case of fulfilling a commandment or an ob-ligation of an ethical nature; it is also a case of satisfy-ing a condition of major importance for God to reveal himself in his mercy to man....

All the subtleties of love become manifest in the Lord's mercy towards those who are his own: he is their Father.... Mercy is the content of intimacy with their Lord, the content of their dialogue with him....

Mercy is in a certain sense contrasted with God's justice, and in many cases is shown to be not only more powerful than that justice but also more profound.... Love, so to speak, conditions justice and, in the final analysis, justice serves love. The primacy and superior-ity of love vis-à-vis justice—this is a mark of the whole of revelation—are revealed precisely through mercy.... Mercy differs from justice, but is not in opposition to it.

– *Dives in Misericordia* 2-4

Saint Maria Goretti

MARIA GORETTI († 1902) was only twelve years old when she died at the hands of Alessandro Serenelli, who was attempting to rape her. "Don't do it!" she had begged her attacker. "It is a sin!" Alessandro stabbed Maria fourteen times—through the lungs, the pericardium, the heart. She survived twenty more hours, suffering a fruitless surgery. The priest who came to hear her confession urged her to forgive Alessandro. A moment of hesitation ended with Maria's declaration: "Yes, I forgive him for the love of Jesus…and I want him to come with me to paradise."

Several years later, Maria came in a dream to Alessandro, as he languished in prison. She was clad in white, with a lily in her hand. Afterward Alessandro wrote to the bishop to confess. He became a model prisoner, earning parole four years before his thirty years were up. Then he went to visit Assunta, Maria's mother, to ask her pardon. And, most amazingly, he testified at the process for Maria's beatification. "I gave myself over to brutal passion," he admitted. "She is a saint. Hers is a true martyrdom."

Alessandro lived out his years working in the garden of a Capuchin friary, praying frequently to his "little saint." She is the protector of girls and the patroness of those who seek forgiveness.

– Lisa Lickona

IN CONFESSION, priests offer every penitent the gifts of pardon and peace. Pardon brings our hearts back into right relationship with the God who created us. This reconciliation makes possible the peace that comes from the right ordering of our lives.

These gifts are offered in every confession, but we can prepare ourselves to receive them more fully by approaching the sacrament with a truly contrite heart and a fervent desire to love God above all things.

To cultivate contrition, we can seek the Spirit's gift of knowledge, which helps us face the truth about our sins. A sincere prayer for the gift of knowledge prepares a penitent for a more fruitful examination of conscience. Awareness of our sins disposes us to appreciate the immeasurable gift of pardon.

To cultivate theological love, we can regularly make acts of love for God, which enkindle the fire of divine love. Saint John Mary Vianney would often pray, "Oh my God, if my tongue is not able to say at every opportunity that I love you, I want at least my heart to repeat it to you as many times as I take a breath!" Such prayers foster the peace that comes from setting our hearts on the only one who will satisfy our longings.

– Father Christopher Seiler

THE PILGRIM DANTE is climbing the mountain of purgatory, a rocky cliff to his left and a sheer fall of a thousand feet to his right. On the roadway ahead he sees people literally relying upon one another, sitting back to back, their heads raised up. Their eyes are sewn shut with iron wire, through which they weep tears of remorse.

They are the souls of the envious, literally, those who looked askance at their neighbor's blessings. It is hard to imagine a more antisocial sin than small-hearted, all-leveling envy. But now the souls must be together, if only to keep from falling from the brink. And they are together for far more than that:

> After we had gone on a little way
> we heard them crying, "Mary, pray for us!"
> and, "Michael!" "Peter!" "All the blessed, pray!"
> (*Purgatory*)

What a fine glance at the true and only community, the communion of saints. We may be apt to think of mercy as what a superior confers upon an inferior. It is hard for us to remember that we will all be—we pray—on that same mountain, where mercy will be our bond of love, and God's way of making us healthy together, and more like him.

– Anthony Esolen

A WEALTHY MAN EAGER FOR ETERNAL LIFE approached
Jesus (Mk 10:17-22). Saint Mark tells us that *Jesus, looking at him, loved him.* What was in that gaze that caused
Mark to write, *Jesus loved him*? When then the Lord tells
the man to sell all he has, give it away and then come and
follow him, *[the man's] face fell, and he went away sad.* I
have envied the sadness of the rich young man, overflowing with the memory of that gaze and a yearning to return
to it if he could but find the courage.

It makes me think of a dying woman who asked me
whether a dog she had once owned would be in heaven,
otherwise she had no interest in going there. I answered,
"That dog looked at you and saw his happiness and was
full of joy just to see you. No one else ever looked at you
that way. But in heaven every person who looks at you will
see the perfected image of Christ in you and will rejoice
just to see you. If every person who looked at you did so
with eternal joy just at seeing you, would you miss your
dog?" She said no.

What filled that young man with sadness as he walked
away was the consciousness that he had never been looked
at like that, looked at by someone who wanted to pass
eternity with him. Who knows what sanctity he lived in
memory of the mercy of that gaze?

– **Father Vincent Nagle**, F.S.C.B.

Lord, I asked you for health to be more effective on earth. You gave me weakness of body so that I would rely more on you than on myself.

Lord, I asked you for responsibilities so that I might bring about the triumph of good ideas and worthy causes. You gave me the grace of being treated as nothing and of being obedient to others so as better to configure me to your obedient and crucified Son.

Lord, I asked you that I might encounter a great love so as to give meaning to my life. You gave me the grace of being able to believe in the goodness of the human heart and the desire to share that faith with all the badly loved persons whom you made me meet.

Lord, I asked you for a faith that would move mountains. You gave me the grace to have uneasy doubts that obliged me to remain prudent and totally abandoned to your Providence.

Lord, I asked you for the well-being of my dear ones. You gave them all kinds of trials, reminding me in this way that Jesus and his dear ones themselves suffered before entering into the joy of your Kingdom.

Lord, I asked you that I might become a saint. You gave me the grace to see my sins better and to be able to rise after each of my grievous falls without despairing.

     – Based on a prayer composed by a Confederate soldier
during the Civil War

Mindy (Lk 10:25-37)

Mindy worked in customer service.
She had a man's voice.
I spoke with her over the phone,
trying to tackle financial affairs
after my husband died.

Mindy felt sorry for me.
She told me so.
She tried to help me
pay my bill.
I cried.

She countered all my worries
with a kind and urgent tone.
I sensed she knew what loss was like.
She took my troubles as her own.

Mindy, with a manly voice,
made me recognize
the One who canceled all I owed
and wrote my name
across the sky.

– Rita A. Simmonds

*T*HE VIRTUE OF MERCY BELONGS TO the cortège of the virtues of love and is its closest helper…. Mercy is a habit of the will which regulates our attitude towards another's ills….

We love our neighbor as something belonging to God and loved by God, as a friend of God, or if he is not his friend as yet, then as someone invited to the friendship of God, who awaits him with eagerness. If the love of neighbor is understood in this manner, it can be extended to all, even to our enemies who, though they have hostile dispositions towards us, do not cease to be an object of God's love and his effort to win their love in return.

Christian mercy should be permeated with the same spirit of love of God; it should have its roots deeply anchored in that spiritual faculty of the soul which is called the will…. It is of the utmost importance that our will be penetrated by mercy so that it may become an instrument of God's holy will pouring out his mercy through us upon the world. Whenever the love of neighbor is alive in the will, it will always find its expression in the sensitive faculties also, and will produce a true compassion for another's suffering.

– Servant of God Father Hyacinth Woroniecki, O.P.

Saint Mary Magdalene

THE GOSPELS TELL US that Mary Magdalene was one from whom *"seven demons had gone out"* (Lk 8:2). Was she really a victim of demonic possession? Or was she mentally ill? Or was Mary, as the Western tradition has it, a woman in the grip of prostitution? Whatever Mary's problem was, it was, to be sure, something dark. And yet she had come to Jesus in her brokenness. Overwhelmed with the desire for something to change, she asked him to heal her. And he did.

From that time, Mary followed him anywhere and everywhere. She stood with the other women at the foot of the cross. And on the morning after the sabbath, she stood outside the tomb, weeping (Jn 20:11-16). There she met the gardener. *"Woman, why are you weeping?"* Sick with grief, Mary said, *"Sir, if you carried him away, tell me where you laid him, and I will take him."* At this, the "gardener" addressed her, *"Mary!"*

All at once she knew that it was Jesus. The one who healed her had conquered death itself! And he called her by name! She was overwhelmed with his love. Meditating upon Mary Magdalene, Pope Benedict XVI taught: "If we seek the Lord with a simple and sincere mind, we too will find him; indeed, he himself will come to meet us; he will make us recognize him, he will call us by name…he will admit us to the intimacy of his love."

– Lisa Lickona

On Penance for Sins: Satisfaction

No Catholic who has gone to confession can forget easily that the priest, before granting the absolution, indicates a penance to be accomplished. Usually we hear words like these: "For your penance, say three Hail Marys and three Our Fathers." Most Catholics who confess regularly have become so accustomed to this practice that they may have forgotten what purpose the penance serves. This forgetfulness would arise especially when the few prayers asked of the penitent seem disproportionate to the many sins for which mercy is asked. Why, then, does the priest assign a penance during confession?

The Sacrament of Penance and Reconciliation plays an essential role in the life of the Catholic. Specifically, the grace that penance imparts puts a sacramental stamp on our efforts to sustain conversion. We need this specialized help that comes from God. Our own good will does not alone suffice. Some Catholics nevertheless wonder why the Church even requires of forgiven sinners a penance. Is not God—such folks might reason—merciful enough just to forgive our past sins and let bygones be bygones? If I am truly sorry for my sins, why do I need to perform a penance? These questions may perplex even devout Catholics who, since their school days, have said the assigned three Hail Marys and three Our Fathers.

To refer to the works of the penitent as penance is an exercise in metonymy. Common usage assigns to one part of the sacrament the name for the whole. The technical term for the "penance" given in confession is satisfaction.

We make satisfaction for our sins because each sin leaves its mark on the sinner and also produces a negative effect on the sinner's community. Sin multiplies disorder. The sinner requires a kind of medicinal remedy to regain full spiritual health and to restore a proper relationship with God and neighbor. When the sins are those against the seventh and eighth commandments, that is, the sins against justice, satisfaction follows restitution. Satisfaction entails more than the return of what was unjustly taken or the correction of what has been said. Satisfaction restores friendship.

Some may still wonder how a few prayers can accomplish so much good, especially when their sins have been serious and of long standing. The answer to this question is easy. Satisfaction gains its salvific value from the penitent's being united with Christ. His preeminent satisfaction on the cross valorizes all the Hail Marys and Our Fathers (and at times, larger penances) that sinners have performed over the centuries.

– **Father Romanus Cessario, O.P.**

DAME MARGOT FONTEYN (1919–1991), prima ballerina, danced her whole career for the Royal Ballet.

Like most of us, she also had a weakness. "She had very bad judgment about people," her former assistant Colette Clark noted.

In 1937, Fonteyn fell madly in love with Panamanian playboy Roberto "Tito" Arias. They were married in 1955.

Fonteyn helped Tito smuggle guns (for which she was once arrested and briefly jailed) and overlooked his incessant philandering.

In 1964, Tito was shot and paralyzed, reputedly by the jealous husband of a lover. Fonteyn nursed him for the next twenty-five years, dancing well into her sixties to pay his debts and support his family. The day he died, another of his mistresses committed suicide by drinking swimming-pool chlorine.

Soon after, Fonteyn was diagnosed with cancer. She converted to Catholicism on her deathbed in order to be buried with him.

Our culture pathologizes such fidelity, labeling it co-dependency or love addiction. But Fonteyn never violated her duty to her vocation. She gave her all to Tito while also giving all to the dance—and thus to us.

The parable of the sheep and the goats reminds us that we will not be judged on our ability to evaluate character. We will be judged on our capacity for mercy. We will be judged on love.

– Heather King

As part of their preparation, candidates for confirmation are asked to write a letter to me. In it they not only request to receive the sacrament, but also write about their service, hobbies, sports, and favorite subject in school. One student wrote a line that caught my attention: *My favorite subject is math because there is only one answer.*

Those of us of a certain age know how much we need the Spirit when there is more than one answer to life's questions. Or when things don't add up and the answer is unclear.

A major focus of the Letter of James is the ethical conduct of Christians, particularly in moments of challenge. Reminiscent of the Sermon on the Mount, his advice is timeless: *mercy triumphs over judgment* (Jas 2:13). James tells us that the moral life is based on mercy.

The mercy God shows to us must be lived with others. In life we are faced with difficult situations and people we do not like or understand. We find ourselves judging others, often harshly, while excusing our indifference and impatience. We insist we have no choice or don't know what to do. There is always one answer: be guided by mercy.

– **Monsignor Gregory E. S. Malovetz**

I want to be completely transformed into your mercy and to be your living reflection, O Lord. May the greatest of all divine attributes pass through my heart to my neighbor.

Help me that my eyes may be merciful, so that I may never suspect or judge from appearances, but look for what is beautiful in my neighbors' souls and come to their rescue.

Help me, that my eyes may be merciful, so that I may give heed to my neighbors' needs and not be indifferent to their pains and moanings.

Help, O Lord, that my tongue may be merciful, so that I should never speak negatively of my neighbor, but have a word of comfort and forgiveness for all.

Help me, O Lord, that my hands may be merciful and filled with good deeds, so that I may do only good to my neighbors and take upon myself the more difficult and toilsome tasks.

Help me, that my feet may be merciful so that I may hurry to assist my neighbor, overcoming my own fatigue and weariness. My true rest is in the service of my neighbor.

Help me, O Lord, that my heart may be merciful so that I myself may feel all the sufferings of my neighbor. I will refuse my heart to no one. I will be sincere even with those who, I know, will abuse my kindness. I will bear my own suffering in silence. May your mercy rest upon me.

O my Jesus, transform me in yourself, for you can do all things.

– Saint Maria Faustina Kowalska

For Mary (Lk 10:38-42)

My sister Mary,
always the contemplative,
has found a permanent place
in the Lord's house.

She sits at the feet of Jesus all day,
knowing Him full well,
and I am a restless Martha
left to this troubled world.

For now this is my part.

She sees Him face to face,
I, but a reflection dim—

yet both of us are fully known
by Him.

– Rita A. Simmonds

*T*HE CHURCH LIVES AN AUTHENTIC LIFE when she… proclaims mercy—the most stupendous attribute of…the Redeemer—and when she brings people close to the sources of the Savior's mercy….

It is precisely because sin exists in the world… that God, who *is love*, cannot reveal himself otherwise than as mercy. This corresponds…to the whole interior truth of man and of the world which is man's temporary homeland. Mercy in itself, as a perfection of the infinite God, is also infinite. Also infinite therefore and inexhaustible is the Father's readiness to receive the prodigal children who return to his home. Infinite are the readiness and power of forgiveness which flow continually from the marvelous value of the sacrifice of the Son.

No human sin can prevail over this power or even limit it. On the part of man only a lack of good will can limit it, a lack of readiness to be converted and to repent, in other words persistence in obstinacy, opposing grace and truth, especially in the face of the witness of the cross and Resurrection of Christ. Therefore, the Church professes and proclaims conversion. Conversion to God always consists in discovering his mercy…. Authentic knowledge of the God of mercy, the God of tender love, is a constant and inexhaustible source of conversion… as a permanent attitude, as a state of mind.

– *Dives in Misericordia* 13

Saint Sharbel Makhlūf

A POOR LEBANESE SHEPHERD BOY, Youssef went often to a lonely cave, where he had placed a statue of the Virgin; he would light incense and kneel in prayer. He longed to follow his two uncles, who were hermits. At the age of twenty-three, he left his home in secret to join a monastery, taking the name Sharbel, after an early martyr.

After fifteen years living according to the strict rule, Sharbel was permitted to go to a hermitage. There his routine was always the same. Before first light he began the prayers to prepare his heart. He said Mass at around eleven. After Mass, his thanksgiving went on into the evening. From morning to night Sharbel begged God's mercy on the world.

Often the peasants came to the hermitage to ask the holy hermit for help. When once a great scourge of locusts was decimating the crops, Sharbel sprinkled holy water on the fields and the locusts were banished.

In 1898, Sharbel suffered a stroke while saying Mass. For the next eight days he lay in bed repeating the prayer he had been saying the moment he was stricken: "Father of truth, behold your son who makes atoning sacrifice to you. Accept the offering: he died for me that I might have life. Behold the offering! Accept it…." Sharbel died on Christmas Eve. His shrine in Lebanon has been the site of numerous healings.

– Lisa Lickona

Vital Participation in Mercy

MERCY APPEARS AS A GREAT MYSTERY in today's world. Friends may encourage us to turn the other cheek, let it go, get over it, and move on. They tempt us with their simplicity. They trap us in their utterance, *"heal thyself"* (cf. Lk 4:23). Weak and imperfect ourselves, we lack the power to conjure this hollow "mercy," and thus fail to receive healing and restoration.

Mercy is not magic. Mercy is hard work, especially the command, *"Be merciful, even as your Father is merciful"* (Lk 6:36)

It is easier to describe mercy in the abstract, but it is challenging to practice at school, at work, and in our lives. Mercy can be even harder to practice in our own homes. People hurt us and those we love. And when they do, I do not like them. I can be tempted to hate them. I may give in to that temptation. The pain is terrible and real. Yet Jesus teaches us, *"Forgive us our trespasses as we forgive those who trespass against us"* (cf. Mt 6:12). God help me to live these impossible words!

Jesus offers a path of restoration. His mercy is not hollow. He plumbs the depth of our hearts, directly touching the great suffering and pain that we carry. He loves us. He forgives us. But first he heals us.

Mercy, to be full, flows not from a self-generated willing but from what the *Catechism* calls "vital participation" (CCC 2842). God does not command from us what he does not first give to us. He invites us into an intimate movement of grace and mercy: he is the Teacher, he is the Healer, he is the Way.

The words of the Our Father strengthen and heal not because they sound nice or I can repeat them back to Jesus. They strengthen and heal because they proclaim my identity: a beloved son of the Father. They draw me to the encounter with Jesus. I meet him on the cross. I meet him in the sacraments. I meet him in confession.

I know how to forgive because I have been forgiven. How quickly then, when I am wronged, do I return to my Lord? I pray, "Jesus, this hurt done to me, how often do I inflict hurt upon you. Yet, you never abandon or hate. You love me and call me repeatedly back into your merciful embrace."

Above our altars hangs an enormous crucifix. From that cross, Jesus declares that nothing—no shame, no suffering, no sin—is greater than his mercy and love. His love is bigger than our biggest sin. His offer to heal is greater than the greatest wound inflicted.

My transformation overflows from the merciful words and embrace of my Savior. I forgive not from my strength but from his. He makes me new. My Savior and my Teacher sends me forth, confident, healed, and unafraid, a missionary of his mercy.

– **Father Eric Cadin**

An old Cumberland beggar trudges down the road, his back bowed, his eyes upon the ground. To the utilitarian mind, there is no point to his life. He cannot even enjoy the rural scenery about him. "One little span of earth/ Is all his prospect," says the poet Wordsworth; "but deem not this man useless."

Statesmen, says the poet, will want to take out their brooms and "rid the world of nuisances," among which they number beggars like the old man. But not "the meanest of created things" is ever divorced from good; so much the less can anyone who

> ever owned
> The heaven-regarding eye and front sublime
> Which man is born to—sink, howe'er depressed,
> So low as to be scorned without a sin;
> Without offense to God cast out of view.
>
> ("The Old Cumberland Beggar")

We can never be but dried flowers that have shed their seeds, or worn out and worthless tools.

But Wordsworth says more. The beggar is meant *for us too*: he calls us into mercy, he stirs in children their "first mild touch of sympathy and thought" in a world of want and sorrow. And he ensures that we will never, as we grow older and less tender, forget that man is finally little more than that poor creature, walking toward the grave.

– Anthony Esolen

IN A COUNTRY AS ETHNICALLY and economically diverse as ours, racism and prejudice seem to be ineradicable. Protests, lawsuits, op-eds, and letters to editors all have their place in these issues, but none seem to burst through the thick walls of ideology or heal the deep wounds of injustice.

The parable of the good Samaritan (Lk 10:29-37) proposes a different method.

Jesus experienced the hostility between Jews and Samaritans. He was once accused of being a Samaritan himself.

His "solution" to this problem is mercy. Not mercy in general, but mercy from one person to another.

Arguments don't seem to change ideologies, but mercy can penetrate the very heart that arguments often harden.

I was once at a play about the Christmas Eve truce of World War I, when enemy soldiers along the front lines came together to celebrate Christmas. A friend who was with me said, "If it were up to those young men, the war would have ended that Christmas Eve."

It was not up to those men. But something happened that night that was so powerful it can move hearts one hundred years later.

Mercy from one person to another seems laughably inefficient to effect large-scale social change, but does any other method get to the heart of the matter, and to the heart of the person, so powerfully?

– Father Richard Veras

Take the most hideous of diseases, under which the body wastes away and corrupts—all is nothing compared with that dreadful sickness of the soul which we call sin. They all are the effects of it, they all are shadows of it, but nothing more. That cause itself is something different in kind, is of a malignity far other and greater than all these things. O my God, teach me this! Give me to understand the enormity of that evil under which I labor and know it not. Teach me what sin is.

In the judgment of the Creator it is that which has marred his spiritual work; it is a greater evil than if the stars got loose, and ran wild in heaven, and chaos came again. But man, who is the guilty one, calls it by soft names. He explains it away. The world laughs at it, and is indulgent to it; and, as to its deserving eternal punishment, it rises up indignant at the idea, and rather than admit it, would deny the God who has said it does. The world thinks sin the same sort of imperfection as an impropriety, or want of taste, or infirmity.

My God, imprint on my heart the infamous deformity of sin. Teach me to abhor it as a pestilence—as a fierce flame destroying on every side; as my death. Let me take up arms against it, and devote myself to fight under your banner in overcoming it.

– Blessed John Henry Newman

Reaching the Kingdom (Lk 11:1-13)

Our father
loved to sing
Malotte's version
of "The Lord's Prayer"
full voice
at Sunday morning Mass.
At the organ's introduction
we knew
our smirk would turn
to shrinking in the pew
when he reached
the "Kingdom
and the power
and the glory."
Looking back
I realize
with pride
there was no one
for miles around
who loved the "Our Father"
with as much fearlessness
and fervor
as our father
who now
looking down
has reached
the Kingdom
he had reached so many times before,
with his powerful and glorious
sound.

– Rita A. Simmonds

*O*PENNESS TO CHRIST, who as the Redeemer of the world fully "reveals man to himself," can only be achieved through an ever more mature reference to the Father and his love. Although God *dwells in unapproachable light,* he speaks to man by means of the whole of the universe….

Through this "making known" by Christ we know God above all in his relationship of love for man…. It is precisely here that "his invisible nature" becomes in a special way "visible," incomparably more visible than through all the other "things that have been made": it becomes visible in Christ and through Christ, through his actions and his words, and finally through his death on the cross and his Resurrection.

In this way, in Christ and through Christ, God also becomes especially visible in his mercy…. Christ confers on the whole of the Old Testament tradition about God's mercy a definitive meaning. Not only does he speak of it and explain it by the use of comparisons and parables, but above all he himself makes it incarnate and personifies it. He himself, in a certain sense, is mercy. To the person who sees it in him—and finds it in him—God becomes "visible" in a particular way as the Father *who is rich in mercy.*

– *Dives in Misericordia* 1-2

Saint Dominic

IN DOMINIC'S († 1221) TIME, princes and prelates led violent crusades against the Cathars, the Manichean heretics of France and Spain. But, having walked among the Cathars, taken dinner at their tables and heard their arguments, the priest Dominic began to imagine a different approach. He wanted to reach souls and bring them out of darkness, not simply to expunge heresy.

Heresy, Dominic knew, flourished where the Gospel seed had not been sown. Preachers were needed to instruct the ignorant. Like monks, they must be grounded in study. But in order for their words to bear fruit, they must impress not by pomp and preening, but by a witness akin to Christ's own. Dominic's preachers would be poor and luminously pure. Above all, these men would draw all their strength from prayer.

Dominic himself was the model of the contemplative man engaged in active ministry. Night fasts and vigils served to refresh him for the day of preaching ahead. Blessed Fra Angelico's image in Saint Mark's in Venice best captures the source of Dominic's strength: like Mary Magdalene, the saint clings to the rough-hewn wood at the feet of the crucified Lord. From such love sprang the Dominicans, the mendicant preachers, who went forth in the spirit of their founder to set the Medieval world on fire.

– Lisa Lickona

The Second Week of the Ignatian *Spiritual Exercises* and the Year of Mercy

IN THE OPENING MEDITATION of the second week of his *Spiritual Exercises*, Saint Ignatius Loyola invites us to ponder a highly imaginative scene. The three Divine Persons look down upon the whole expanse of all the earth, filled with human beings. All of these human beings are going down to hell. The three Divine Persons decree, in their eternity, that the Son, the Second Person of the Blessed Trinity, should become man to save the human race.

This act, this decree, is the primal act of divine mercy. In the words of the Creed, "for us men and for our salvation he came down from heaven, and by the Holy Spirit was incarnate of the Virgin Mary and became man." The Incarnation is the source from which flow all the rest of Christ's life and actions in one great torrent of mercy.

Mercy is forgiveness. Mercy means not demanding repayment of a debt or exacting revenge for an injury, but canceling the debt and restoring harmony. Saint Ignatius does not write of mercy in the second week of the *Exercises*, but he invites us to contemplate mercy in action. The second week of the *Exercises* is a series of meditations on the mysteries of Christ's life, from the Incarnation to Palm Sunday. These mysteries make present and efficacious the supreme act of mercy, the Incarnation. Christ's teachings are mercy for minds, his cures of the sick are mercy for bodies, his exorcisms are mercy for souls, his raising the dead is mercy triumphing over death, his institution of baptism and the Eucharist are sacramental gifts of mercy. God's mercy is to be pondered in each event of our Lord's life, in every detail of the Gospel narratives.

There is also another dimension to the second week: meditating on a fitting response to the Incarnation. If God has done so much for us in Christ, what should we do in return? In a series of meditations, Saint Ignatius invites me to consider the state of life I should choose; he has me contemplate two standards, the standard of Satan: riches, honors, pride; and the standard of Christ: poverty, humiliations, humility. A meditation on the three classes of men is meant to spur me to act on my resolutions and not procrastinate. Finally, I contemplate three kinds of humility. The third and highest kind is to be poor with Christ poor, insulted with Christ insulted, even accounted a fool for Christ. "So Christ was treated before me."

These meditations are thus the mirror image of the Incarnation: as I meditate on the Gospels, I ponder what Christ did for me; then, following Saint Ignatius, I ask God to help me respond rightly: to imitate Christ, even to be Christ.

– Father Joseph T. Lienhard, s.j.

There are times when writing songs feels like a routine day job: like showing up to a cubicle and sending faxes or making copies. But there are other moments when it feels mystical—divinely appointed. In those moments I feel as though I am reaching up to a cloud above me to pick out notes and melodies that exist independently of me—I feel I am merely stewarding them as Adam stewarded creation in the garden.

In making music, the artist is attempting to delve fearlessly into her human experience and emerge from the depths, however splutteringly, with some glittering glimpse of what lies beyond her. Artists are deep-sea divers in search of a pearl to enjoy and display: whether or not an artist recognizes the ocean as the divine mercy of God does not change the fact that it is so. The mercy of God in art is apparent in the fact that our work may be imperfect or lazy or even bad—and yet there is something mystical in all art, because those who make it are looking beyond what is visible to communicate something invisible.

It is an immutable reality that we live in a state of yearning. Art reflects that perhaps most poignantly, because the very act of creating it is a search: and in listening, we search to encounter ourselves, and perhaps there we may encounter God and his divine mercy.

– Audrey Assad

"*SON OF DAVID, have pity on us!*" The two blind men in Matthew's Gospel (9:27-31) broadcast in stereo a firm messianic faith. Christ is not addressed simply as "Hey Mister." He is recognized as the embodiment of the promised mercy of the Lord. When the blind man in Jericho calls out the same words, Jesus asks, "*What do you want?*" (Lk 18:41) and with good reason. "Have mercy!" was a pan-handling formula.

Like us, most beggars surely asked far too little of the Lord: a dime for a cup of coffee, when the Creator of all things stood ready at their service. As the beggars in Matthew call out, however, the Lord simply asks, "*Do you believe that I can do this?*" When we cry out for mercy, we must not be so cramped in our expectations that we make God parsimonious with his gifts. *[The Lord] became poor although he was rich, so that by his poverty you might become rich* (2 Cor 8:9). The Lord longs to lavish upon us *everything* he has—to empty his pockets in proportion to our belief. "*Let it be done for you according to your faith*" (Mt 9:29). Let us, then, beg for a full flood of light to heal our darkness.

– Father Anthony Giambrone, O.P.

We have gone astray.
We are weary and cold.
Mother of Mercy, once again you have not left us alone
in the days of sorrow and affliction.
Again from heaven
you descended in the brightness
of refulgent light
to visit our bloodstained land.

Mother, to whom shall we flee,
to whom shall we appeal
in abandonment, affliction, and distress?
Cast your glance, O Mother,
at our hearts, bruised
by sorrow and longing;
at our lips, blue from hunger and cold.
Bring us back to the land
that heaven itself
has given us; to the land
adorned with churches
and wayside crosses;
to the land you have loved
from the very beginning.
Allow us to see again
the pictures and shrines
abounding in grace.
Permit us to sing again the hymns
of gratitude and love
to merciful Jesus
and to you, O Mother of Pity,
to you who have promised
to obtain remission of all transgressions. Amen.

– Servant of God Adelė Dirsytė

Vanity's Cure (Eccl 1:2; 2:21-23)

W hat does it mean to fall asleep?

To throw my body from the mountain of worries
that form the backdrop of my days?
To slide like an avalanche into bed
and hide beneath the brambled darkness
that chokes the seeds of striving peace?
To slip on the stairs that lead to success,
and bump my head on each concrete step
until I am unconscious of the glory I want to reach?

What does it mean to fall asleep?

To resign my days to sleepless nights,
and place my head of worry
into Your arms of mercy,
and never dream of sleep.

                                    – Rita A. Simmonds

*I*F WE LIVE OUT OUR OWN NATURE as an image of the mystery that created us and participate in this mystery, if we understand that this mystery is both mercy and goodness, then we will try to live that mercy, goodness, and brotherhood as if it were our own nature, no matter how difficult or challenging the task....

We are so much the objects of this affection that we are made, created, saved, and kept alive by it. We have been created by this affection; it is now our turn to make it our self, acting from within this mercy, failing which we shall betray our deepest nature....

It does not matter what level of perfection you reach. What others think or don't think of how much you do does not matter, nor does your judgment of yourself. All that matters is that mercy has taken you for ever, from the very origin of your existence. Mercy called you to love, because mercy loved you.

Holiness means always affirming—before everything else, in everything else—the embrace of the Father, the merciful, pitying movement of Christ, his gesture....

Nothingness, destruction, exile is the life proper to the world...without this covenant.... Grace holds fast because God leads me to discover what he is and to understand that from my destruction he makes something new bud forth as identification with him and the Father.

– Servant of God Monsignor Luigi Giussani

Saint John Vianney

WHEN HE WAS SIXTEEN, John, the farmer's son from Dardilly, France, decided to become a priest. He had to study philosophy and theology, and all of it in a foreign tongue—Latin. Father Balley, the curé of Ecully, taught John's Latin class. John, the oldest student, was at the bottom of the class, but Father Balley patiently tutored him. Even so, when John took his seminary exams, he froze up. Father Balley convinced the examiner to hear the answers in French, and John passed.

In 1815, John went to Écully as Father Balley's associate. Now the older priest tutored him in fasting and prayer. So, when John received his own parish, becoming the curé of Ars, he immediately stormed heaven for his people. He slept on an old mattress. He donned a hair shirt and subsisted on moldy potatoes. He preached and said Mass and, above all, heard confessions. In ten years, the priest who had barely made it out of the seminary had revived the faith of the entire parish.

Then the world came. The faithful and the desperate traveled from all parts of France to confess to him. Sixteen to eighteen hours a day John sat in the confessional box. He suffered with them, often wracked with headaches, always wearing his hair shirt. After he died in 1859, he became the help of all parish priests.

– Lisa Lickona

Among the synonyms suggested for the word "daunting" are: challenging, intimidating, and formidable. But the *Catechism of the Catholic Church* uses "daunting" to describe the obstacles we must overcome to receive God's mercy. Why is seeking forgiveness so daunting? Because we must admit—to God, to ourselves, to others, and then to a priest—that we are less what we claim to be. "In refusing to forgive our brothers and sisters, our hearts are closed and their hardness makes them impervious to the Father's merciful love" (CCC 2840).

Consider the rich young man in Mark's Gospel, so eager to be a disciple that he runs to Jesus and spills his life's story. Jesus looks at him with love, says Saint Mark, and that loving look reveals to the young man who he truly is, not who he claims to be. Despite all the good he has done, something is lacking (see Mk 10:17-22). But rather than asking Jesus to fill up what is missing, the young man goes away sad. His possessions, his self-importance, his reluctance to forgive others have hardened him; he is "impervious" to Jesus' offer.

In his song "Anthem," the singer-songwriter Leonard Cohen sings, "There is a crack in everything; that's how the light gets in." Let us pray to be cracked open every day to forgive and to seek forgiveness.

– Father Tim S. Hickey

ÉLISABETH LESEUR, Servant of God (1866–1914), a French mystic, is known for the spiritual diaries she wrote while married to a doctor who scorned her devotion to Christ. Her husband, Félix, lost his Catholic faith shortly before their 1889 wedding and became a publicly vocal atheist.

The Leseurs frequently entertained. Élisabeth, a gracious and lively hostess, came to see that enduring the anti-Catholic jibes of her husband—whom she loved deeply—and his friends could be a hidden form of mortification.

She developed a rich interior life. She quietly remained faithful to her prayers—especially for Félix—works of mercy, and daily devotions. She carried on a wide-ranging correspondence, mostly unbeknownst to her husband, throughout her life.

"Look around oneself for proud sufferers in need," Élisabeth counseled, "find them, and give them the alms of our heart, of our time, and of our tender respect."

By July 1913 she was bedridden with breast cancer. She offered up her sufferings for the conversion of Félix's soul.

Shortly after her death, he found a letter she had written to him praying that he would turn to Christ.

Félix was ordained a Dominican priest in 1923. He spent much of his last twenty-seven years promulgating the writings, and advancing the cause for beatification, of his wife.

– Heather King

GROWING UP IN THE CULTURAL MOVEMENTS of the sixties, I gained ideas about morality that I considered to be infinitely more tolerant and therefore more loving than— as I considered it at the time—the often "backward and repressive" moral teachings of the Catholic Church.

It was an act of mercy that opened me up to a different criterion of judgment. At university I found myself facing people proposing Catholic views that I found outrageous. I went against these people and their teachings with all my might. Yet they never went against me; when I was in a real financial bind, it was the leader of this Catholic group who took the initiative to help me. Then when it was time for me to graduate, it was again he who intervened with the university to help me overcome an obstacle. When I tried to thank him, he said, "We need more students like you here, asking the tough questions." He mercifully did not add, as he did years later, that my presence had been very painful.

When Jesus healed a man's withered hand on the sabbath (Mt 12:9-13), he was trying to open up his detractors to a new criterion: it is lawful to do good on the sabbath. The real criterion for what is good comes from what brings life. The miracle of mercy shows us where life comes from, and opens us up to a true judgment of what is good.

– Father Vincent Nagle, F.S.C.B.

I feel intimately, O my God, that, whenever I am left to myself, I go wrong. As sure as a stone falls down to the earth if it be let go, so surely my heart and spirit fall down hopelessly if they are let go by you. You must uphold me by your right hand, or I cannot stand. How strange it is, but how true, that all my natural tendencies are towards sloth, towards excess, towards neglect of religion, towards neglect of prayer, towards love of the world, not towards love of you, or love of sanctity, or love of self-governance. I approve and praise what I do not do. My heart runs after vanities, and I tend to death, I tend to corruption and dissolution, apart from you.

My God, I have had experience enough what a dreadful bondage sin is. If you are away, I find I cannot keep myself, however I wish it—and am in the hands of my own self-will, pride, sensuality, and self-ishness. And they prevail with me more and more every day, till they are irresistible. In time the old Adam within me gets so strong that I become a mere slave. I confess things to be wrong which neverthe-less I do. I bitterly lament over my bondage, but I cannot undo it. O what a tyranny is sin! It is a heavy weight which cripples me. By your almighty power, I entreat you, O my Lord, to give me life and sanc-tity and strength!

– Blessed John Henry Newman

Ill-Gotten Grace (Lk 12:48)

It's true what is written:
"To the one who has, more will be given":
The worker whose day is brief,
the lost and found son,
the Kingdom-bound thief.
We may protest such success
yet ill-gotten Grace
we have all received,
gain that is murder-based
where Mercy hangs in ruin
but tears through veiled space,
annihilates the tomb.
(Betrayal will not stay
to see the final proof.)
The one the Master trusts,
must trust the Master's wounds.

– Rita A. Simmonds

I KNOW WELL THAT, because the soul is imperfect before she is perfect, her prayer is imperfect as well....

She should make an effort to concentrate on my love, pondering at the same time her own sins and the blood of my only-begotten Son. There she will find the expansiveness of my charity and forgiveness for her sins. Thus self-knowledge and the consideration of her sins ought to bring her to know my goodness to her and make her continue her exercise in true humility.

Now I do not want her to think about her sins individually, lest her mind be contaminated by the memory of specific ugly sins. I mean that I do not want her to, nor should she, think about her sins either in general or specifically without calling to mind the blood and the greatness of my mercy. Otherwise she will only be confounded. For if self-knowledge and the thought of sin are not seasoned with remembrance of the blood and hope for mercy, the result is bound to be confusion.

And along with this comes the devil who, under the guise of contrition and hatred for sin and sorrow for her guilt, leads her to eternal damnation. Because of this—though not this alone—she would end in despair if she did not reach out for the arm of my mercy.

– Saint Catherine of Siena

Saint Maximilian Mary Kolbe

THE FRANCISCAN FRIAR Maximilian Mary Kolbe died in the Auschwitz concentration camp on August 14, 1941. Two weeks earlier, a prisoner had gone missing. The commandant, Karl Fritsch, announced the penalty to the entire camp: ten men would die in the starvation bunker. As his name was called, Franciszek Gajowniczek cried out, "My wife, my children!" Father Maximilian stepped forward and offered to take his place. He and the other nine men were tossed naked into a concrete hole in Building 13.

The camp prisoners waited to hear the howls of anguish coming from the bunker. Instead, they heard feeble voices raised in prayer and hymns of praise. Maximilian was encouraging the men. A Pole assigned to serve at the bunker later told how at each inspection the priest was always in the middle of them, standing or kneeling in prayer. After two weeks, only Maximilian remained alive. When the SS men entered the cell, he offered his arm for their lethal injection.

One prisoner later said his death was "a shock filled with hope, bringing new life and strength…. It was like a powerful shaft of light in the darkness of the camp." Maximilian is a patron of families, for he gave his life for the father of a family. He is a patron of prisoners, for he gave hope to the condemned.

– Lisa Lickona

GOD, the Father of mercies, through the Death and Resurrection of his Son, has reconciled the world to himself and sent the Holy Spirit among us for the forgiveness of sins; through the ministry of the Church, may God give you pardon and peace, and I absolve you from your sins in the name of the Father, and of the Son, and of the Holy Spirit.

These are the words of absolution that every penitent hears as his or her sins are forgiven when going to confession. What would a Jubilee Year of Mercy be without hearing these same words ourselves?

God is the Father of mercies, and as a prayer in the liturgy of the Church reminds us: "O God, who manifest your almighty power / above all by pardoning and showing mercy...." (CCC 277). He extends that mercy to us constantly. No matter how far we have gone astray, no matter how distant we feel, no matter what we have done, God extends his mercy to us constantly in the confessional.

We need to hear the words of absolution in our lives because we need the human confirmation of God's forgiveness and mercy. Married couples know that they love each other, but imagine how that knowledge might fade when neither spouse speaks the words "I love you" any longer.

– Father James M. Sullivan, O.P.

ALYOSHA KARAMAZOV and a gang of boys are standing by a grave.

"Boys, we shall soon part. I shall be for some time with my two brothers, of whom one is going to Siberia and the other is lying at death's door. But soon I shall leave this town, perhaps for a long time, so we shall part. Let us make a compact, here, at Ilusha's stone that we will never forget Ilusha and one another. Whatever happens to us later in life, if we don't meet for twenty years afterwards, let us always remember how we buried the poor boy at whom we once threw stones...and afterwards we all grew so fond of him. He was a fine boy, a kindhearted, brave boy, he felt for his father's honor and resented the cruel insult to him and stood up for him. We will remember him, boys, all our lives."

For that one brave memory of courage and mercy, says Alyosha, may keep them all someday from great evil. They may reflect, and say, "Yes, I was good and brave and honest then!"

"Ah, children, dear friends," says Alyosha, "don't be afraid of life! How good life is when one does something good and just!"

"Yes, yes," cry the boys in reply.

– Anthony Esolen

She looked at it, and then at me. The cashier at a small family grocery did not know the item I was purchasing. "It's an onion," I informed her. A veteran cashier nearby shook her head in disbelief and suggested the rookie cashier study the produce aisle. Learning it was her first day I said, "I'm sure you'll be a pro the next time I see you." Embarrassed by her co-worker, she answered: "Thanks for being patient, and I did remember it was a vegetable."

The author of the First Letter of Peter wrote to rookie Christians living in Asia Minor. He wrote to encourage them in the midst of persecution, reminding them that through baptism God *in his great mercy gave us a new birth* (1 Pt 1:3). What saves us from despair is not information or knowing facts, but remembering that in baptism we become God's children.

Even veterans in the faith still make mistakes or worse. There is never a moment when we do not need the encouragement that is the tender mercy of God. That truth gives us the strength to be kinder when people make rookie mistakes, and merciful to those whose failures are greater than not recognizing an onion.

– **Monsignor Gregory E. S. Malovetz**

Only for today, I will seek to live the livelong day positively without wishing to solve the problems of my life all at once.

Only for today, I will dress modestly; I will not raise my voice; I will be courteous in my behavior; I will not criticize anyone; I will not claim to improve or to discipline anyone except myself.

Only for today, I will be happy in the certainty that I was created to be happy, not only in the other world but also in this one.

Only for today, I will adapt to circumstances, without requiring all circumstances to be adapted to my own wishes.

Only for today, I will devote ten minutes to some good reading, for good reading is necessary to the life of the soul.

Only for today, I will do one good deed and not tell anyone about it.

Only for today, I will do at least one thing I do not like doing; and if my feelings are hurt, I will make sure that no one notices.

Only for today, I will make a plan for myself: I may not follow it to the letter, but I will make it. And I will be on guard against two evils: hastiness and indecision.

Only for today, I will firmly believe, despite appearances, that the good providence of God cares for me as no one else who exists in this world.

Only for today, I will have no fears. In particular, I will not be afraid to enjoy what is beautiful and to believe in goodness.

– Saint John XXIII

Division (Lk 12:49-53)

This peace that passes understanding
begins with division:
Christ and wickedness at war within.
And sometimes the battle is so fierce
my only recourse
is to release
the enemy
through my own lips.
It's no pleasure
to hear myself speak dark deeds—
Hushed
rushed
they run from me
and linger in the box.
They will not leave
until they are crushed
by the Rock
so ancient
and immediate!

Peace begins
with the two-edged sword—
it is the anguish of the Lord
that burns
and brings my baptism forth
to spring my soul
again.

– Rita A. Simmonds

*I*T IS AT THIS POINT that we ought to recall
that God has not created us for human loving
but for that eternal awesome love
with which he loves everything
that he has ever created.

We should also accept this love
not as a large-hearted magnificent partner
but as the idiot beneficiary of it that we are,
devoid both of charm and basic loyalty.

And in this adventure of Mercy
we are asked to give whatever we can
until we have nothing left.
We are even asked to laugh
when the gift that we make is defective
whether because of failure, filth, or impurity.

But we are asked also to be full of wonder
with tears of thanksgiving and joy
before this inexhaustible treasure
that flows into us from God's heart.

It is at this intersection
of laughter and joy
that we find a peace
beyond all confusion.

– Servant of God Madeleine Delbrêl

Saint Augustine

AUGUSTINE WAS NOT A SIMPLE PLAYBOY. He was a young man of unparalleled gifts who took a concubine and fathered a son with her and then found himself a narrow religious system, Manicheism, to justify his behavior. Eventually, he went to Italy to find a decent job and threw off the Manichean philosophy. He made a show of sending away his partner of fourteen years to find a respectable wife. But when the marriage stalled, he took up with someone else.

By now Augustine had heard the majestic, brilliant sermons of Saint Ambrose. He became convinced of the Christian truth, but still could not resist the downward pull of the flesh. One day, having met some simple, pure monks, he became terribly distressed at his own inability to change. In this moment he heard through the open window a child's voice chanting a rhyme: "Take up and read, take up and read." Augustine opened the Scriptures to Romans 13: *Let us conduct ourselves properly as in the day, not in orgies and drunkenness, not in promiscuity and licentiousness, not in rivalry and jealousy. But put on the Lord Jesus Christ, and make no provision for the desires of the flesh* (13-14).

God's Word healed Augustine; chaste continence enveloped him. He was baptized and became a prolific and profound writer, bishop, holy Doctor, and saint.

– Lisa Lickona

Is IT POSSIBLE TO HAVE TOO MUCH CONFIDENCE in God's mercy? No, obviously. God is without limit and so his goodness is without limit and so his mercy (which is one of the ways his goodness shows itself) is also without limit. You can't possibly have too much trust in it.

Nevertheless, it *is* possible to trust wrongly in God's mercy. How so? Quite simply, you can freely and seriously sin, believe that God is merciful, and conclude from God's mercy that you can expect heaven while continuing to sin freely and seriously. God's love means you never have to change.

This sinful attitude is really more about the sinner than it is about God. It's not about estimates of God's power. It's about the sinner's absurdly inflated conception of his value. The sinner is assuming that she is so important to God that God could not imagine being happy in heaven without her. The sinner knows that God makes noises about punishments for unrepented sin but then assumes that God is bluffing. The sin is smugness.

This sort of smugness should not be confused with the authentic hope of a sinner who knows that she needs to change, knows that she is not yet willing to change, and continues to hope that through God's grace she will turn away from her sin and turn toward her Lord.

– Father John Dominic Corbett, O.P.

DANTE IS CLIMBING THE LOWER CLIFFS of the mountain of purgatory when a group of souls, learning that he is alive, race up to him to beg a favor. When Dante returns to this life, they want him to remember them to their loved ones, lest they've given up hope for their salvation, as they might well have:

> "O soul who go your journey to be blessed
> with the same limbs you had when you were
>   born,"
> they came and cried, "here pause awhile and rest.
> Look! Tell if you can bring back any news
> of one of us you may have seen before.
> Why must you go? Why can't you stop for us?
> We all were sinners till our latest hour
> and all in violent manner met the grave,
> when light from Heaven made us wise to see
> Our sins, and we repented and forgave,
> leaving our lives at last in peace with God,
> who now torments our hearts with the desire
> To see His face."

Most sorrowful is a young man who died in battle, pierced in the throat, spattering the plain with blood. But he insists that his story be told! "I ended with 'Maria' on my lips," he says. For one little tear—*una lagrimetta*—the angel of God snatched him from the devil as he fell. One tear!

– Anthony Esolen

IN THAT STORY OF THE LOST SHEEP who wanders away (Lk 15:3-7), isn't that the sheep you want to be?…the one that gets to be carried so tenderly on Jesus' shoulders?

Has anyone ever heard this parable and not, in their heart of hearts, wanted to be the one?

Why did people flock to the Curé of Ars, or Padre Pio, or Mother Teresa? Why is personal confession so healing? Because mercy is not generic!

Often when someone speaks to a person in whom Christ is palpable, they will tell you, "He looked at me as if I were the most important person in the world."

Christ knows we want to be the one. He has put that desire into our hearts. He wants us to acknowledge our sin and so receive his mercy.

John writes that if we pretend not to have sin, we deceive ourselves; but if we acknowledge our sins, he will forgive us (see 1 Jn 1:8-9). Jesus attracts us with the image of that one lost sheep, begging us not to be afraid to admit our sins.

"There will be more joy in heaven over one sinner who repents than over ninety-nine righteous people who have no need of repentance" (Lk 15:7).

Those ninety-nine do not exist! It is only that one who can truly represent each of us sinners. And when we sorrowfully and realistically admit our sins, each of us can experience the mercy and the joy of being that one!

– **Father Richard Veras**

When at last I cling to you with my whole being there will be no more anguish or labor for me, and my life will be alive indeed, because filled with you. But now it is very different. Anyone whom you fill you also uplift, but I am not full of you, and so I am a burden to myself. Joys over which I ought to weep do battle with sorrows that should be matter for joy, and I do not know which will be victorious. But I also see griefs that are evil at war in me with joys that are good, and I do not know which will win the day.

This is agony, Lord, have pity on me! It is agony! See, I do not hide my wounds; you are the physician and I am sick; you are merciful, I in need of mercy. In adverse circumstances, I long for prosperity, and in times of prosperity I dread adversity.

On your exceedingly great mercy rests all my hope. Give what you command, and then command whatever you will. You order us to practice continence. A certain writer tells us, *I know that no one can be continent except by God's gift, and that it is already a mark of wisdom to recognize whose gift it is.* By continence the scattered elements of the self are collected and brought back into the unity from which we have slid away into dispersion; for anyone who loves something else along with you, but does not love it for your sake, loves you less. O Love, ever burning, never extinguished, O Charity, my God, set me on fire! You command continence: give what you command, and then command whatever you will.

– Saint Augustine

The Iris of His Eye (Heb 12:11-13)

Your being colors my vision
with beams of collapse and rebuild.
The weight of your dependence,
the rawness of your pain,
the sincerity of your struggle,
the dignity of your way
have made your soul a spectrum for my life.

I want you to see what I see:
the smile that waits to welcome me
despite the battle in vain;
The light in dark circles that shines
at the revelation of a new day.

Still, what can buttress the crooked columns
that quaver and crack beneath your skin?
Where is the hand that will close the gap
that has stolen your wholeness within?

Life is a drama
and you speak your hope
to an actor whose face you cannot see.
He enters the stage while you turn in your sheets
in tension toward rest or release.

If, in broad daylight,
I could play His part,
I would look at you and love you,
the iris of His eye,
the tinted window of His heart!

– Rita A. Simmonds

*S*OCIETY CAN BECOME EVER MORE HUMAN only if we introduce into the many-sided setting of interpersonal and social relationships, not merely justice, but also that "merciful love" which constitutes the messianic message of the Gospel.

Society can become "ever more human" only when we introduce into all the mutual relationships which form its moral aspect the moment of forgiveness, which is so much of the essence of the Gospel. Forgiveness demonstrates the presence in the world of the love which is more powerful than sin. Forgiveness is also the fundamental condition for reconciliation, not only in the relationship of God with man, but also in relationships between people. A world from which forgiveness was eliminated would be nothing but a world of cold and unfeeling justice, in the name of which each person would claim his or her own rights vis-à-vis others; the various kinds of selfishness latent in man would transform life and human society into a system of oppression of the weak by the strong, or into an arena of permanent strife between one group and another.

For this reason, the Church must consider it one of her principal duties…to proclaim and to introduce into life the mystery of mercy…. This mystery is the source of a life different from the life which can be built by man.

– *Dives in Misericordia* 14

Saint Joseph of Arimathea

JOSEPH OF ARIMATHEA († 1ˢᵗ century) was the "good and just man" who offered his own tomb for the body of Jesus after it was removed from the cross. Joseph was a member of the Sanhedrin, one of the few who had refused to condemn Jesus (see Lk 23:50-51). At first he followed Jesus in secret, *for fear of the Jews* (Jn 19:38). But after the crucifixion, Joseph became audacious. He went directly to Pilate and asked for Jesus' body.

Joseph's reverence for the pierced and broken body of the Lord was a mercy not only to the dead but also to the living. His interference probably prevented Jesus' corpse from being interred in the public grave reserved for criminals. The remains would have stayed there for a year before family members could collect them. Jesus' body went instead to Joseph's private tomb. Thus, thanks to Joseph, on Easter morning Mary Magdalene and Mary Salome could hurry to anoint the body with holy oil.

But the one who was most deeply struck by Joseph's kindness to Jesus' body was the Mother of the Lord. Medieval storytellers, wanting to express Mary's gratitude, told of how, in her final days of life, Mary called Joseph of Arimathea to her bedside. They say that Joseph saw the Son, who took his Mother by the hand, and the angels, who bore her body into heaven.

– Lisa Lickona

W E ARE ALL CHILDREN OF POVERTY. Not just material-
ly, but metaphysically bereft. We exist only as a word spoken by Another, without whom the alphabet of being will
not begin. To what do we owe so extraordinary an exercise in largesse? Mercy. It was not justice that moved God
to make a world, filling it with impossible people like us.
"From nothing to being," says William James, "there is no
logical bridge." Only God can satisfy on the score of why
there is being rather than nothingness.

Yet even so gratuitous a gesture as this does not exhaust the possibilities of divine generosity. Because when
it all came to grief, what prodigies of mercy did he not
work to undo the wreckage wrought by sin!

We thus find ourselves beneficiaries of two distinct
blessings, neither of which we deserve. Given in nature,
forgiven in grace. And while birth was God's work, rebirth
will require us to work as well. Why? Because the mercy
on which eternal life depends, happens only to those who
hunger and thirst for the righteousness they do not yet
have. "To receive his mercy," the *Catechism* reminds us,
"we must admit our faults" (CCC 1847).

– **Regis Martin**

ONE DAY A LAD NICKNAMED FRENCHY, sprightly and popular, met a very sick man passing by him on the road. Frenchy shied away. It was a natural reaction, especially as he loved dapper clothing and sweet scents and all things bright and beautiful. But the Lord wrung his heart with a pang of guilt and shame, so he turned around, caught up with the leper, embraced him, and kissed him.

That was Saint Francis and Jesus.

François Mauriac had that great moment in mind when he wrote his novella *A Kiss for the Leper*, about a young woman urged into marriage with a sickly, lonely, frail, and ugly man, Jean, whose body could never beget a child, and who silently regrets having blighted her youth for ever. She sets herself to love him, as a virgin of old might have set herself to meet the beasts in the arena. He knows it too well.

What mercy can touch him? It is mercy directed outward, for others. They take to visiting people in the hospital, each pretending that it was the other's idea. And they say their prayers side by side: "Enemies in the flesh, they found union in their nightly supplications. Their voices at least could mingle. Kneeling there together, each in a world apart, they met in the infinite."

– Anthony Esolen

"*Ephphatha!*" (Mk 7:34). We open doors and cans and windows and stores, but Jesus alone opens us. When he speaks his command to the deaf man, *"Be opened!"* he unlocks the poor man's prison of silence. The first words the deaf man hears are the words of the Word. Magnificent! The creating Word rings through the air and shatters the awful stillness; a man alien to music, to the song and sounds of nature, a man sealed in solitude, is inwardly touched by a mysterious power. A new dimension and world suddenly open up before him.

In the Book of Amos, the Lord forecasts a coming famine: *"Not a famine of bread, or thirst for water,/ but for hearing the word of the LORD"* (Amos 8:11). In sin the world is robbed of its hearing. God in heaven seems to sit in unsearchable silence. When he speaks his Word, the Lord tears open the iron heavens, like the sweet mercy of rain showers falling after a drought. To outsiders, God's Word, in Scripture and the Tradition of the Church, is merely lips moving without any music or meaning. To those opened, however, a new sense is awaked in the hearing of faith.

– **Father Anthony Giambrone, O.P.**

Let me know you, O you who know me; then shall I know even as I am known. You are the strength of my soul; make your way in and shape it to yourself, that it may be yours to have and to hold, free from stain or wrinkle. As for the rest of this life's experiences, the more tears are shed over them the less are they worth weeping over, and the more truly worth lamenting the less do we bewail them while mired in them.

But the abyss of the human conscience lies naked to your eye, O Lord, so would anything in me be secret even if I were unwilling to confess to you? I would be hiding you from myself, but not myself from you. But now that my groans bear witness that I find no pleasure in myself, you shed light upon me and give me joy, you offer yourself, loveable and longed for, that I may thrust myself away in disgust and choose you, and be pleasing no more either to you or to myself except in what I have from you.

To you, then, Lord, I lie exposed, exactly as I am. I have spoken of what I hope to gain by confessing to you. My confession to you is made not with words of tongue and voice, but with the words of my soul and the clamor of my thought, to which your ear is attuned; for when I am bad, confession to you is simply disgust with myself, but when I am good, confession to you consists in not attributing my goodness to myself, because though you, Lord, bless the person who is just, it is only because you have first made him just when he was sinful.

– Saint Augustine

Atoning Butterfly (Sir 3:20, 29)

Butterfly,
both busy and beautiful,
you are so at home
in the garden of flowers,
undisturbed by the larger world,
the infinite sky,
the expanding space.

You stay all day
paying visits
from pink to purple petal,
waving white wings
between tall green weeds,
now and again,
landing on a stem.

You flutter without falsehood,
atoning for sins,
offering alms
to finespun limbs,
never wishing to leave
the world you love
for things above
you cannot attend.

– Rita A. Simmonds

*T*HE WORK OF FORGIVENESS AND MERCY is costly. Its success depends chiefly on the grace of God, which alone can convert hearts. It depends also on others. To touch a man, it is not enough to forgive him once. Christ told Peter to forgive seventy times seven times. Through forgiveness, we give to God and to others the best of ourselves, dearly acquired at the price of our rebellious self-love, and we leave them to draw the profit from it, knowing that we shall not always see the results, and that our kindness may even be abused. Once the gift of pardon is given, it is no longer ours. We should even risk losing the grace, were we to cling to it and claim a reward.

However this may be, forgiveness has opened up in our own depths a source of mercy which will never run dry if we let it flow and refrain from placing obstacles in its way. This is the abundance signified by the number seventy times seven given to Peter. It means, "Never stop forgiving, if you want the fountain of mercy to flow always for you. Do not forget that you yourself sin seven times a day."…

The beatitude of the merciful is offered to us daily as we choose between a justice that suits our impressionable and often peremptory taste, and a generous, kind, and understanding justice. The struggle for mercy goes on unceasingly in our hearts.

– Father Servais Pinckaers, O.P.

Saint Jeanne Jugan

AT TWENTY-FOUR, JEANNE († 1879) refused a marriage proposal: "The good Lord is keeping me for work not yet begun," she told her mother. For several years she worked as a nurse. Then she became a servant to a pious wealthy woman. After twelve years, the woman died, and Jeanne moved in with two friends. She continued to maintain her rhythms of prayer and service, conforming her heart to Christ, waiting for her work to begin.

One day, Jeanne came upon an old, blind woman living in a freezing hovel. Jeanne brought her home and placed her in her own bed. "Where will you sleep?" the woman objected. "Don't worry," Jeanne replied. Soon another elderly woman came. And then another. From that time, Jeanne seemed to know where to find the old people and how to care for them. This was the work! She drew others into it, and the Little Sisters of the Poor began to take shape. At fifty-one, Jeanne became Sister Mary of the Cross.

Jeanne found a priest to help guide her fledgling order. One day he removed Jeanne from her post, sending her to beg for the community. With humility, Jeanne accepted. Years went by. Jeanne was ordered into retirement. She went to live at the motherhouse in obscurity, unknown to the novices. She taught them, nevertheless: "Little, very little, be very little before God."

– Lisa Lickona

WHEN IS THE BEST TIME to cry out to Jesus, to the One whose Name bespeaks the very presence of God himself? Any time. A wise woman I know, her days filled with torment, tells me that her arms are always outstretched, her nothingness lifted up as an oblation before God: "Jesus, I trust in thee. Have mercy on me." By that prayer, the *Catechism* assures us, "the heart is opened to human wretchedness and the Savior's mercy" (CCC 2667).

And where is the best place to meet Jesus? "The privileged place of encounter," Pope Francis tells us, "is within the caress of his mercy." Like the money-mad Matthew, whom Christ came to call, pointing his finger at him. Not an accusatory look, but one marked by mercy. And Matthew could hardly believe his eyes, could scarcely credit the message in that finger pointed at him. It was, says Francis, who would often go to the Caravaggio painting to pray, "the message in those eyes that looked at Matthew with mercy," that made all the difference.

What a strange blessing sin provides when accompanied by a misery so heartfelt as to melt God's own merciful heart.

– Regis Martin

Trying to live Catholic Christianity by ourselves leaves us vulnerable, and our faith tends to be reduced to just another of the many "things" in our life. Thus, the experience of a genuine friendship in Christ is mercy, because we need to see that faith gives meaning to human life and invests it with joy.

My brother and I were raised Catholic and received great support within our family, but we grew up in a social milieu in which people were becoming estranged and isolated. Then something new happened when, at my parents' insistence, my brother went to a very small and totally unknown Catholic college in 1979. We didn't know what to expect when he began.

What we found was something completely different from anything in this world.

My brother's life was changed for ever in 1979, and when I visited him in October of that year, I was struck by something wonderful. I encountered a friendship that can only be described by one word: *Catholic*. These kids went to Mass, but they also studied, worked, made trouble, played pranks, and had hilarious fun together every day. It didn't need to be said that Christ was the reason for all these things and the joyful bond they nourished. It was *evident*. What a great mercy it was to meet Jesus living within a real friendship.

– John Janaro

WHEN JESUS IS MOVED WITH COMPASSION for the crowds (Mk 6:34-44), the Scriptures tell us exactly why. *They were like sheep without a shepherd.* This is not an incidental comment—as if anything in the Scriptures were. In the Book of Numbers, this phrase is found in Moses' mouth. Because of his sin at Meribah, Israel's leader could not bring the people into the Promised Land. He thus prayed that the Lord would raise up a new man to go before the people, so *"the LORD's community may not be like sheep without a shepherd"* (Nm 27:17). The Lord in response elects Joshua, son of Nun, to be Israel's new leader.

But Jesus Christ is the true Joshua (in Greek, "Jesus"), and when he sees the crowds, he sees that they are indeed, since the death of Moses, like sheep without a shepherd. Today, too, sadly, we often see that the sins of Church leaders leave the flock of God as wandering, unguarded prey for wolves in the world. In the miracle of the loaves, however, we have a hint of the Lord's merciful promise, *"I am with you always"* (Mt 28:20). In the Eucharist he says, *"I myself will be their shepherd"* (cf. Ez 34:15).

– **Father Anthony Giambrone, O.P.**

Blessed are you, Father, who, in your infinite love, gave us your only-begotten Son. By the power of the Holy Spirit he became incarnate in the spotless womb of the Virgin Mary and was born in Bethlehem. He became our companion on life's path and gave new meaning to our history, the journey we make together in toil and suffering, in faithfulness and love, towards the new heaven and the new earth where you, once death has been vanquished, will be all in all.

Father, by the power of the Spirit, strengthen the Church's commitment to the New Evangelization and guide our steps along the pathways of the world, to proclaim Christ by our lives, and to direct our earthly pilgrimage towards the City of heavenly light. May Christ's followers show forth their love for the poor and the oppressed; may they be one with those in need and abound in works of mercy; may they be compassionate towards all, that they themselves may obtain indulgence and forgiveness from you.

Father, grant that your Son's disciples, purified in memory and acknowledging their failings, may be one, that the world may believe. May dialogue between the followers of the great religions prosper, and may all people discover the joy of being your children.

– Saint John Paul II

The Road of Discipleship (Lk 14:25-33)

The road of contradiction
bids that we carry
what's overbearing.
It takes everything we have,
so we leave our possessions
and come with empty hands.
It is the path to our fulfillment
if we only hate ourselves.
It is not a road one glides along;
our feet must beat the ground.
And only when we turn to leave
we know we've neared the end,
for Mercy meets our breaking point—
the place where we begin!

– Rita A. Simmonds

[OD'S] LOVE FOR US LED CHRIST…TO CALVARY. Sin did it, our sin and the sins of the world. Sin still does it….

God is not being loved and honored as he should by the race he has elevated to the sublime dignity of adopted sons. There is a gap, and God is looking for someone to stand in the gap before him on behalf of this race and beg that he may not destroy it….

We do all that we can do just to make God forget the ingratitude of man in return for his boundless love and to make him remember his mercies. He hangs before us on the cross crying out, "I thirst!"… We are truly blessed in having a little share in the following of the cross.

See the compassion of Christ toward Judas, the man who received so much love, and yet betrayed his own Master, the Master who kept the sacred silence and would not betray him to his companions. Jesus could have easily spoken in public and told the hidden intentions and deeds of Judas to the others, but he did not do so. He rather showed mercy and charity; instead of condemning him, he called him a friend. If Judas had only looked into the eyes of Jesus as Peter did, today Judas would have been the friend of God's mercy. Jesus always had compassion.

– Blessed Teresa of Calcutta

Saint Pius of Pietrelcina

Pɪᴜs ᴏꜰ Pɪᴇᴛʀᴇʟᴄɪɴᴀ (†1968), or Padre Pio, as he is affectionately known, was a Catholic media sensation of the twentieth century. His fame was based on the stigmata, the wounds of Christ, that appeared on his hands, his feet, and his side. Thousands saw him in person and millions more have seen the pictures. He had other gifts, too: the ability to read hearts in the confessional, a proclivity to mystical prayer during the consecration, and the grace of bilocation. After his fame spread, his friary in San Giovanni Rotondo, Italy, was inundated with visitors.

With all the attention came a host of sufferings: alienation from those in his order, suspicion, and repeated investigations. And after his name was cleared, Pius was given more to suffer. At the end of his life he entered a "dark night" in which all meaning was hidden from him. Nothing made sense anymore. "I go forward almost miraculously," he said, "but I understand nothing. Living like that is quite painful." But, he professed, "I let Jesus Christ take care of it all."

The mystic and stigmatist was borne along not by extraordinary manifestations, but by trust, childlike and pure. "Pray, hope, and don't worry. Worry is useless. God is merciful and will hear your prayer," he taught.

– Lisa Lickona

BASEBALL, perhaps more than any other sport, is heavy on ritual. Consider the player in the on-deck circle. He swings the bat a few times to loosen up. He adjusts his helmet. Perhaps he scans the infield or tries to get a read on the pitcher. He may even make a hurried sign of the cross. Only then is he prepared to step into the box.

In the words of Pope Francis, the Sacrament of Reconciliation is a "moment of intense prayer" and "source of true interior peace" (*Misericordiae Vultus* 17). Since that is what the sacrament offers us, perhaps before we "step into the box" for confession we should do two things: "Stop" and "Go."

Stop: Stop lying to ourselves that we aren't in need of confession—regardless of whether it's been two weeks or twenty years. Stop making excuses: "Father's too busy. Father's too mean! I went when I made confirmation. Confession's only for little old ladies." Stop pretending that our sinful actions are just bad habits, idiosyncrasies, or justified responses to how others treat us.

Go: Go get a guide to confession, especially if it's been a while. Next, *"Go to your inner room,"* says Jesus (Mt 6:6). In prayer, ask the Father for the honesty you need to examine your conscience and to make a good confession. Finally, just go, running like a batter rounding third into home, or like the prodigal son into the arms of our all-forgiving Father.

– **Father Tim S. Hickey**

In the book *The Interior Castle*, Saint Teresa of Ávila writes:

> This Beloved of ours is merciful and good. Besides, he so deeply longs for our love that he keeps calling us to come closer.... For now, his voice reaches us through words spoken by good people, listening to spiritual talks, and reading sacred literature.... Through illnesses and suffering and sorrow he calls to us....

I came to understand the truth of God's mercy and his desire for us to become closer after a fall I had taken that paralyzed the right side of my body temporarily. Already known by my friends to have great faith in God and trust in him with all things, it seemed he wanted even more of me. My desire for him in an instant became urgent and necessary, and fortunately it followed with incredible divine mercy.

A group of friends organized a schedule in their already busy lives to care for me day and night. I recuperated most of my movement within a couple weeks, and it was all because I saw Christ in my friends and God's mercy pouring out on all of us.

On about the tenth day I was left alone for a couple of hours and had to take medicine, but I was still trying to relearn to lift my arm to my mouth to drink. This task was painful and difficult and seemed impossible until I literally said, "Jesus, I know you are here with me. Please help me, I need you!" Suddenly I felt warmth around my wrist. I knew it was his hand giving me the strength. From that moment I was and still am able to drink on my own. (He is a real and merciful God.)

Sometimes God's love seems surreal and intangible, but it isn't. Jesus will carry our burdens just as he said he would. And God's plans are so much bigger and more detailed than we can imagine. Jesus is taking me on a journey and carrying me through pain and suffering, and will ultimately lead me to rejoicing and true thanksgiving!

We often forget that he wants us to love him, and the mercy is that, even with the judgment that we deserve, God still pours out his mercy on us. I've experienced firsthand through real life experiences that there is nothing and no one who can fulfill our deepest needs and give us what we need with such love and mercy, regardless of our worthiness. May God be praised!

– **Mary Joseph**

THE VOICE OVER THE MARINE RADIO was firm, but urgent. While I was staying at a friend's beach house, the Coast Guard reported that two kayaks were overturned in the nearby bay. Those who had been in them were missing. A flurry of conversation continued, and then silence. I said a quick prayer, continued reading my book, but periodically wondered about the outcome. Then came the voice of the Coast Guard dispatcher: *They have been found safely.*

It is easy to get lost in life. The voice of the author of the First Letter of Peter speaks a message not only to the ancient world but to us as well. He tells us that God never tires of looking for us when we are lost in the sea of life. It is God's mercy that not only finds us but reminds us of who we are.

Referencing the prophet Hosea, the author tells those who have found mercy that *now you are God's people* (1 Pt 2:10). More often than not life offers us a choice. We can remain lost or allow God to find us even in the turbulent waters of life. Those who know they are God's children embrace a mercy that understands that even in the silence, someone is trying to find the way home.

– **Monsignor Gregory E. S. Malovetz**

Let us ask God for forgiveness, a thousand times a day, for these faults into which we fall every day. Let us tell him with a great feeling of pain and of humility:

Lord, I recognize all my miseries in your presence; my life is nothing but an endless series of sins and acts of ingratitude. I forever fall from one into the other. I commit them at all times and in my holiest actions. I would be incapable of doing anything that does not give you some reason to complain. And God wants that even this prayer, which I offer you at present, draw to a close without my having displeased you in anything! I do not know how you can put up with me for so long. For it begins again every day, at every hour.

However, I hope in your mercy and I dare to ask you for one more grace. I do not refuse to be punished; but, my God, you have thousands and thousands of scourges in hand with which you can strike me: *Many are the scourges of the sinner.* Punish me, my God, either by sorrow or by confusion, or by the loss of those whom I love, or if you want by all of these together. But do not punish my sins with other sins, my slight faults with serious faults. I fear only this from your justice; all the rest seems to me rather to come from your mercy.

– Saint Claude La Colombière

Forgiveness (1 Tm 1:15)

Two tall towers,
a traded target
twin and twisted
forever enflamed.

A serene September sky
stained, exploded
stories stolen
panic high
rescue low to vain.

Abraham and Edward
Mohammad and Welles
Mychal and Wesley,
Moira, Anil.
Souls upon souls
rose as they fell.

Death is an instant,
Dying, each second.
"Father, forgive them!"—
Humanity's sentence.

– Rita A. Simmonds

H UMAN WRETCHEDNESS stirs the mercy of God. For when the faithful and merciful God saw that the enemy had by trickery caused the downfall of humanity, his thoughts of it were thoughts of peace. It was due to incitement by another that human beings were overthrown and so fell. Now, because the enemy fell due to his own wickedness, this wickedness became an object of hate. But the Father of mercies was moved by the straits of imprisoned human beings, who lamented their own wretched state and begged for mercy, crying out constantly: *Bring my soul out of prison and be pleased, O Lord, to deliver me, for I was stolen away from my own land, and here without any fault was cast into a dungeon.*

I admit indeed that I am guilty, but I am innocent by comparison with the one who dishonestly led me astray. Let your grace help me, for it is the wickedness of another that has harmed me; let your mercy and truth come to my aid, for it was the wicked lies of another that overthrew me. O Lord Jesus Christ, I have already rotted completely in this prison; when shall I see your face? When shall you come, my Savior? O Lord God of my salvation, do quickly, I beg, that which you are coming to do. Come, Lord, and do not delay. Show your face and we shall be saved. We are waiting for you; be our arm in time of trouble.

– Father Peter of Blois

The Blessed Virgin Mary, Untier of Knots

IN THE CHURCH OF Saint Peter am Perlach, in Augsburg, Germany, hangs a picture of Mary who is undoing the many knots in the ribbon she holds—a reference to the wedding ribbon, a part of the traditional German marriage ceremony symbolizing the unity of bride and groom. It is said that this painting was commissioned by a young priest around the year 1700 in gratitude for the miraculous healing of his grandparents' troubled marriage some years before.

Father Jorge Mario Bergoglio, s.j., was studying in Germany in the 1980s when he discovered this painting. When he returned to his native Argentina, he promoted the devotion to "Mary, Untier of Knots." In a 2013 speech, Bergoglio, now Pope Francis, elaborated on the idea of the "knot": "When we do not listen to [God], when we do not follow his will, we do concrete things that demonstrate our lack of trust in him—for that is what sin is—and a kind of knot is created deep within us…. Many knots can form a tangle that gets more and more painful and difficult to undo."

In the Church's tradition, Mary is the one "whose 'yes' opened the door for God to undo the knot of the ancient disobedience." We can bring her our tangled knots. "She leads us by the hand as a Mother, our Mother, to the embrace of our Father, the Father of mercies."

– Lisa Lickona

MANY TIMES IN ACTION MOVIES, when the hero does not kill the villain at the end, it is somehow seen as a sign of weakness. At least that's what the boos would seem to indicate. The complete opposite, however, is true for God. His being all-powerful or almighty is *proved* by his forgiveness and mercy. The *Catechism* (270) even goes so far as to say that "by his infinite mercy…he displays his power at its height by freely forgiving sins."

God maintains each one of us in existence. If he were somehow to "forget" any one of us for just one instant, we would cease to be. God loved us before he even created us. His love brought us into existence. Can we even imagine our life without the mercy of God, or where we would be without him?

Our sins are never stronger than the power of God's mercy. As Pope Francis teaches us: "God never ever tires of forgiving us." We may get tired of confessing our sins, but he never tires of forgiving them. The power of God over our sins, though, does recognize one force greater, and that is our own will. When we refuse to confess our sins, when we refuse to repent, that is when we begin to boo at the end of the movie when the hero tries to save the life of the villain yet again.

– Father James M. Sullivan, O.P.

W E ARE IN ROBERT BROWNING'S GREATEST WORK, *The Ring and the Book*.

A man in prison awaits execution. He has butchered three innocent people: the innocent young wife he suspected of adultery, and her parents, who tried to protect her. Since he once took minor orders, he appeals to the dying pope to commute his sentence. Innocent XIII considers every feature of the case, every mitigating and aggravating circumstance. He denies the appeal, for the sake both of justice and, it seems, of mercy. The murderer Guido must be beheaded on the morrow:

> For the main criminal I have no hope
> Except in such a suddenness of fate.
> I stood at Naples once, a night so dark
> I could have scarce conjectured there was earth
> Anywhere, sky or sea or world at all:
> But the night's black was burst through by
>   a blaze—
> Thunder struck blow on blow, earth groaned
>   and bore,
> Through her whole length of mountain visible:
> There lay the city thick and plain with spires,
> And, like a ghost disshrouded, white the sea.
> So may the truth be flashed out at one blow,
> And Guido see, one instant, and be saved.

Meanwhile, says the pope, "let there be incessant prayer."

Even should we save a guilty man's forfeited life, what final good is it to him, unless his soul too should be saved?

– Anthony Esolen

FOR THOSE FIRST TWO SERVANTS in Jesus' parable of the talents (see Mt 25:14-30), the coins they received from the master were precious. They were signs of his trust in them, his personal attention to them, his invitation to cooperate with him.

The sense of their master's presence and love propels them forward to trade. The task he gives them is easy, the burden is light, because the very task is itself a sign of his merciful and personal love for them.

For the third servant, the talent didn't mean much. He forgot the one who had entrusted it to him. The task seemed too heavy, so he buried it.

When I recognize my priestly assignments as entrusted to me by our merciful Father, then the tasks that they require of me are lighter. The very work becomes a way of relating to the Lord who loves me.

When I rip my daily work out of context by forgetting from whose hand it is given, the task becomes heavy. In my distraction, I approach work as if everything depends on me alone, with nothing but my strength and strategy. I am now yoked to my measures of failure and success.

When I recall that God is the source of the tasks before me, then I recognize that everything does not depend upon me, but rather that any lasting fruits of my daily work stem from God's mercy at work in me.

– Father Richard Veras

Through your grace, your intercession, and your example, deliver us from all evil, our Lady, and untie the knots that prevent us from being united with God, so that we, free from sin and error, may find him in all things, may have our hearts placed in him, and may serve him always in our brothers and sisters.

Holy Mary, full of God's presence during the days of your life, you accepted with full humility the Father's will, and the devil was never capable of tying you up with his confusion.

Once with your Son you interceded for our difficulties, and full of kindness and patience, you gave us example of how to untie the knots in our life.

By remaining forever our Mother, you put in order and make more clear the ties that link us to the Lord.

Holy Mother, Mother of God and our Mother, to you who untie with a motherly heart the knots of our life, we pray to you to receive in your hands N. and to free [him/her] of the knots and confusion with which our enemy attacks.

– Pope Francis

He Lifts Up the Poor (Ps 113)

Even in my sleep I feel Your breath so light
    against my ear,
for just last night, in a dream, someone asked,
"How do you pray?"
And I had in waiting the words to say!
"I beg as I sleep,
not to be rich,
but to be poor,
and I hold out my hand,
and always my King
places not diamonds or gold,
but His very self
WHOLE
into the palm of my hand.
And I take Him again,
and I ask to be poor,
so that He will always come to me
and I will always wait for Him."

– Rita A. Simmonds

ORGIVENESS IS A POWER that counteracts, that serves as an antidote to the energy of the pain that directs me. Forgiveness is a power that says that as deep as the pain may be, there is a strength and a comfort that goes beneath the pain so that I am finally led not by the wound but by a force more commanding than the hurt.

A great degree of consciousness is required here. We are not asked to bypass our grief or to count it as inconsequential. We are asked to confront it, to discern its origin, to feel it, and then to forgive with all our wits about us. That kind of conscious, deliberate confrontation lets me go to the very bottom of my hurt and, metaphorically, cleans out the wound and cauterizes it. Only then can healing begin.

Forgiveness is an event, not an idea, and it comes full circle at the moment I discover myself and claim myself as a sinner. At that moment, we receive divine forgiveness as "that 'making right' of our lives which occurs when we turn away from fighting ourselves, and others, and the truth itself, and turn trustfully toward the divine power which surrounds us and can work through us." Through this extraordinary experience of reconciliation, our past failures and unsolved current problems notwithstanding, we are actually made "more lovable, more discerning, more capable of devoting [ourselves] to goods which enrich humanity" (David E. Roberts).

– Doris Donnelly

Saint Thomas of Villanova

IN 1565, THOMAS, an Augustinian canon, preacher, and scholar, was appointed archbishop of Valencia, Spain. A bishop had not been in residence there for a century, and disorder reigned among the people and the clergy. Thomas started with the people. He went from town to town to meet them. He saw where they lived, looked at them with eyes of mercy, and then preached to them of hope for eternal salvation.

Thomas started many "programs." His bishop's palace became a veritable soup kitchen for upwards of 500 people a day, where he served food and wine. He provided dowries for women who wanted to marry but could not. He gave tools to tradesmen who had fallen on hard times. Foundlings were his favorites; Thomas paid a finder's fee to anyone who brought him an abandoned child.

Some complained that the poor took advantage of Thomas. He answered that it was not his job to find the cheats among them—that was for the authorities. His job was to give when asked. In his life they called him "the almsgiver," "the father of the poor," and "the model of bishops." Not a few miracles of multiplication were attributed to him. His energy came from prayer, fervent and frequent, the habit of his youth. He died in prayer, succumbing to a heart attack after Mass had been said in his quarters.

– Lisa Lickona

Why Mercy and Omnipotence
Go Together

THE COLLECT FOR the Twenty-Sixth Sunday in Ordinary Time includes this opening invocation: "O God, who manifest your almighty power above all by pardoning and showing mercy, bestow, we pray, your grace abundantly upon us." These words are meant to comfort us. At the same time, they also require some explanation. Think about it! Were the highest expression of the divine omnipotence to appear in God's pardoning and his showing mercy, then would not the maximum expression of God's power somehow remain tied to human failure? Paradoxically, God would become more powerful the more humans sinned. When we profess the Creed, however, we affirm that God's power begins with his own initiatives: "I believe in one God, the Father almighty, maker of heaven and earth." The almighty God can do whatever does not entail contradiction. Some things though cannot be done. For example, God cannot make a square circle. He can, however, make another world.

The Collect speaks the truth. God's omnipotence does manifest itself in a unique way when he pardons and shows mercy. In fact, when we receive mercy for our transgressions, God reveals himself as the Highest Truth. He alone can forgive the creature's rebellion against the supreme norm for human life. What is better, God not only pardons, he also perfects. By the absolution that the priest pronounces, the forgiven sinner finds not only mercy but also new life. That God raises sinful humanity to share in his own life reveals an essential dimension of the divine omnipotence. Mercy, like everything else God accomplishes, comes to us as an unmerited gift of the divine bounty. This leads some people to wonder why God does not forgive everybody for everything wrong they have done.

Some things not even God can do. For example, God cannot show mercy to the person who resolutely refuses the invitation to live a new life of virtue. God may overcome our indispositions to repent. He cannot, however, bestow mercy on the unrepentant sinner. The reason for this apparent limitation is not a weakness in God. Mercy no more becomes impenitence than does squareness a circle. No one should court the dangerous state of rebellious isolation. Pope Francis has announced a Jubilee of Mercy to persuade the world that, even when we feel trapped in sin, God still manifests above all his almighty power by pardoning and showing mercy. The sheer gift that comes from the divine omnipotence helps the human creature approach, confidently, the very good God. Put otherwise, mercy appears as the crowning effect of God's power.

– Father Romanus Cessario, O.P.

There is a balm in Gilead,
To make the wounded whole;
There is a balm in Gilead,
To heal the sin-sick soul.

MARILYNNE ROBINSON IS, to my mind, the greatest Christian novelist alive. Her novel *Gilead*, set in the 1950s, in a dusty Iowa village by that name, is a long letter written by an old man with a heart condition, who knows he is going to die soon. He is writing it for his little boy, so he will know a little about the father he won't remember, and his grandfather and great-grandfather, all ministers of God.

Reverend Ames has a mercy for all of this sad and lovely life of ours. He'll soon be made immortal, "in the twinkle of an eye," he says, meditating upon Saint Paul's charming phrase. But he loves the world too. It is God's creation, worthy of reverence and love, and he can't believe we will ever forget it entirely. "In eternity this world will be Troy, I believe," he writes, "and all that has passed here will be the epic of the universe, the ballad they sing in the streets." Hence he loves the small place where he was born, and where he'll be buried, in a last act of love. Even in Gilead "there is more beauty than our eyes can bear."

– Anthony Esolen

I HAD JUST ARRIVED FOR A VISIT to a Middle Eastern town when a man passed in front of me, and, when I said that I was a visiting priest, his next words were, "Come and eat at my house!" That culture places great store by hospitality, both as a duty and as a chance to increase the honor of one's house. This helps me understand Jesus' encounter with Zacchaeus (Lk 19:1-10), a famous sinner made rich by betraying his people.

The Lord *intended to pass through* Jericho. In the crowd that formed around him, there must certainly have been some respectable men who, as was their duty and opportunity, entreated Jesus to stop and rest at their homes. But Jesus refused them all till he caught sight of Zacchaeus. The hostility of the crowd must have flamed at the sight of this hated traitor. But their curses stopped short when Jesus shouted out to him, *"Come down quickly, for today I must stay at your house!"* After having refused this honor to the good men of the city, Jesus now invites himself to the house of their wealthy persecutor.

Zacchaeus ceased to be the object of their anger, for Jesus had now drawn it upon himself, bearing their hatred in Zacchaeus' place. Zacchaeus, fully aware of the unprecedented mercy of this act, welcomed the Lord, never having imagined that on earth any such thing could exist.

– **Father Vincent Nagle, F.S.C.B.**

By your noble and glorious blood,
offered unceasingly to please God who sent you,
may the dangers be lifted from me, the condemned,
may my transgressions be forgiven,
may my vices be pardoned,
may my shamelessness be forgotten,
may my sentence be commuted,
may the wailing stop,
and the gnashing of teeth fall silent.
Let the laments lessen and tears dry.
Let mourning end and darkness be banished.
May the vengeful fire be tamped out
and torments of every kind be exiled.

May you who grant life to all be compassionate now.
Let your light dawn, your salvation be swift,
your help come in time, and the hour of your
arrival be at hand.
May the dew of your mercy quench the parched field
where my bones have fallen into the pit of death.
Prepare the earth for the day of light
and let the soil bloom and bring forth fruit,
heavenly cup of life-giving blood,
ever sacrificed, never running dry
all for the salvation and life of the souls in eternal rest.
And though my body die in sin,
with your grace and compassion,
may I be strengthened in you, cleansed of sin
through you, and renewed by you with life everlasting,
and at the resurrection of the righteous
be deemed worthy of your Father's blessing.

– Saint Gregory of Narek

Time Is for Mercy (Lk 16:19-31)

Dear Lazarus,
what could you have done
to sponge our sullied hearts
as you lay in our doorway
day after day
begging for crumbs,
your skin sick with sores
and dogs' tongues?

What more could you have done
to loose our stringent souls
as you writhed and rolled
in the threshold we set
and stepped over
again and again?

No amount of nothingness was ever enough
to turn us from our revelry
and make us regret
the day you left on angels' wings.

Only when our throats were dry
did we cry for our neglect.
But mercy is delivered in time
and squandered at death.

– Rita A. Simmonds

W E EXPERIENCE A…WONDER whenever we are suddenly faced with something great, and even though it does not present any evil or danger to us, yet its magnitude and unexpected appearance awakens in us a certain rapture, amazement, and fear. Such a state will endure forever within the souls enjoying the sight of God. There will be nothing unpleasant about it. Rather, it will be a motive for a deeper worship and love of God who, in spite of all his awe-inspiring greatness, will irresistibly attract them by his goodness and by the fullness of his mercy.

Filial fear is, therefore, something sublime and perfect, without any negative element in it.…

It is evident that the sentiment of filial fear is the best protection against a light-minded approach to God's mercy and disrespect for the law of God.… The more [filial fear] permeates the soul, the more the soul sees how much God in his wisdom and omnipotence condescends to it with his mercy.… It is in contemplation of [God's] works that filial fear in our hearts should draw its daily food. Since the greatest among these is the Word Incarnate and his divine heart…it should become a center of all our filial fear, ever watchful that we do not wound but rather console and gladden it with our every act, with our every word, and with every beat of our hearts.

– Servant of God Father Hyacinth Woroniecki, O.P.

Saint Maria Faustina Kowalska

HELENA († 1938) KNEW SHE WAS MEANT for Christ, but her poor parents could not pay the convent's dowry. So she sought to drown out the voice of her heart. She was at a dance with her sister when Christ appeared suddenly beside her. In that moment, "there was no one but Jesus and me," she later said. That night Helena was told in prayer, "Go to Warsaw."

In Warsaw, she joined the Congregation of the Sisters of Our Lady of Mercy. Helena received her habit and took the name Maria Faustina. A long period of spiritual dryness followed. At the end of it, Jesus appeared again, now clad in white, his heart exposed, white and red rays issuing from it. "Paint this image," he told her. He kept coming to her, asking that the image be painted and teaching Faustina its meaning. "My daughter," he said, "say that I am love and mercy personified." "The greatest sinners could become the greatest saints if they trusted in my mercy." "My mercy is drawn from only with the cup of confidence."

Faustina's spiritual director worked to have the image of Jesus painted. It was displayed in public for the first time on the Sunday after Easter, 1935. Faustina died October 5, 1938, of tuberculosis. In 2000, Pope John Paul II canonized her and named the Second Sunday after Easter in honor of Divine Mercy.

– Lisa Lickona

An Examination of Conscience

THIS YEAR OF MERCY, dare to believe and to live this truth: Jesus longs to forgive us. Prepare for confession in a new and heroic way.

It is easy, safe, and sufficient to use the Ten Commandments as the guide for examining our own conscience. Sin is found whenever we fall short of living any of the Ten. So this is the place to *start*.

Pope Francis challenges us to go deeper. In his letter on the Year of Mercy (no. 17), the pope instructs all priests to carry the longing and the heart of the father who runs to kiss, embrace, and lavishly forgive his prodigal son.

For all of us sinners, this is great joy. We already know how God desires to write our life story. Without fear, we can examine our lives boldly and courageously, and bring to Jesus *all* our sins.

We now ask our Mother, Mary, to accompany us through our conscience and help us to hear the quiet whisper of God's merciful voice:

- Show me where and how I worship idols of power, fame, possessions.
- Show me where and how I seek my selfish desires, my advantage, my convenience.
- Show me where and how I long to control, to possess, to use others.
- Show me where and how my heart lusts after food, sex, comfort.
- Show me where and how my mind judges, boasts, condemns.
- Show me where and how I loathe, I harm, I hate myself, my neighbors, and you, my God.

– Father Eric Cadin

BISHOP JAMES EDWARD WALSH (1891–1981) served twelve years of a twenty-year prison sentence under the Communist regime.

He was ordained a priest in 1915 at the then-fledgling Maryknoll Seminary in Ossining, New York, a community committed to serving the poor. He traveled to China as a missionary in 1918, becoming first a bishop, then executive secretary of the Catholic Central Bureau for all of China. He was arrested as a spy in 1958 and subjected to a sham trial. He was sixty-seven when the sentence was handed down.

In *Zeal for Your House*, he described an important tool that enabled him to endure the monotony of prison life: the rosary, his "lifeline" he called it, he would pray as many as eighteen times daily.

Of his unexpected release in 1970, he wrote: "I felt that I would not live long enough to complete my sentence of twenty years, and that I would die in prison. It is a bit hard for me to believe even now that I have been released. I have no bitterness toward those who tried and condemned me. I just could never feel angry with the Chinese. I felt that way almost from the day I first set foot in China in 1918, and it has just grown stronger with the years, even during my imprisonment."

"I love Chinese people."

He returned to Maryknoll and lived there until his death.

– Heather King

HIS WORLD IS GRADUALLY becoming smaller. Living with Alzheimer's disease, my father is suffering the fading away of his memory. Faces once familiar are now strangers. What gives me joy in the midst of this terrible disease is that he consistently remembers two things: his son is a priest, and cocktail hour is at 5 PM. And raising his small glass of wine, he offers a toast: "To our family and our friends, and to all we love."

The Second Letter of John is not a theological teaching but a personal response to problems in a particular local church. The author advises that in the midst of life's challenges, they must not forget Jesus' great commandment of love. Using a traditional biblical greeting, he adds the word mercy to *grace and peace* (2 Jn 3). The author says mercy is a blessing that enables us to remember what is important.

Whose face in your life has become strange because of hurt or disagreement? Where has the world become smaller because of your pride or stubbornness? At what hour of the day do you need mercy to guide you? Perhaps the raised glass of a man for whom the light is fading might help us remember the power and importance of love.

– Monsignor Gregory E. S. Malovetz

O my God! Most Blessed Trinity, I desire to love you and make you loved, to work for the glory of Holy Church by saving souls on earth and liberating those suffering in purgatory. I desire to accomplish your will perfectly and to reach the degree of glory you have prepared for me in your Kingdom. I desire, in a word, to be a saint, but I feel my helplessness and I beg you, O my God! to be yourself my sanctity!

Since you loved me so much as to give me your only Son as my Savior, the infinite treasures of his merits are mine. I offer them to you with gladness, begging you to look on me only through the face of Jesus and in his heart burning with love.

I offer you, too, all the merits of the saints, their acts of love, and those of the holy angels. Finally, I offer you, O Blessed Trinity! the love and merits of the Blessed Virgin, my dear Mother. It is to her I abandon my offering, begging her to present it to you. Her divine Son told us in the days of his mortal life: *"Whatsoever you ask the Father in my name he will give it to you!"* I am certain, then, that you will grant my desires; I know, O my God! that the more you want to give, the more you make us desire. I feel in my heart immense desires and it is with confidence I ask you to come and take possession of my soul.

– Saint Thérèse of Lisieux

The Mulberry Sea (Lk 17:5-6)

Forgiveness takes the mustard seed of faith—
a sigh, a speck
packed with hope,
to say to the gnarly tree in your soul,
"I can't feed you anymore!
Don't torture me! Be gone!"
And feel it extract itself,
taste its strange fruit
as it leaves through your mouth
to be planted in the dark valley
of the sea.
Its branches,
tired of the weight,
will sway in the salty waves
and be at peace.
The ocean goes an open length
to bare the messy mulberry.

                                        – Rita A. Simmonds

*A*T THE EXTREME LEFT OF [A] PHOTO [of the nuns of the Carmel of Lisieux (1895)] Sister Saint John the Baptist seems very pensive. Her spirituality was the opposite of Thérèse's. Always serious, she wanted to acquire sanctity by the strength of her own efforts, by multiplying prayers and penances. She found that Thérèse [of the Child Jesus] relied too much on God's mercy and in the end neglected his justice.

Thérèse remarked one day that she saw Sister Saint John the Baptist as the "image of God's severity." Imposing in presence and an expert embroideress, Sister Saint John the Baptist nursed the secret hope of one day becoming prioress, as she had been led to believe. Yet in 1893, at the age of forty-six, she was still working in the laundry.

She had difficulty accepting that Thérèse was entrusted, so young, with the care of the novices. "If I were novice mistress," she said, "I would not put up with a single black hair on the fleece of my lambs." She thought that Thérèse was not severe enough, and told her this in recreation one day: "You need to direct yourself more than to direct others!" With her customary gentleness Thérèse replied: "Ah! Sister, how right you are. I am even more imperfect than you think."

– Father Pierre Descouvemont

Saint Francis of Assisi

ACCORDING TO THOMAS OF CELANO's *First Life of Saint Francis*, the great saint from Assisi (†1226) did not go all at once from rich, carefree youth to passionate lover of the poor. He became charitable bit by bit, "for it is very hard to forsake accustomed things, nor is it easy to sap the force of what has once been put into the mind." And prayer was not second nature for Francis. He had to learn to remove "himself for a while from the bustle and busyness of the world" and to seek "to lay up Jesus Christ in the inward man."

In his early life, Francis had a great repugnance for lepers, such that "he would look at their houses only from a distance of two miles and he would hold his nostrils with his hands." But, as the young man drew deeply into intimacy with Christ, he "was beginning to think of holy and useful things." One day, as Francis was riding along the road, he saw a leper, and this time he did not recoil, but "made stronger than himself, he kissed him." Francis later said that this was the moment when he left the world.

But Francis was not yet perfect. Shortly thereafter he met a poor beggar and fell to lecturing him. Francis caught himself and made a vow never to refuse the request of the poor—another step on his journey with our Lord.

– Lisa Lickona

THE GREATEST TRUTH about going to confession is that God made it all possible for us to be there. It is possible not only because the sacrament itself is the working of Jesus Christ, his Risen Son, who was crucified for our salvation. God made it all possible for us to be in that confessional, kneeling or sitting, behind the screen or face to face. God made all of that possible by putting in our heart the desire to be forgiven. This is his first grace (of many) that he bestows upon us when we go to confession.

Who but a loving and merciful Father puts that desire in the heart of a sinner?—in the soul of one who has chosen to be disobedient, time and time again?—in the mind of one who has closed his thoughts to God repeatedly? Only the God of mercy can call us back to himself. Even the movement of guilt in our conscience is an echo of his voice calling us back!

Saint Augustine, a man who knew well the reality of sin, guilt, and mercy, consoles us: "Whoever confesses his sins…is already working with God" (CCC 1458). People who come to confession seeking only freedom from guilt don't understand the fullness of mercy. People who leave the confessional thanking God for his mercy understand the purpose of guilt. The work with God has already begun.

– Father James M. Sullivan, O.P.

Stanley Joseph Ott (1927–1992) served as bishop of Baton Rouge, Louisiana, from 1983 until his death.

Bishop Ott was a vocal champion of the pro-life movement. To that end, he spoke out against abortion, and he also celebrated the funeral Mass of Elmo Patrick Sonnier, who was convicted of rape and murder, and was executed by the state of Louisiana in 1984.

Though Elmo had been present, the actual crimes were very possibly committed by his brother Eddie, who confessed to them after his brother had been sentenced to the electric chair, and who attended Elmo's funeral in chains.

"'Blessed are the merciful, for they will obtain mercy,'" Bishop Ott reminded the mourners, and, "At the cross, Jesus said to the thief, 'Today you will be with me in paradise.'"

He then saw to it that Sonnier was buried in a part of Roselawn Memorial Park that was normally reserved for nuns, across a gravel drive from the graves of bishops.

In the aftermath, he was severely criticized. But the mercy Bishop Ott showed toward Sonnier reminds us that to be pro-life means to be for life—all life.

Bishop Ott was diagnosed with terminal cancer in 1991. He continued to work for the end of the death penalty. On one of his last public appearances he was seen to be praying before a local abortion clinic.

– Heather King

Put yourself in the position of that poor, prodigal, and penniless pig feeder (Lk 15:11-32).

You are coming back from your failed venture. Your speech is ready, you've rehearsed it a hundred times. You've convinced yourself that you can live as a slave and no longer as a son. What other choice have you? After the way you've thrown away your sonship, to ask for it back is inconceivable.

Your thoughts are interrupted by a man running toward you. You are stopped in your tracks, not out of fear, but confusion. Everything you ever thought about how things are supposed to be is trampled by the joyful footsteps of your father.

You can't get your prepared speech out because his embrace will not allow it. And the more he embraces you, the more you see the fallacy of your speech.

When your brother refuses to celebrate, that seems to you totally justified. You want to stop your father from correcting him. Your brother's reaction is understandable to your old way of thinking, and your father's celebration embarrassingly undeserved.

But nothing stops your father. And you are beginning to discover that mercy is not a band-aid on sin. Mercy is an invitation to leave your childish measure behind and to see reality as it truly is: the fatherly expression of God, who is Love.

– **Father Richard Veras**

The Joyful Mysteries of the Rosary

◖ *The Annunciation* – The angel's announcement to Mary was the breakthrough of mercy in a nightmarish world. The Blessed Virgin's response was equally a mercy. Her *Fiat* set off the re-creation of everything from the nothing of human evil. If undone by our sin, may we bear Mary's confidence toward mercy: *Let it be done!*

◖ *The Visitation* – The proof that Mercy is alive in Mary's womb is her compelling desire to share that gift with others. Mercy is the bridge that connects God and human beings, opening hearts to a hope of being loved for ever. Our Lady brings that bridge. She models for us how the Mercy-filled becomes merciful.

◖ *The Nativity of Jesus* – The birth of Jesus is the first exercise of a corporal work of mercy: visiting the imprisoned. With eyes fixed on Jesus and his merciful gaze, we come to know a love impossible for us to imagine, held captive in sin: Mercy-with-Us. Christ's Presence issues a call, breaking our cage: *Follow me*.

◖ *The Presentation* – We share in Mary and Joseph's sacred act of presenting Jesus in the Temple by presenting to the poor and needy our acts of mercy. The gift of Jesus we have received must be given in turn to the Father as a gift. Every merciful work done in faith is an oblation—a desire to offer Christ's saving self.

◖ *The Finding in the Temple* – The anguish of losing Jesus confirms how critical to the spiritual works of mercy is the act of comforting the afflicted. Mary and Joseph seek this comfort as they search for Jesus. And that is the point: they are one and the same. In our loss, mercy shows us that we seek Someone. Or else we are lost.

– Father Peter John Cameron, O.P.

Tree-ness (2 Tm 2:10-13)

Seeing you so exposed
all leafy life dead and blown,
your tiny twigs raw nerves in wind
that rocks you while you live.

There is something sad and something sure
in seeing you so stripped and bare,
yet would I say
you're not the same
without the green of spring
and the many nests abundance brings,
and the way the wind would grab your limbs
and set your leaves to wave and spin?
And in your autumn years
with grace you slowly twirled,
in brightest face your life unfurled.
Yet even then, I saw, I knew
what nature could not promise you.

Then what is there of beauty now?
Your chipping bark? Your barren bough?

All this, and yet no less a tree.
Your tree-ness lives eternally.

– Rita A. Simmonds

*H*ow I would like to make you understand the tenderness of the Heart of Jesus, what he expects from you. Your soul…is called to raise itself to God by the ELEVATOR of love and not to climb the rough *stairway* of fear….

I would like to try to make you understand…how much Jesus loves even imperfect souls who confide in him.

I picture a father who has two children, mischievous and disobedient, and when he comes to punish them, he sees one of them who trembles and gets away from him in terror, having, however, in the bottom of his heart the feeling that he deserves to be punished; and his brother, on the contrary, throws himself into his father's arms, saying that he is sorry for having caused him any trouble, that he loves him, and to prove it he will be good from now on, and if this child asks his father *to punish* him with a *kiss*, I do not believe that the heart of the happy father could resist the filial confidence of his child, whose sincerity and love he knows. He realizes, however, that more than once his son will fall into the same faults, but he is prepared to pardon him always, if his son always takes him by his heart…. I say nothing to you about the first child…. You must know whether his father can love him as much and treat him with the same indulgence as the other.

– Saint Thérèse of Lisieux

Saint Vincent de Paul

VINCENT DE PAUL († 1660) had neither youthful mystical experiences nor a dramatic conversion. During his first years as a priest he was primarily concerned with finding a position that would enable him to live comfortably and support his elderly mother. At last he landed a job as an almoner, the one in charge of handing out money to the poor on behalf of a wealthy woman.

Now Vincent found himself face to face with the poor every day. He began to pray in earnest, led by Father Bérulle, the great French spiritual director. When doubts began to creep in, he sewed the Creed into the lining of his coat so that he could remind himself of that which he professed. And he committed himself to concrete acts of charity in the local hospital. The trial ended when Vincent made the decision to give himself totally in the service of the poor—the beginning of his many extraordinarily fruitful apostolates bringing God's mercy to others. The Confraternities of Charity, the Congregation of the Mission, and the Daughters of Charity were all Vincent's foundations.

"The great secret of the spiritual life," Vincent once said, "is to abandon all that we love to him by abandoning ourselves to all that he wishes, with perfect confidence that everything will turn out for the best."

– Lisa Lickona

BEING ABLE TO GO TO CONFESSION is a great blessing. That doesn't mean it's easy. First of all, we have to name our sin. Secondly, we have to say we are sorry to the priest. Finally, we have to promise to make up for our sins and to change.

Naming our sin can be hard for many reasons. We can lose the habit of examining our conscience and then gradually lose our grasp of the difference between right and wrong. Or we can be so ashamed of our sins that we cannot even bear to speak of them.

Going through the commandments is a good reality check. Have I been going to Mass on Sundays? Do I tell the truth? Do I use bad language? Do I pray? These sorts of questions can help us to name our sins.

Next we have to be sorry. This doesn't necessarily require a great storm of emotion. All it requires is a sober recognition of the wrongness of our action coupled with a firm intention not to repeat it and a real desire to make up for it.

This last bit can be tricky. We may think that we can never really change and we might think that nothing we do in the future could make up for our past.

Here we need great confidence in God's love for us. The practice of gazing upon a crucifix can convince us of this as nothing else can. See the price he paid for us and believe again in his love.

– Father John Dominic Corbett, O.P.

On October 18, 1982, Dennis Hinds was shot in a Los Angeles convenience store holdup. The bullet lodged in his spinal cord. He was eighteen years old.

He was hospitalized for seven months. He never walked again.

He has never met, nor has he ever resented, the man who shot him. "There's nothing I could do, think, or say that's going to hurt that guy more than he's already hurt himself," says Dennis. "Hate destroys the hater."

For years, he celebrated October 18 as a birthday. "I wasn't celebrating that I got shot. I was celebrating that I lived. I never thought 'Why me?' I have three brothers. I'd rather it happened to me than to one of them."

Then, eighteen years after he was shot, he got sober. "Most people don't get a second chance. I got a third." He is widely known and loved in his area of Los Angeles for helping other alcoholics stay sober.

"We all have our crosses. A friend was once telling me about an ingrown toenail. Suddenly he stopped, embarrassed, and said, 'Look who I'm talking to!' But my situation doesn't diminish anyone else's suffering one iota."

He scoffs at any suggestion that his capacity to forgive is a special gift. "I can take about as much credit for that as I can for my blue eyes."

He thanks God and his mother, whom he lived with and cared for until the day she died.

– Heather King

THE DISTRESSING DISCOVERY of our true nature and the recognition of the Savior go together. There are moments in our lives when our daydreams about our noble innocence shatter to reveal a soul darkened by fear and rage. This kind of painful self-discovery and knowledge of Christ are intimately linked.

In the Gospel of Luke we find Peter coming to this self-knowledge. After declaring *"Lord, I am prepared to go to prison and to die with you"* (22:33), Peter followed his arrested Lord and observed his trial from the courtyard. Accused of being with Jesus, he angrily denied it, *"I do not know what you are talking about."* Then *the Lord turned and looked at Peter; and Peter remembered the word of the Lord, how he had said to him, "[...] today, you will deny me three times"* (Lk 22:60-61).

Peter suffered the shock of seeing that despite his good intentions he had indeed denied his Lord, and in that sudden meeting of Christ's merciful gaze upon him it dawns on Peter who Jesus really is: Jesus is the Savior who saves us from our sins and the damnation we have merited. Peter's truest identity is as the one entreating merciful salvation, and Jesus' merciful gaze offers this salvation. In discovering who we are, we see who Jesus is, and in seeing who Jesus really is, we see who we really are.

– **Father Vincent Nagle, F.S.C.B.**

The Sorrowful Mysteries of the Rosary

◖ *The Agony in the Garden* – Agony moves Jesus to pray aloud *Abba, Father*. Merciless suffering assures us of a merciful love—unfailing, ever close, father-like, embracing us. Agony helps us to hand ourselves over to the Father, so rich in mercy. Let me be that rock in the middle of the garden. Let the one in agony lean on me.

◖ *The Scourging* – Scourging is the opposite of mercy, the slave of corruption—a work of darkness, fed by suspicion and intrigue. We beg to bear patiently with those who do us ill. May we lash out only with gentleness, tenderness, compassion. In the wounds we refuse to impose, and in those we receive, may others be healed.

◖ *The Crowning with Thorns* – Those who press down the crown of thorns in mockery of Christ's majesty are unimpressed with the man. One spiritual work of mercy is to instruct the ignorant. We teach others by the humiliations we endure. Paradoxically, it is Pontius Pilate who publishes the truth for all the world to read: *Jesus, the King*.

◖ *Jesus Takes up His Cross* – The ardor with which Jesus embraces his instrument of torture is a scandal. How can he love it? No increase of cruelty can lessen his resolve to carry out Calvary. For only Christ's devotion to the cross is sufficient to admonish sinners. They see: he takes up the cross to take away their curse.

◖ *The Crucifixion* – Every act on Golgotha—the forgiving of the crucifiers, the praying of Psalm 22, the refusal to come down, the offer of paradise to the thief, the appointment of Mary as our Mother, the commending of his spirit—bespeaks a Mercy that men can't kill. Christ's pierced side will ever be our way to it.

– Father Peter John Cameron, O.P.

A Song to the Sun (Ps 121)

New Sun,
Can I say I cannot see you
this day
when from behind you hold before me
trees in gold and glimmer,
a love at first sight of morning?

Noon Sun,
Scorching, stellar,
in your prime.
I cannot look you in the eye.
You tinge my skin,
expose and singe.
Your shadows show me where to hide.

Late Sun,
Red circle soon to set,
you hush the cares
that glared all day.
For me you blush
with shame?
Your kindest hour
has begun.

Good night,
Dear Sun,
remember me,
and not what I forgot
this day.

– Rita A. Simmonds

THROUGH HOPE WE EXPECT GOD FROM GOD, that is, we trust that we will reach God, the highest Good, owing to the supernatural help which he is granting us. What attracts us to God is his infinite goodness, which we see in him and which alone is able to satisfy our hunger for infinite happiness constantly crying within our souls. However, our confidence that we shall not lack the strength to achieve it is not based on the attribute of God's goodness, but on his mercy flowing from his goodness, his mercy being that attribute of his will which…is the most eloquent testimony of his wisdom and omnipotence in his exterior activity….

Although hope is concerned with our own happiness, God forfeits nothing through it; indeed, every act of hope is an acknowledgment of God's supreme attribute in his relation to us. Whence everyone living in the fullness of hope does not cease to sing a hymn of praise to divine mercy throughout all his life, and thus to adore God in his attribute most worthy of our gratitude and adoration.

We need not fear that hope would soil our soul or lower its flight, that it would make it self-centered or prevent it from a complete surrender to God.

– Servant of God Father Hyacinth Woroniecki, O.P.

Saint Pedro de San José Betancur

Pedro († 1667) was born at Chasna de Vilaflor on Tenerife, one of the Canary Islands, off the coast of Morocco. His family was poor, and from his earliest days he busied himself caring for the sheep. In the fields, he developed a deep life of prayer.

When he heard of the needs of the indigenous peoples and the enslaved blacks in the New World, Pedro made up his mind to go to them. His mother resisted, but a devout aunt told him: "You must go to meet God like Peter on the water." He crossed the Atlantic, finally reaching Guatemala. His first thought was to become a priest, but he could not keep up with the studies at the Jesuit college. He went instead to the Franciscans as a tertiary, desiring to devote his life to prayer and the care of the abandoned of Guatemala City.

Soon Pedro began his little works: feeding the hungry, visiting the prisons, praying with the desolate. He found a poor shack and turned it into a home for convalescents and a school for street children, "Our Lady of Bethlehem." A little order grew up around Pedro, the Bethlehemites. He made them a simple rule. "We serve God better," he said, "by carrying a sick person from one room to another, than by submitting ourselves to excessive penances." After his death, they called him the "Saint Francis of the Americas."

– Lisa Lickona

THE CATECHISM OF THE CATHOLIC CHURCH teaches, "The Gospel is the revelation in Jesus Christ of God's mercy to sinners" (1846). Where this sentence occurs is crucial: under "Life in Christ," on the moral life; in chapter one, "The Dignity of the Human Person"; and in the first article of the last chapter, "Sin." The article on sin begins with this sentence. In other words, it is in only Jesus Christ that we truly understand what the dignity of the human person is. And sin is a reality in human life—not the first reality, but the last. God did not create us in sin or guilt. Evil is not part of our nature, or of nature itself. Free choice brought about evil, and free choice can reject it, as God has revealed in the Gospel.

God's mercy is revealed in Christ to sinners: far from being abstract, that statement tells us that mercy is like a lighthouse seen by a lost sailor, like a strong hand reached out to one about to fall, like a word of hope to one on the brink of despair.

True mercy also has another dimension: surprise. We may not expect mercy, and surely we may not demand it. The revelation of mercy is a surprise in the profoundest sense of that term: grace beyond imagining, deliverance that I could not merit, joy that can never turn to sorrow. Ponder it: mercy as joyful surprise.

– Father Joseph T. Lienhard, s.j.

DOROTHY DAY died in New York on November 29, 1980. The following day, Saint John Paul II issued his second encyclical, *Dives in Misericordia* (*Rich in Mercy*).

Five years later, in November 1985, I was in Rome, having spoken at a Catholic event in Turin, Italy. I had arranged to go to the Wednesday papal audience with my friends Robert and Jane Orsi and their newborn infant Clare. I wanted to present the holy father with a copy of Dorothy Day's spiritual autobiography, *The Long Loneliness*, and they wished to have the pope bless their baby.

The holy father came over to us and I gave him the book, which his valet took and put in a sack filled with bouquets of flowers. The pope blessed Clare. He continued walking down the aisle and then stopped and turned to the valet, apparently asking him what the book was. The valet showed it to the pope, who then turned around. What was happening? All in the hall were bewildered, but the cheers continued. The pope walked all the way back to me, and looking at me directly in the eye, smiling, took my left hand and gently but firmly tapped it three times in gratitude.

Dorothy Day, Servant of God, centered her life on living the corporal and spiritual works of mercy, the expression of the "rich in mercy" proclaimed by Saint John Paul II.

– Geoffrey Gneuhs

WALKING MY FRIEND'S GOLDEN RETRIEVER, we meet a woman standing outside her store. Seeing the dog, she invites us in for a biscuit. He takes it gratefully and eats while we talk. Moments later she asks whether he would like another. I jokingly ask if she thinks he deserves it. To which she replies, "Of course he does, he's a loveable sweet boy."

Paul's Letter to Titus was written to encourage him as a Church leader in Crete. The letter is among the readings heard at Christmas. We hear it at a time of year when we are giving presents as signs of our friendship and love. Paul writes that God offers the gifts of friendship and love not just once but every day of the year. And then the startling truth: it is offered *not because of any righteous deeds we had done/ but because of his mercy* (Ti 3:5).

At the heart of God's mercy is the truth we can never forget. God's love for us is neither given because of a great thing we have done nor withheld because of our sins. There is no scorecard kept to assess who deserves the merciful love of God. It is continually offered because God is that good and, appearances to the contrary, we are that loveable.

– Monsignor Gregory E. S. Malovetz

The Luminous Mysteries of the Rosary

❨ *The Baptism of the Lord* – Vast crowds mass for the mercy of baptismal water. Jesus joins them. The mercy of God is a concrete thing. Through it he reveals the love of a Father, moved to the very depths out of love for his child. Mercy longs for us to hear and believe: *You are my beloved child. On you my favor rests.*

❨ *The Wedding Feast of Cana* – One of the corporal works of mercy is giving drink to the thirsty. The Mother of God, seeing the store of wedding wine spent, identifies human need with her Son. The blessed guests who taste Christ's lavish new outpouring look for that look of Mary toward her Son never to end. They thirst for it.

❨ *The Preaching of the Kingdom* – The spiritual works of mercy include counseling the doubtful, instructing the ignorant, and admonishing sinners. One word of grace helps us escape the doubt that leads to despair and crippling loneliness. I will preach by being a devoted listener. The preaching of Jesus is made visible by my witness.

❨ *The Transfiguration* – I will pray for the living and the dead with unswerving certainty, because the Transfiguration blazons that everything is susceptible to change. Appearances are not what they seem. Mercy wants to transfigure us. I will devote myself to prayer, especially for those in darkness and for the holy souls.

❨ *The Institution of the Eucharist* – The consummate act of Christ's life is a return to a corporal work of mercy: feeding the hungry. On the verge of your death, Jesus, you know how prone we are to deny you, to forget you. You, Mercy-Made-Flesh, leave your Presence in a form we can never mistake: in the Food without which we would perish.

– Father Peter John Cameron, O.P.

Confession (Lk 18:9-14)

Bless me, Father, for I have sinned.
I am Pharisee and publican.
I pray to a person who does not exist:
a graven image of myself.
But I smell a sinful leper
pining in my cell.
He calls to me unceasingly.
His whining sears my ears.
He interrupts my litany.
I cannot keep my prayer.
I despise this groping publican.
His growth is my decay.
If I offer him a morsel,
he'll rally for the plate.
If I offer him a sip,
his lips will curse my cup.
He offers me his pity!
That's all I can recall.

– Rita A. Simmonds

*S*INCE WE ARE CREATURES, we do not have being of ourselves, but our whole existence depends on God. And since we do not have our being in ourselves or of ourselves, we cannot satisfy our longing for it and give ourselves happiness by our own resources, but we should seek it in its inexhaustible source which is God. The desire to appease our hunger for happiness in God has nothing evil or debasing in itself; on the contrary, it is a necessity of our nature, and as such it is something that we need not renounce. God himself arouses and strengthens such desires in us by infusing the supernatural virtue of hope into our souls. In doing this he does not lose anything, for every act of hope is also homage to his mercy....

Grounded in the faith which teaches us that God is our ultimate end, and assures us of his help in reaching him, hope is a force impelling us to a constant search for God and giving us confidence that we shall never run short of strength, for God places his unfailing power at our disposal.

Thus, we realize that hope not only strengthens our longing to obtain the infinite Good, but also confirms our confidence of obtaining it.

– Servant of God Father Hyacinth Woroniecki, O.P.

Saint Martin de Porres

"I'M ONLY A POOR MULATTO, and I'm the property of the Dominican Order. Sell me!" The speaker was Martin de Porres, the illegitimate son of a freed slave and a Spanish nobleman. In 16th-century Peru, Martin was, indeed, property. He could be bought, sold, branded, or brutalized. And yet, by all accounts—and we have many—Martin was sweet-tempered and full of joy from his youth. When his poor, overworked mother became angry with him, Martin turned to Mother Mary. When sometimes his mother could not feed him, Jesus did, in the Sacrament of the Altar. Martin saw Jesus everywhere—in the other poor, in the children, in the sick people whom he, as a barber's apprentice, was learning to treat. It was natural for him to go to work for the Dominicans and even more natural that, after nine years, they bent the rules so that he, a black man, could take vows as a lay brother.

Martin's mercies were famous throughout Lima. The poor, the desolate, the forgotten, all received what they needed—bread, shelter, prayers. Even the rats could expect something from Martin. And he did indeed offer himself to satisfy a debt for the order, although they did not take him up on it. When Martin died, the entire city came. The most illustrious personages vied for the chance to carry the casket of the poor mulatto.

– Lisa Lickona

"FATHER, why do I have to go to confession?" Why did Jesus give us the Sacrament of Confession? Why did he make his mercy available in this unique way? I could point to Scripture, the *Catechism*, or many great books on this topic, but I would like to reflect with you on just one simple but important reason.

When we sin, whether it's big or small, all the time or just that once, we can begin to hear that voice. You know that voice. It taunts our mind and aches in our heart. At times it is even uttered by those around us. It condemns, it mocks: "You put on a good and holy front, but this sin, this is who you *really* are. You can't be forgiven." We hear it, and sometimes we believe it.

When we whisper our sins to the priest, we speak what we did and how often we did it. Our fear, that voice, awaits the certain condemnation. It never comes. We hear, instead, the truth. You are loved. You are forgiven. *"Behold, I make all things new"* (Rv 21:5).

The fear and the condemnation, they are lies. Every time we approach the place of mercy, we hear those beautiful and efficacious words of absolution. More than hope, more than wish, we know, with certainty, because we hear it: I am forgiven. These words of Jesus, spoken through the priest, we hear…and they silence the lies.

And we go in peace.

– **Father Eric Cadin**

Full fathom five thy father lies,
Of his bones are coral made,
Those are pearls that were his eyes.
Nothing of him that doth fade,
But doth suffer a sea-change
Into something rich and strange.
(Shakespeare, *The Tempest*)

THAT'S THE MYSTERIOUS SONG Prince Ferdinand hears as he roams the island. He believes his ship has been wrecked and his father, King Alonso of Naples, drowned. The song seems to confirm him in sorrow.

But the key of the music is not sadness but wonder. In this last of Shakespeare's plays, vengeance gives way to forgiveness, and justice, fulfilled, is crowned by mercy. Alonso, who also believes that Ferdinand is dead, is alive and searching the island for his son. He has been a wicked man, and he must be reborn in grace, as a little child. So it will be.

In the final scene, Alonso not only sees Ferdinand safe and sound. He sees him together with the girl he loves and has promised to marry, a girl whom Alonso had tried to murder many years before, along with her father, Prospero. Her name is Miranda: worthy of wonder.

Alonso falls before her. His words show us the transience of worldly power, and the solemn joy of being born anew:

I am hers.
But, O, how oddly will it sound that I
Must ask my child forgiveness!

A sea-change indeed.

– Anthony Esolen

Aꜰᴛᴇʀ ʜᴀᴠɪɴɢ ɪɴᴠɪᴛᴇᴅ ᴛʜᴇ Lᴏʀᴅ to dine at his house
(Lk 7:36-50), Simon the Pharisee dispenses with every traditional sign of welcome. An uninvited woman intrudes,
witnesses this belittling treatment, and sets to remedy-
ing Simon's behavior with tears and kisses. The host holds
Jesus in contempt for not dismissing such a person, for, as
Simon knows, *"she is a sinner."*

Then the Lord does something interesting and unexpected: *He turned to the woman and said to Simon....* Jesus
speaks to his host while facing, not his host, but the weeping, sinful woman. He is inviting Simon to look with him
at this woman, to gaze upon her with the Lord's own gaze.
And what does the Lord see that he wants Simon and us
as well to see? He wants us to see that this woman's truest
identity is not defined by her sin but by something that
goes even deeper: her need. She needs forgiveness, something that the sinful woman herself tearfully acknowledges.

This is the path of faith: living with Jesus, learning to
see what he sees. And what he sees in us is our deepest
need: God's mercy. This has been the path of our life and
vocation, born from a community that gives us our communion with the Lord and teaches us not to respond to
the sin of the other, or even our own, but to answer the
need that even our sin expresses: Mercy.

– Father Vincent Nagle, ꜰ.ꜱ.ᴄ.ʙ.

The Glorious Mysteries of the Rosary

◖ *The Resurrection* – Mercy's might consists in bringing non-being into being. This is the miracle of the Resurrection of Jesus. My wrongdoing, my failures, my fatalism, my regrets no longer have the last word. A new beginning pulses in every betrayal, every misdeed. Mercy risen from the dead repairs what is broken.

◖ *The Ascension* – With Jesus ascended into heaven go the wounds that for ever adorn his resurrected flesh. These marks of beauty Jesus perpetually shows to the Father as a testimony that mercy has triumphed over justice. Mercy frees the world from its slavery to corruption. Mercy ascended into heaven restores hope.

◖ *The Descent of the Holy Spirit* – Mercy is the ultimate act by which God comes to meet us. Pentecost is a glorious meeting of divine mercy in the Person of the Spirit. All goodness descending from the Father through the Son reaches us in the Holy Spirit. The Spirit comes so that we can make Christ and his mercy more and more our own.

◖ *The Assumption* – The arms that cradled Jesus as an infant, that reached out to him on the cross, and that caressed his corpse on Calvary are carried up to heaven in the Assumption as a promise that they will one day embrace us. Our Lady's presence in heaven is a mercy for us: the assurance that one day we will join her.

◖ *The Coronation of the Blessed Virgin Mary* – The majesty of the Blessed Virgin Mary's Queenship is the mercy she mediates. Our Lady uses her royal authority to dispense the graces of heaven to us who, left to ourselves, are so unworthy of them. When grief and fear drive us to lose hope, we find in our Queen and Mother of Mercy ultimate refuge.

– Father Peter John Cameron, O.P.

Never Alone (Wis 11:22–12:2)

There is joy
in the order
of the universe.
One spark explodes.
You won't see it.
You won't feel it.
You'll never even perceive it
unless
pushing your grocery cart
or baby carriage
or wheel barrel full of earth and stones
you ask yourself
how it all is
how you came to be
from nothing to
never alone.

– Rita A. Simmonds

*S*INCE WE ARE UNITED TO CHRIST in the Mystical Body and form one organism with him, any achievement in our spiritual life has a supernatural value, not only for us as individuals, but also for the entire Church. The dogma of the Communion of Saints makes the social solidarity of people something real in a very profound way. Because of it our merits are a common good and can be exchanged or transferred to others. This refers to prayer as well as all acts of mercy, and most of all to suffering.

Christ himself, sitting at the right hand of God the Father...cannot suffer. However, as the Head of the suffering Body he too suffers. That suffering is borne in his stead by countless individuals into whom sanctifying grace flows as a life-giving sap, and who thus fill up those things that are wanting of the sufferings of Christ for his Body which is the Church (Col 1:24).

In this way they partake of the mercy brought to the world by the sufferings of Christ. At times, after they have paid out to God the debt for their own faults, they are permitted the great honor of suffering with Christ for the sins of others.... The countless chosen souls who...through their saintly life, prayer, mortification, Christian apostleship and suffering, appease the wrath of God and obtain his mercy for the world.

– Servant of God Father Hyacinth Woroniecki, O.P.

Saint Elizabeth of Hungary

ELIZABETH OF HUNGARY († 1231) was fourteen when she was wed to Ludwig of Thuringia. Ludwig cherished Elizabeth; he supported whatever she loved. And Elizabeth loved the poor. She could not keep away from them; she was always stealing from the castle with bread and meat, blankets and tunics—whatever they needed. The tongues of the courtiers wagged constantly about Elizabeth and her "excessive" piety. And it is said that, one time, Ludwig believed them. He intercepted Elizabeth as she was hurrying yet again from the castle with food for some poor starving woman. Asked to open her apron, Elizabeth readily obeyed. Instead of bread, roses, red and abundant, fell out. Ludwig never questioned Elizabeth again.

On another occasion, Elizabeth entered the cathedral for Mass and spontaneously knelt down and placed her crown at the foot of the crucifix. Her royal relations were incensed, but she said that she "couldn't bear" to wear a crown of gold while Christ wore his of thorns.

Elizabeth was twenty when Ludwig died while on crusade, a great grief. Afterward, she left Marburg Castle, found safe haven for her three little ones, then pledged herself to follow Saint Francis in poverty, penance, and prayer. She died when she was only twenty-three, a living icon of charity.

– Lisa Lickona

GROWING UP CATHOLIC IN A WORLD where everything
to save your soul was steeped in sacrament, there was never
an excuse for falling short. When you missed the mark, the
solution was straightforwardly simple. You went to confession. There, amid the dark anonymity of the box, the
whispering voice unburdening itself of its own brokenness, you discovered *life*. The impossible gift of renewal,
offered as often as you fell. An occasion of grace, no less,
your soul wholly drenched in divine mercy. Not therapy.
Not an exercise in moral accounting, as if God were taking
inventory of our iniquities. God is not a number cruncher.

"At its best," writes Monsignor Lorenzo Albacete, confession "is the affirmation that the ultimate truth of our interior life is our absolute poverty, our radical dependence,
our unquenchable thirst, our desperate need to be loved."
In going to confession, we carry all the broken pieces of
our lives to God, asking in humility and trust for his forgiveness, of which we feel perfectly confident thanks to
the transparency of the priest standing *in persona Christi*.
In asking God to put all the pieces back together, we give
him reason to smile.

– Regis Martin

In 2008, Lou Resciniti, fifty-eight at the time, drove drunk one night and crashed his car. A twenty-five-year-old mother of three was killed.

Lou had been raised Catholic but had renounced the faith long before. He'd refused to have his three children baptized. Back at home awaiting trial, he was depressed, almost suicidal. But one day he was seized by "a mysterious sudden concern for the state of my soul." Though his recovery was still a long way off, he had a very strong sense, in the form of a "voice," asking: "Are you ready *now*?"

He was sentenced to ten years in a Florida prison.

His twenty-seven-year-old son Keith had become a member of the Church but, knowing his father's virulent anti-Catholicism, had kept it to himself.

But now Keith prevailed upon a priest, Father Caulfield, to visit his father. Father suggested that Lou read the Gospel of John, chapter six.

It was on the third reading, over a period of time, that the words burst through like a thunderbolt: *"I am the bread of life"* (Jn 6:48).

"It is through the Eucharist that I have found his Church," Lou writes. He knows "the loving, forgiving Father who embraces his penitent prodigal son."

In prison, he prays for lost souls, especially those who have been wounded by tragedies perpetrated by others.

His release date is set for October 11, 2017.

– Heather King

SHE LEARNED AT HER FAMILY'S TABLE. The daughter of Hungarian and Slovak parents, my mother grew up believing there was always room at the table. That belief followed her through all the years as a mother, grandmother, and today as a great-grandmother. There is always room at the table to squeeze in another person at Christmas, Easter, or other occasions. When the number grows from eleven to nineteen people, her response is always the same: "How could I say no?"

Paul's Letter to the Romans is his longest, written to introduce himself and present his message to them. One of the great themes of this letter is the universal call of Jesus to follow him. Jews and Gentiles alike are offered the invitation to sit at the table.

There is something both touching and challenging when we realize that he can never say no. Anyone with a sincere heart is welcomed. Paul writes *he has mercy upon whom he wills* (Rom 9:18), insisting that in God there is always the spirit of welcome. The followers of Jesus, to live that mercy, must cultivate a spirit of welcome. We must be willing to confront the hard truth: whom do we exclude not only from our dining tables but from the table of the human family? We can understand God's mercy only when we are challenged by the question, "How could I say no?"

– Monsignor Gregory E. S. Malovetz

O Jesus, Lover of souls, we recommend unto you
the souls of all those your servants who have departed with the sign of faith and sleep the sleep of peace.
We beseech you, O Lord and Savior, that, as in your
mercy to them you became man, so now you would
hasten the time, and admit them to your presence
above. Let their souls rejoice in your light, and im-
pute not to them their former iniquities, which they
committed through the violence of passion, or the
corrupt habits of their fallen nature.

O Gracious Lord, we beseech you, remember
not against them the sins of their youth and their
ignorances; but according to your great mercy, be
mindful of them in your heavenly glory. May the
heavens be opened to them, and the angels rejoice
with them. May all the saints and elect of God, who in
this world suffered torments for your name, befriend
them; that, being freed from the prison beneath, they
may be admitted into the glories of your Kingdom.

Come to their assistance, all you saints of God;
gain for them deliverance from their place of punishment; meet them, all you angels; receive these holy
souls, and present them before the Lord. Eternal rest
give to them, O Lord. And may perpetual light shine
on them.

May they rest in peace. Amen.

– Blessed John Henry Newman

In the Space (Ps 17)

W hat is there in the space
between a saint's gaze
and the Infant's face?
or between fleshy lips positioned to kiss?
or two hands coming towards clasp?
or a hand and a head that waits to be blessed?
What is there in the space
between a secret sigh
and God's wide ear
that gets compressed
as meeting draws near—
vacant to the naked eye,
magnified in prayer?

– Rita A. Simmonds

*M*AY YOUR LOVE DRAW DOWN upon you the mercy of the Lord, and may he let you see that within your soul a saint is sleeping. I shall ask him to make you so open and supple that you will be able to understand and do what he wants you to do. Your life is nothing; it is not even your own. Each time you say, "I'd like to do this or that," you wound Christ, robbing him of what is his. You have to put to death everything within you except the desire to love God. This is not at all hard to do. It is enough to have confidence and to thank the little Jesus for all the potentialities he has placed within you. You are called to holiness, like me, like everyone; don't forget….

Don't count on yourself, for alone you can do nothing. It is not you who must act, but Christ in you. And then you will taste the marvels of divine love, prayers filled with honey…and your soul will climb, without you noticing it, to the summit of love. But for this, you must put self-love to death…become like the slave of others…. Be like the clay which the divine potter can shape as he wills. The one who abandons himself to God in this way no longer has a heart of flesh in his breast, but a ball of fire…. When the Lord begins to kindle the fire of his love, his victim is quick to cry for mercy, for the joy is beyond our human strength to bear.

– Servant of God Jacques Fesch

Saint John XXIII

ANGELO GIUSEPPE RONCALLI was born of a very large, poor, but happy family—thirteen children in all. When he became a priest, he attached himself to two saints who are known for their constant prayer and their presence among the people—Francis de Sales and Charles Borromeo. And when he was made a delegate for the Holy See, first in Bulgaria, and then Turkey and Greece, he made friends with Orthodox, Muslims, and Jews.

When Angelo became John XXIII, he brought his charism for friendship to the world stage. In four short years, he became known as "the good pope," his arms always open wide. John's best-known work was the calling of the Second Vatican Council. The day after the Council opened, John recalled his time with his friends in Turkey and Greece: "We did not debate; we spoke; and though we did not discuss, we loved each other." And then he added, "How my heart burns with a desire to work and to suffer for the coming of that hour when Jesus' prayer at the Last Supper will be realized for all men."

Jesus prayed that *"they may all be one, as you, Father, are in me and I in you"* (Jn 17:21). This was John's prayer, too. Of Saint John XXIII, Saint John Paul II taught: "Even amid many difficulties, the elderly pontiff opened a season of hope for Christians and for humanity."

– Lisa Lickona

On the Papal Motto of Pope Francis

POPE FRANCIS' MOTTO, *Miserando atque eligendo*, "by having mercy and by choosing," puzzled many. But Jorge Mario Bergoglio recounted that at the age of seventeen, on September 21, 1953, the feast of Saint Matthew, he experienced the loving presence of God in his life and sensed the mercy of God calling him to religious life. Francis' motto is found in a homily by Saint Bede the Venerable read in the liturgy of the hours on Saint Matthew's day: "So Jesus saw the publican [Matthew], and because he looked upon him by having mercy and by choosing, he said to him, *'Follow me'*" (Mt 9:9).

The translation is meant to provoke reflection. "He looked upon him by having mercy and by choosing." There are different kinds of looking: a looking that is indifferent: staring at the floor; or a looking that is also seeking: the shelves of a bookstore. Saint Bede suggests still another kind of looking: one that communicates and elects. We need to imagine the gaze of Christ, God made man. It is a powerful gaze: Christ's looking acts upon me. From his eyes I experience mercy. By sin I am in debt. Mercy forgives that debt and wipes out what I cannot repay.

But further: "and choosing." For Matthew sitting at the tax office, Christ's gaze chooses and elects him. Perhaps the young Jorge experienced that same gaze.

– Father Joseph T. Lienhard, s.j.

FOR THE MEN AND WOMEN WHO, in their human weakness, have contravened not only the moral laws of God but also the criminal laws of the state, the date of their conviction is generally seen as the only pertinent fact of their existence. Nothing about them is worth recognizing except the black stain of their offense: they've been found guilty, and guilty they shall remain in perpetuity, shackled as they are to an inexpungable criminal record.

How different is the divine mercy!

To the woman caught in adultery (Jn 8:3-11)—a criminal offense in that day, requiring not imprisonment but death—Jesus never uses the words *adultery* or *adulterer*, never asks, "How could you?" She doesn't need her sin thrown back in her face; she needs a new beginning; and that's what he gives her—not only on the day recounted in John's Gospel, but in every moment of every day of the rest of her life. She is changed, not through the imposition of a scarlet letter, not through imprisonment or lifetime social banishment, but rather through what Pope Francis has memorably termed "the caress of Christ's mercy" on her sins.

We are united to men and women in prison because our hearts have the same needs as theirs, among which are truth, beauty, goodness—and a new beginning made possible only through mercy.

– Joshua Stancil

Day 1 – Feed the Hungry and Give Drink to the Thirsty

"We cannot escape the Lord's words to us, and they will serve as the criteria upon which we will be judged"

(Misericordiae Vultus *15*).

THE DISCIPLES APPROACHED [Jesus] and said, "…Dismiss the crowds so that they can go to the villages and buy food for themselves." [Jesus] said to them, "There is no need for them to go away; give them some food yourselves."

Matthew 14:15-16

Loving Father, rich in mercy, you give us your entire self, always, freely, asking nothing in return. Through mercy you reach out to the sinner, offering a new chance to reflect, convert, and believe. Your mercy opens our hearts to a hope of being loved forever despite our sinfulness. Free us to let go of anger, wrath, violence, and revenge—a necessary condition for living joyfully.

Help us to see the wounds of our brothers and sisters who are denied their dignity. May we refrain from judgment and envy toward others. Enable us to accept the good in every person. It is time to bear the weaknesses and struggles of our brothers and sisters. Let us help others escape the doubt that causes them to fall into despair. May the flesh of your Son—visible in the tortured, the scourged, the malnourished, and the exiled—be acknowledged, touched, and cared for by us.

With our eyes fixed on Jesus' merciful gaze, let us experience the love of the Most Holy Trinity. Through Christ our Lord.

(Based on *Misericordiae Vultus*)

Day 2 – Clothe the Naked and Welcome the Stranger

"Mercy [is] the ultimate and supreme act
by which God comes to meet us"
(Misericordiae Vultus 2).

WHEN [JESUS] CAME ashore a man from the town who was possessed by demons met him. For a long time he had not worn clothes; he did not live in a house, but lived among the tombs. When he saw Jesus, he cried out and fell down before him.   Luke 8:27-28

Loving Father, rich in mercy, you give us your entire self, always, freely, asking nothing in return. Through mercy you reach out to the sinner, offering a new chance to reflect, convert, and believe. Your mercy opens our hearts to a hope of being loved forever despite our sinfulness. Free us to let go of anger, wrath, violence, and revenge—a necessary condition for living joyfully.

Help us to see the wounds of our brothers and sisters who are denied their dignity. May we refrain from judgment and envy toward others. Enable us to accept the good in every person. It is time to bear the weaknesses and struggles of our brothers and sisters. Let us help others escape the doubt that causes them to fall into despair. May the flesh of your Son—visible in the tortured, the scourged, the malnourished, and the exiled—be acknowledged, touched, and cared for by us.

With our eyes fixed on Jesus' merciful gaze, let us experience the love of the Most Holy Trinity. Through Christ our Lord.   (Based on *Misericordiae Vultus*)

Day 3 – Heal the Sick

"The mercy of God…is a 'visceral' love. It gushes forth from the depths…full of tenderness and compassion"
(Misericordiae Vultus 6).

SIMON'S MOTHER-IN-LAW LAY sick with a fever. They immediately told [Jesus] about her. He approached, grasped her hand, and helped her up. Then the fever left her.   Mark 1:30-31

Loving Father, rich in mercy, you give us your entire self, always, freely, asking nothing in return. Through mercy you reach out to the sinner, offering a new chance to reflect, convert, and believe. Your mercy opens our hearts to a hope of being loved forever despite our sinfulness. Free us to let go of anger, wrath, violence, and revenge—a necessary condition for living joyfully.

Help us to see the wounds of our brothers and sisters who are denied their dignity. May we refrain from judgment and envy toward others. Enable us to accept the good in every person. It is time to bear the weaknesses and struggles of our brothers and sisters. Let us help others escape the doubt that causes them to fall into despair. May the flesh of your Son—visible in the tortured, the scourged, the malnourished, and the exiled—be acknowledged, touched, and cared for by us.

With our eyes fixed on Jesus' merciful gaze, let us experience the love of the Most Holy Trinity. Through Christ our Lord.   (Based on *Misericordiae Vultus*)

Day 4 – Visit the Imprisoned

"[God] envelops [justice] and surpasses it with an even greater event in which we experience love"
(Misericordiae Vultus *21*).

"'WHEN DID WE see you ill or in prison, and visit you?' And the king will say to them in reply, 'Amen, I say to you, whatever you did for one of these least brothers of mine, you did for me.'"   Matthew 25:39-40

Loving Father, rich in mercy, you give us your entire self, always, freely, asking nothing in return. Through mercy you reach out to the sinner, offering a new chance to reflect, convert, and believe. Your mercy opens our hearts to a hope of being loved forever despite our sinfulness. Free us to let go of anger, wrath, violence, and revenge—a necessary condition for living joyfully.

Help us to see the wounds of our brothers and sisters who are denied their dignity. May we refrain from judgment and envy toward others. Enable us to accept the good in every person. It is time to bear the weaknesses and struggles of our brothers and sisters. Let us help others escape the doubt that causes them to fall into despair. May the flesh of your Son—visible in the tortured, the scourged, the malnourished, and the exiled—be acknowledged, touched, and cared for by us.

With our eyes fixed on Jesus' merciful gaze, let us experience the love of the Most Holy Trinity. Through Christ our Lord.   (Based on *Misericordiae Vultus*)

Day 5 – Counsel the Doubtful and Instruct the Ignorant

*"We are called to gaze even more attentively on mercy
so that we may become a more effective sign
of the Father's action in our lives"*
(Misericordiae Vultus 3).

"AFTER MY DEPARTURE savage wolves will come among you…. So…remember that for three years…I unceasingly admonished each of you with tears. And now I commend you…to that gracious word of [God's] that can build you up."
Acts of the Apostles 20:29, 31-32

Loving Father, rich in mercy, you give us your entire self, always, freely, asking nothing in return. Through mercy you reach out to the sinner, offering a new chance to reflect, convert, and believe. Your mercy opens our hearts to a hope of being loved forever despite our sinfulness. Free us to let go of anger, wrath, violence, and revenge—a necessary condition for living joyfully.

Help us to see the wounds of our brothers and sisters who are denied their dignity. May we refrain from judgment and envy toward others. Enable us to accept the good in every person. It is time to bear the weaknesses and struggles of our brothers and sisters. Let us help others escape the doubt that causes them to fall into despair. May the flesh of your Son—visible in the tortured, the scourged, the malnourished, and the exiled—be acknowledged, touched, and cared for by us.

With our eyes fixed on Jesus' merciful gaze, let us experience the love of the Most Holy Trinity. Through Christ our Lord. (Based on *Misericordiae Vultus*)

Day 6 – Admonish Sinners

"When faced with the gravity of sin,
God responds with the fullness of mercy"
(Misericordiae Vultus 3).

THEN JESUS STRAIGHTENED up and said to her, "Woman, where are they? Has no one condemned you?" She replied, "No one, sir." Then Jesus said, "Neither do I condemn you. Go, [and] from now on do not sin any more."

John 8:10-11

Loving Father, rich in mercy, you give us your entire self, always, freely, asking nothing in return. Through mercy you reach out to the sinner, offering a new chance to reflect, convert, and believe. Your mercy opens our hearts to a hope of being loved forever despite our sinfulness. Free us to let go of anger, wrath, violence, and revenge—a necessary condition for living joyfully.

Help us to see the wounds of our brothers and sisters who are denied their dignity. May we refrain from judgment and envy toward others. Enable us to accept the good in every person. It is time to bear the weaknesses and struggles of our brothers and sisters. Let us help others escape the doubt that causes them to fall into despair. May the flesh of your Son—visible in the tortured, the scourged, the malnourished, and the exiled—be acknowledged, touched, and cared for by us.

With our eyes fixed on Jesus' merciful gaze, let us experience the love of the Most Holy Trinity. Through Christ our Lord. (Based on *Misericordiae Vultus*)

Day 7 – Comfort the Afflicted

"Jesus reveals the nature of God as that of a Father who never gives up until he has...overcome rejection with compassion and mercy"
(Misericordiae Vultus 9).

AND THEN A leper approached, did [Jesus] homage, and said, "Lord, if you wish, you can make me clean." He stretched out his hand, touched him, and said, "I will do it. Be made clean."

Matthew 8:2-3

Loving Father, rich in mercy, you give us your entire self, always, freely, asking nothing in return. Through mercy you reach out to the sinner, offering a new chance to reflect, convert, and believe. Your mercy opens our hearts to a hope of being loved forever despite our sinfulness. Free us to let go of anger, wrath, violence, and revenge—a necessary condition for living joyfully.

Help us to see the wounds of our brothers and sisters who are denied their dignity. May we refrain from judgment and envy toward others. Enable us to accept the good in every person. It is time to bear the weaknesses and struggles of our brothers and sisters. Let us help others escape the doubt that causes them to fall into despair. May the flesh of your Son—visible in the tortured, the scourged, the malnourished, and the exiled—be acknowledged, touched, and cared for by us.

With our eyes fixed on Jesus' merciful gaze, let us experience the love of the Most Holy Trinity. Through Christ our Lord.   (Based on *Misericordiae Vultus*)

Day 8 – Forgive Offenses and Bear Wrongs Patiently

"Touched by [God's] compassion,
we also can become compassionate towards others"
(Misericordiae Vultus 14).

AFTER RECALLING THE apostles, they had them flogged, ordered them to stop speaking in the name of Jesus, and dismissed them. So they left the presence of the Sanhedrin, rejoicing that they had been found worthy to suffer dishonor for the sake of the name.   Acts 5:40-41

Loving Father, rich in mercy, you give us your entire self, always, freely, asking nothing in return. Through mercy you reach out to the sinner, offering a new chance to reflect, convert, and believe. Your mercy opens our hearts to a hope of being loved forever despite our sinfulness. Free us to let go of anger, wrath, violence, and revenge—a necessary condition for living joyfully.

Help us to see the wounds of our brothers and sisters who are denied their dignity. May we refrain from judgment and envy toward others. Enable us to accept the good in every person. It is time to bear the weaknesses and struggles of our brothers and sisters. Let us help others escape the doubt that causes them to fall into despair. May the flesh of your Son—visible in the tortured, the scourged, the malnourished, and the exiled—be acknowledged, touched, and cared for by us.

With our eyes fixed on Jesus' merciful gaze, let us experience the love of the Most Holy Trinity. Through Christ our Lord.   (Based on *Misericordiae Vultus*)

Day 9 – Bury the Dead and Pray for the Living and the Dead

"Mercy is the force that reawakens us to new life
and instills in us the courage
to look to the future with hope"
(Misericordiae Vultus *10*).

MARTHA SAID TO Jesus, "Lord, if you had been here, my brother would not have died. [But] even now I know that whatever you ask of God, God will give you." Jesus said to her, "Your brother will rise." John 11:21-23

Loving Father, rich in mercy, you give us your entire self, always, freely, asking nothing in return. Through mercy you reach out to the sinner, offering a new chance to reflect, convert, and believe. Your mercy opens our hearts to a hope of being loved forever despite our sinfulness. Free us to let go of anger, wrath, violence, and revenge—a necessary condition for living joyfully.

Help us to see the wounds of our brothers and sisters who are denied their dignity. May we refrain from judgment and envy toward others. Enable us to accept the good in every person. It is time to bear the weaknesses and struggles of our brothers and sisters. Let us help others escape the doubt that causes them to fall into despair. May the flesh of your Son—visible in the tortured, the scourged, the malnourished, and the exiled—be acknowledged, touched, and cared for by us.

With our eyes fixed on Jesus' merciful gaze, let us experience the love of the Most Holy Trinity. Through Christ our Lord. **(Based on *Misericordiae Vultus*)**

Lord Jesus, mercy is the ultimate and supreme act by which God comes to meet us. Mercy, as regards external works, is the greatest of all the virtues. It is proper to God to have mercy. Through mercy God's omnipotence is manifested to the greatest degree. The very salvation that God offers us is itself the work of his mercy.

God's mercy is great, forgiving us by caressing us. The steadfast love of God never ceases; his mercies never come to an end. They are new every morning.

Divine Savior, your invitation to mercy is intended to draw us into a deeper imitation of God our Father: *"Be merciful, as your Father is merciful"* (cf. Lk 6:36). Your gaze, O Jesus, makes us feel an interior wonder, and makes us hear you beckon: Follow me.

Mercy is the bridge that connects God and the human being, opening our hearts to a hope of being loved forever, despite our sinfulness. Mercy brings us peace!

To become merciful, we must first acknowledge that we have done many things wrong: we are sinners! I need to know how to say: *Lord, I am ashamed of what I have done in life.* With this attitude of repentance I will be more capable of being merciful, because I will feel God's mercy for me.

To become merciful, I need an openness to expanding my heart. Shame and repentance expand a small, selfish heart, since they give space for God to forgive us. A big heart does not get entangled in other people's lives. It does not condemn, but forgives and forgets.

The way of mercy is the way of life. A Christian must necessarily be merciful, because this is the center of the Gospel. Mercy overcomes every wall, every barrier, and leads us always to seek the face of the other—of the person. And it is mercy that changes one's heart and one's life—that can regenerate a person and allow that person to integrate into society in a new way.

True mercy takes the person into one's care, listens to the other attentively, approaches the situation with respect and truth, and accompanies that person on the journey of reconciliation. Love can never be just an abstraction. Mercy first means treating others' wounds. And mercy means neither generosity nor rigidity. Whenever we have an opportunity to perform a work of mercy, we should rejoice as if a fountain has been let loose so that a fire might be extinguished.

And you, our Lady, through your grace, your intercession, and your example, deliver us from all evil and untie the knots that prevent us from being united with God, so that we, free from sin and error, may find him in all things, may have our hearts placed in him, and may serve him always in our brothers and sisters.

– Based on the talks and writings of Pope Francis

Brief Biographies of Contributors

Audrey Assad is a wife, mother, musician, and writer living in Nashville with her husband, her son, her books, and her coffeemaker.

Father Eric Cadin is a priest of the Archdiocese of Boston, where he serves full time in the Vocation Office.

Father Peter John Cameron, o.p., is editor-in-chief of MAGNIFICAT and editor of *Prayers for the Moment* (MAGNIFICAT).

Father Romanus Cessario, o.p., serves as senior editor for MAGNIFICAT and teaches theology at Saint John's Seminary in Boston, MA.

Father Ryan Connors serves as associate pastor of Our Lady of Mercy Parish in East Greenwich, RI. After studies at the Pontifical North American College in Rome, he was ordained a priest in 2012.

Father John Dominic Corbett, o.p., teaches moral theology at the Pontifical Faculty of the Immaculate Conception in Washington DC. He also assists in formation work and spiritual direction and preaches retreats.

Father Cajetan Cuddy, o.p., is a priest of the Dominican Province of Saint Joseph. He currently serves as parochial vicar at Saint Joseph's Church in New York City (Greenwich Village).

Anthony Esolen is professor of English at Providence College, a senior editor of *Touchstone Magazine*, and a regular contributor to MAGNIFICAT. He is the translator and editor of Dante's *Divine Comedy* (Random House) and author of *The Beauty of the Word: A Running Commentary on the Roman Missal* (MAGNIFICAT).

Justin Fatica is co-founder of Hard as Nails Ministries, a non-profit Catholic/Christian organization that has impacted over one million young people in the last decade.

Father Michael Gaitley, M.I.C., is director of Evangelization for the Marians of the Immaculate Conception, head formator for the Marian Missionaries of Divine Mercy, and author of several bestselling books, including *33 Days to Morning Glory*. He lives and works in Stockbridge, MA, home of the National Shrine of the Divine Mercy.

Father Anthony Giambrone, O.P., is a Dominican priest of the Province of Saint Joseph and a professor of Sacred Scripture at the École biblique in Jerusalem.

Geoffrey Gneuhs is an artist and writer. His most recent publication is *Saint Thomas Aquinas: A Biography for Young Readers* (New Priory Press, 2014). He is a member of the advisory board of the Dorothy Day Guild.

Father Donald Haggerty is a priest of the Archdiocese of New York, and serving at Saint Agnes Church in New York City.

Father Tim S. Hickey, a priest of the Archdiocese of Hartford, is administrator of Blessed Sacrament Parish and the Shrine of Saint Anne, both in Waterbury, CT. Prior to becoming a priest, he was editor of *Columbia* magazine, the monthly publication of the Knights of Columbus.

Jennifer Hubbard resides in Newtown, CT. The younger of her two children, Catherine Violet, was a victim of the Sandy Hook Elementary School shooting.

John Janaro is associate professor emeritus of theology at Christendom College and author of *Never Give Up: My Life and God's Mercy* (Servant Books). He blogs at www.johnjanaro.com.

Father William M. Joensen, a priest of the Archdiocese of Dubuque, IA, is dean of Campus Spiritual Life at Loras College, where he also teaches philosophy and is spiritual director for seminarians.

Mary Joseph, a composer and choreographer, was working for a financial corporation near the World Trade Center on September 11, 2001. She contracted an incapacitating illness as a result.

Heather King is a contemplative laywoman and author of several books. She blogs at www.heather-king.com.

Barbara Ann La Porte is the mother of Matthew Joseph La Porte, Air Force Cadet, who lost his life in the Virginia Tech shooting on April 16, 2007. Her son was declared a national hero upon receiving the Airman's Medal for his brave act, credited with saving lives.

Priscilla La Porte is the younger sister of Matthew La Porte, who was killed in the 2007 shootings at Virginia Polytechnic Institute and State University. Today, she is a high school counselor in northern New Jersey.

Lisa Lickona is a wife and mother to nine children whom she schools on a farm in upstate New York.

Father Joseph T. Lienhard, s.j., teaches patristic theology at Fordham University in the Bronx and Saint Joseph's Seminary in Yonkers, NY. He is currently translating Saint Augustine's commentaries on the Old Testament.

Monsignor Gregory E. S. Malovetz, a priest of the Diocese of Metuchen, is the pastor of Saint Charles Borromeo Church in Montgomery Township, NJ.

Father Guy Mansini, o.s.b., is pastor of Saint Isidore the Farmer and Holy Cross parishes in southern Indiana and teaches theology at Saint Meinrad Seminary.

Regis Martin is professor of theology at Franciscan University in Steubenville, OH, and the author of more than a half-dozen books, including most recently *The Beggar's Banquet: A Personal Retreat on Christ, His Mother, the Spiritual Life, and the Saints* (Emmaus Road Publishing).

Father John P. McIntyre († 2014) was a Jesuit theologian, professor, and writer in residence at Saint Mary's Hall, Boston College.

Father Vincent Nagle, F.S.C.B., is a member of the Priestly Fraternity of the Missionaries of Saint Charles Borromeo. He works as a traveling preacher and has his residence in Milan, Italy.

Father George William Rutler is pastor of the Church of Saint Michael in Manhattan, NY. His latest book is *Hints from Heaven* (Sophia Institute Press).

Father Christopher Seiler is a priest of the Archdiocese of St. Louis. He is the associate pastor at Saint Gabriel the Archangel Parish in St. Louis, and teaches Dogmatic Theology at Kenrick-Glennon Seminary.

Rita A. Simmonds is an award-winning poet. She lives in Brooklyn, NY, with her two sons.

Joshua Stancil is a writer living in North Carolina. His work has appeared in MAGNIFICAT and *Traces*.

Father James M. Sullivan, O.P., serves as director of the Institute for Continuing Theological Education at the Pontifical North American College in Rome.

Father Richard Veras is the director of Pastoral Formation at Saint Joseph's Seminary in New York and a regular contributor to MAGNIFICAT. He is author of *Jesus of Israel: Finding Christ in the Old Testament* (Servant Books) and *Wisdom for Everyday Life from the Book of Revelation* (Servant Books).

Biographies of Authors of Meditations and Prayers

Saint Anselm († 1109) was an abbot, bishop, philosopher, and theologian.

Saint Augustine († 430) is called the Doctor of Grace.

Saint Catherine of Siena († 1380), Doctor of the Church, was a Dominican, stigmatist, and papal counselor.

Blessed Charles de Foucauld († 1916) was a desert hermit and the inspiration for the community known as the Little Brothers of Jesus.

Saint Claude La Colombière († 1682) was a French Jesuit priest and the spiritual director of Saint Margaret Mary Alacoque.

Servant of God Madeleine Delbrêl († 1964) was a French laywoman, writer, and mystic devoted to caring for the poor and to evangelizing culture.

Father Pierre Descouvemont is a priest of the Diocese of Cambrai, France, a theologian, and the author of several books.

Servant of God Adelė Dirsytė († 1955) was a devoted school teacher and minister to the poor. Sentenced to a concentration camp for participating in the organized resistance of the Soviet occupation of her native Lithuania, she served as a true spiritual leader there, even amidst appalling persecution and torture.

Doris Donnelly is a professor of religious studies at John Carroll University.

Servant of God Jacques Fesch († 1957) was a murderer who experienced a profound conversion in prison before his death.

Pope Francis was elected to the See of Saint Peter in 2013.

Servant of God Monsignor Luigi Giussani († 2005) was a priest from Milan, Italy, who was the founder of the ecclesial movement Communion and Liberation.

Saint Gregory of Narek († 1003) was an Armenian monk, poet, mystical philosopher, and theologian. He is a Doctor of the Church.

John Janaro is associate professor emeritus of theology and the author of *Never Give Up: My Life and God's Mercy*.

Blessed John Henry Newman († 1890) established the Oratory in Birmingham, England, and was a preacher of great eloquence.

Saint John Paul II († 2005) reigned as pope from 1978 until 2005.

Saint John XXIII († 1963) reigned as pope from 1958 until 1963.

Saint Leo the Great († 461) reigned as pope from 440 to 461. He is a Doctor of the Church.

Venerable Louis of Granada († 1588) was a Spanish Dominican priest, the composer of a catechism for the use of missionaries in the New World, and a friend of Saint Charles Borromeo.

Blessed Margaret Ebner († 1351) was a Dominican nun at Maria Medingen, Germany.

Saint Maria Faustina Kowalska († 1938) was a sister of the Congregation of Sisters of Our Lady of Mercy in Cracow, Poland.

Saint Maximilian Mary Kolbe († 1941) was a Polish Conventual Franciscan priest who was martyred in Auschwitz.

Sister Briege McKenna, O.S.C., is a Sister of Saint Clare from Ireland who is dedicated to a worldwide apostolate of healing through conferences and retreats.

Father Peter of Blois († 1212) was born near Tours, France, and served as archdeacon of London.

Father Servais Pinckaers, O.P., († 2008) was professor of moral theology at the University of Fribourg, Switzerland.

Venerable Marthe Robin († 1981) was a French mystic and stigmatist who was bedridden most of her life.

Blessed Teresa of Calcutta († 1997) won the Nobel Peace Prize and founded the Missionaries of Charity.

Saint Thérèse of Lisieux († 1897) was a French Carmelite nun. She was declared a Doctor of the Church in 1997.

Saint Thomas Aquinas († 1274), Doctor of the Church, was a Dominican priest from Italy.

Jean Vanier is the founder of L'Arche, an international network of communities for people with developmental disabilities.

Servant of God Hyacinth Woroniecki, O.P., († 1949) was a Polish Dominican priest, the rector of the Catholic University of Lublin, a professor of theology at the Angelicum, and the founder of the Congregation of the Dominican Sister Missionaries of Jesus and Mary.

BIBLIOGRAPHY FOR PRAYERS

AUTHOR		PAGE
Anselm (Saint)	From *The Prayers and Meditations of Saint Anselm*. Copyright © 1973, Penguin Classics, London. All rights reserved.	272
Augustine (Saint)	From *Confessions*, Book 10, Dame Maria Boulding, o.s.b., Tr. © 1997, Augustinian Heritage Institute. Published by New City Press, Hyde Park, NY. Used with permission.	331, 338
Catherine of Siena (Saint)	From *The Prayers of Catherine of Siena*, 2nd Edition, Suzanne Noffke, o.p., Ed. and Tr. © 2001, Authors Choice Press, iUniverse.com, Inc. www.iuniverse.com. Used with permission.	168, 175, 256
Charles de Foucauld (Blessed)	From *Come Let Us Sing a Song Unknown*. © 1977, Dimension Books, Inc., Denville, NJ. All rights reserved.	53
Claude La Colombière (Saint)	From *Claude La Colombière Sermons*, Vol. I; Christian Conduct. William P. O'Brien, trans. © 2014, Northern Illinois University Press, DeKalb, IL. Used with permission.	353
Confederate Soldier	Cited in *Prayers for Urgent Occasions*. © 2008, Catholic Book Publishing Corporation, NJ. Reproduced with permission. All rights reserved.	286
Dirsytė, Adelė (Servant of God)	From *Mary Save Us*, Rev. Kestutis A. Trimakas, s.j., Tr. © 2005, Our Sunday Visitor, Inc., Huntington, IN. www.osv.com. 1-800-348-2440. Used with permission.	310
Francis (Pope)	From *Prayer to Mary Undoer of Knots*. www.catholiccompany.com/content/Mary-Untier-of-Knots-Prayers.cfm. All rights reserved.	425
Francis (Pope)	From Prayer to Mary after the Profession of Faith with the Bishop of the Italian Episcopal Conference, Vatican Basilica, May 23, 2013. Used with permission of the Libreria Editrice Vaticana. www.vatican.va.	183, 360
Gregory of Narek (Saint)	From *St. Grigor Narekatsi: Speaking with God from the Depths of the Heart*, The Armenian Prayer Book of St. Gregory of Narek, Prayer 54, Thomas J. Samuelian, Tr. © 2002, Vem Press, Yerevan, Armenia. www.vem.am. Used with permission.	45, 368

Author		Page
Janaro, John	From *Never Give Up: My Life and God's Mercy.* © 2010, John Janaro, Servant Books, an imprint of Franciscan Media, 28 W. Liberty St., Cincinnati, Ohio. To order copies call 1-888-322-6657 or visit www.servantbooks.org. Used with permission.	109
John Henry Newman (Blessed)	From *Prayers, Verses, and Devotions.* © 1989, Ignatius Press, San Francisco, CA. www.ignatius.com. Used with permission.	61, 77, 160, 279, 302, 317 410
John Paul II (Saint)	From prayers for the celebration of the Great Jubilee of the Year 2000. Used with permission of the Libreria Editrice Vaticana. www.vatican.va.	191, 249, 345
John XXIII (Saint)	From *The Decalogue of Pope John XXIII.* www.appleseeds.org/Decalogue_John-23.htm. All rights reserved.	324
Margaret Ebner (Blessed O.P.)	From *Major Works*, translated and edited by Leonard P. Hindsley. © 1993 by Leonard P. Hindsley, Paulist Press, Inc., New York/Mahwah, NJ. Reprinted by permission of Paulist Press, Inc. www.paulistpress.com.	102
Maria Faustina Kowalska (Saint)	From *Diary: Divine Mercy in My Soul.* © 2000, Marians of the Immaculate Conception, Stockbridge, MA. All rights reserved.	151, 294
Robin, Marthe (Venerable)	From *The Cross and the Joy*, Rev. Raymond Peyret, Tr. © 1983, The Fathers and Brothers of the Society of St. Paul, ST. PAULS / Alba House, Staten Island, NY. www.albahouse.org. Used with permission.	94, 241
Thérèse of Lisieux (Saint)	From *The Prayers of Saint Thérèse of Lisieux: The Act of Oblation*, Aletheia Kane, O.C.D., Tr. © 1997, ICS Publications, Washington, DC. Used with permission.	375
Thomas Aquinas (Saint)	From *The Aquinas Prayer Book: The Prayers and Hymns of St. Thomas Aquinas,* Robert Anderson, Johann Moser, Eds., Trs. © 2000, Sophia Institute Press, Manchester, NH. www.sophiainstitute.com. Used with permission.	69

ACKNOWLEDGMENTS

Most Scripture selections are taken from the *New American Bible with Revised New Testament and Psalms*. Copyright © 1991, 1986, Confraternity of Christian Doctrine, Inc., Washington, DC. Used with permission. All rights reserved. No portion of the *New American Bible* may be reprinted without written permission from the copyright holder.

The formatting of some texts may be altered in keeping with guidelines required by the USCCB.

Some Scripture selections are taken from *The Holy Bible: Revised Standard Version, Catholic Edition*, copyright 1946 (New Testament), copyright 1965 (The Catholic Edition of the New Testament) by Division of Christian Education of the National Council of Churches of Christ in the United States of America.

Published with the approval of the Committee on Divine Worship, United States Conference of Catholic Bishops.

© MAGNIFICAT Inc., New York, 2015.

Printed in Germany by CPI-CLAUSEN & BOSSE.

Cover: *The Holy Trinity* (c. 1754), Corrado Giaquinto (1703–1765), Prado Museum, Madrid, Spain. © akg-images/Album/Joseph Martin.

The Magnificat®
Year of Mercy Companion

Publisher: **Pierre-Marie Dumont**

Vice President, Publishing: **Romain Lizé**

Editor-in-Chief: **Father Peter John Cameron, o.p.**

Senior Editor: **Father Romanus Cessario, o.p.**

Assistant Editors: **Susan Needham, Anne Needham**

Editorial Assistants: **Catherine Kolpak,
Nora Macagnone, Claire Gilligan**

Senior Managing Editor: **Frédérique Chatain**

Permissions: **Diaga Seck-Rauch**

Cover and Inset: **Solange Bosdevesy**

Iconography: **Isabelle Mascaras**

Translator: **Janet Chevrier**

CONTRIBUTORS:

Audrey Assad	**Mary Joseph**
Father Eric Cadin	**Heather King**
Father Peter John Cameron, o.p.	**Barbara Ann La Porte**
Father Romanus Cessario, o.p.	**Priscilla La Porte**
Father Ryan Connors	**Lisa Lickona**
Father John Dominic Corbett, o.p.	**Father Joseph T. Lienhard, s.j.**
Father Cajetan Cuddy, o.p.	**Monsignor Gregory E. S. Malovetz**
Anthony Esolen	**Father Guy Mansini, o.s.b.**
Justin Fatica	**Regis Martin**
Father Michael Gaitley, m.i.c.	**Father John P. McIntyre**
Father Anthony Giambrone, o.p.	**Father Vincent Nagle, f.s.c.b.**
Geoffrey Gneuhs	**Father George William Rutler**
Father Donald Haggerty	**Father Christopher Seiler**
Father Tim S. Hickey	**Rita A. Simmonds**
Jennifer Hubbard	**Joshua Stancil**
John Janaro	**Father James M. Sullivan, o.p.**
Father William M. Joensen	**Father Richard Veras**

YEAR OF MERCY COMPANION

ORDER EXTRA COPIES

as low as $1.99 per copy!

- The essential page-a-day guide for living the Extraordinary Jubilee of Mercy
- Meditations, poetry, Scripture, witness, catechesis, saints, and more
- A stirring way to walk with the Church in this year-long celebration

Ref: YOM

ONLY AVAILABLE IN THE UNITED STATES AND CANADA	
QUANTITY	**PRICE PER COPY**
1-4	US $7.99
5-9	US $6.99
10-49	US $4.99
50-99	US $3.99
100-499	US $2.99
500+	US $1.99

In Him Alone Is Our Hope

Ref: IHO

By Pope Francis

✎ Get an in-depth glimpse into the mind of Pope Francis as he calls the faithful to renew their commitment to holiness, and to place their hope in Christ alone

Only $11.95

Special price from MAGNIFICAT
20% off the suggested retail price

144 pages — Size: 5.4 x 8 inches — Softcover
Also available as an eBook

Holy Days and Gospel Reflections

By Heather King

Ref: HDGR

✎ Thought-provoking reflections on select Gospel readings, feast days, and notable women in the Bible

Only $7.95

Special price from MAGNIFICAT
20% off the suggested retail price

160 pages — Size: 5 x 7.75 inches
Softcover

ORDER CARD

REF OR TITLE	UNIT PRICE	QUANTITY	TOTAL
....	US $	....	....
....	US $	....	....
....	US $	....	....
....	US $	....	....
....	US $	....	....
....	US $	....	....
....	US $	....	....
....	US $	....	....
....	US $	....	....
		TOTAL:	....
+ Shipping and handling (see chart below)			....
		GRAND TOTAL:	....

If you live in Colorado or New York, please include sales tax

SHIPPING AND HANDLING

PER ORDER	USA	CANADA
Up to US $7.99	US $1	US $2
US $8 to US $15.99	US $2	US $4
US $16 to US $49.99	US $5	US $10
US $50 to US $99.99	US $8	US $16
US $100 to US $299.99	US $16	US $32
US $300 and more	6% of the order	9% of the order

MY INFORMATION

TITLE .... FIRST NAME ....

LAST NAME ....

ADDRESS ....

....

....

CITY .... STATE .... ZIP ....

COUNTRY .... PHONE ....

EMAIL ....

METHOD OF PAYMENT

☐ CHECK ENCLOSED (CHECK PAYABLE TO MAGNIFICAT, US $ ONLY)

☐ MASTERCARD ☐ VISA ☐ DISCOVER

CARD No └──┴──┴──┴──┘ └──┴──┴──┴──┘ └──┴──┴──┴──┘ └──┴──┴──┴──┘

EXPIRATION DATE └──┴──┘/└──┴──┘ SECURITY CODE └──┴──┴──┘

NAME ON CARD ....

SIGNATURE ....

Please mail this completed order card with payment to:

MAGNIFICAT–BCR
1331 RED CEDAR CIRCLE
FORT COLLINS, CO 80524
or call (970) 416-6670 or fax (970) 224-1824
or email bookstore@magnificat.com
or visit www.magnificat.com

If you are uplifted by your daily walk
with the *Year of Mercy Companion*…
walk with MAGNIFICAT all year long!

Continue to be accompanied in your
daily encounter with Jesus, his Blessed
Mother, and his Church

Read more personal accounts of lives
forever changed in Christ

Enter more fully into the prayer of the
Church and her liturgical rhythm

Participate more fervently at Mass

Every day,
the treasures of the Church

Prayer

◆ Morning, evening, and night prayers inspired by the Liturgy of the Hours and adapted to your busy schedule

◆ Compelling spiritual and biblical essays

Eucharist

◆ Readings and prayers of each daily Mass
◆ Liturgical insights

Saints

◆ Every day, the inspirational life of a saint, providing a model for daily living

Spiritual Life

◆ Carefully selected daily meditations drawn from the very best writings of the Fathers of the Church as well as from recent spiritual masters

Sacred Art

◆ Inspiring award-winning covers that draw you more deeply into the mysteries of our Faith

◆ Full-color reproductions of great works of sacred art, complete with commentary

$\mathcal{M}$AGNIFICAT has inspired the prayer lives of millions all over the world....

Why not yours?

$\mathcal{M}$AGNIFICAT is such a blessing! Once a month I go to the mail box and it's "Christmas." I unwrap each issue and delight in the artwork, the Gospels, and the commentaries written centuries ago as well as those written today. May this joyous, beautiful publication never cease, and may it remain profoundly "Catholic."   Mary L. K.

$\mathcal{I}$ just turned 90 in February, but still optimistic, so renewed for another 4 years. Hope God lets me live that long to do his work.   Markee B.

$\mathcal{I}$ love my $\mathcal{M}$AGNIFICAT. I'm not even Catholic (yet) but $\mathcal{M}$AGNIFICAT is making me want to be. I can't get enough of $\mathcal{M}$AGNIFICAT. It is the only thing I do read every day. The print version makes it handy for me and my lifestyle with little kids. Thank you.   Jennifer S.

Ask for a complimentary copy and begin reading and praying with $\mathcal{M}$AGNIFICAT

Visit www.magnificat.com/freecopy
or subscribe today

Receive a **FREE COPY** *of*

MAGNIFICAT

Please fill out the form below or visit
www.magnificat.com/freecopy

❏ Regular edition
(4.5 x 6.7 inches)

❏ Large print edition
(5 x 7.7 inches)

MY INFORMATION

TITLE   FIRST NAME

LAST NAME

ADDRESS

ADDRESS

CITY

STATE   ZIP   YEAR OF BIRTH

PHONE NUMBER

EMAIL _____ YOM15

Offer valid in the US only

Please return this form to
MAGNIFICAT
PO Box 822 – Yonkers, NY 10702

To subscribe for only $44.95 a year,
please visit www.magnificat.com